D1807116

# Modernity, Memory and Identity in South-East Europe

Series Editor
Catharina Raudvere
Department of Cross-Cultural and Regional Studies
University of Copenhagen
Copenhagen, Denmark

This series explores the relationship between the modern history and present of South-East Europe and the long imperial past of the region. This approach aspires to offer a more nuanced understanding of the concepts of modernity and change in this region, from the nineteenth century to the present day. Titles focus on changes in identity, self-representation and cultural expressions in light of the huge pressures triggered by the interaction between external influences and local and regional practices. The books cover three significant chronological units: the decline of empires and their immediate aftermath, authoritarian governance during the twentieth century, and recent uses of history in changing societies in South-East Europe today.

More information about this series at
http://www.palgrave.com/gp/series/15829

Zlatko Jovanovic

# A Cultural History of the 1984 Winter Olympics

## The Making of Olympic Sarajevo

Zlatko Jovanovic
The Many Roads in Modernity
University of Copenhagen
Copenhagen, Denmark

ISSN 2523-7985          ISSN 2523-7993   (electronic)
Modernity, Memory and Identity in South-East Europe
ISBN 978-3-030-76597-2          ISBN 978-3-030-76598-9   (eBook)
https://doi.org/10.1007/978-3-030-76598-9

This Palgrave Macmillan imprint is published by the registered company Springer Nature
Switzerland AG.
The registered company address is: Gewerbestrasse 11, 6330 Cham, Switzerland

*To my mom*

# Acknowledgments

I was caught by surprise with, even overwhelmed by, the magnitude of the task of writing these acknowledgements. As I sat down to write them, I quickly realised that it is impossible to acknowledge everyone who has helped me conduct the research and write this book. Simply put, too many people extended me their hospitality and cooperation, and while being grateful to all of them, I at the same time fear that I in the following may forget some. Should I do so, I apologise for it now.

This project has been in progress for several years. It started in 2014 with a generous grant from the Carlsberg Foundation and is now materialising into this monograph on the 1984 Sarajevo Winter Olympics. I first arrived at this topic while still working on my dissertation in 2012. It was through my interest for Socialist Yugoslavia's urban history as well as through my participation in the research network "The Many Roads to Modernity" that I arrived at the topic of the Sarajevo Olympics. Originally conceived to cover different (sub)processes of modernisation in post-WWII Sarajevo, the project was subsequently narrowed by my newfound research interest in the relationship between modernity and the Olympic Games.

Arriving at the topic of history of sport—from a perspective of cultural historian previously focusing on youth subcultures and cultural memory—I soon found myself outside my comfort zone in terms of the research background. Fortunately, being a part of the research centre "The Many Roads in Modernity" at the University of Copenhagen, I was able with my dear colleague Selma Bukovica Gundersen and unlimited support from Catharina Raudvere to establish—even if only for a few years—a

Scandinavian network dealing with Yugoslav and post-Yugoslav history and society. While existing, the network managed to organise several seminars and workshops, some of which covered the topic of sport in Yugoslavia and its successor states. Among others we had Dario Brentin and Nicolas Moll as key speakers. From them I drew some important insights and perspectives concerning sports scholarship. Soon I was invited by Dario to contribute to a special issue on sport in Socialist Yugoslavia in the *International Journal of the History of Sport*. For that I remain deeply indebted to Dario and his co-editor Dejan Zec.

Meanwhile, I had the privilege of working with some exceptional researchers at the University of Copenhagen and at the Weiser Centre for Europa and Eurasia at the University of Michigan during my residency there. I am profoundly grateful to my colleagues and students at the Saxo Institute of the University of Copenhagen. I am also eternally grateful for the vibrant atmosphere and warm collegiality I have experienced at University of Michigan in Ann Arbor. Especially to Zana Kwaiser and Krisztina Fehérváry who included me as a presenter in the Weiser Center's lecture series. Finally, I want to thank my colleagues at the mentioned research centre "The Many Roads in Modernity", Catharina and Selma, Mogens Pelt, Trine Stauning Willert, Abdullah Simsek, Christoffer Stoerup and Niels Reeh. They have offered considerable advice and criticism, as well as moral support.

I also highly appreciate the ever-helping staff at numerous archives and institutions in the former Yugoslavia. Among them, I should mention Sarajevo Historical Archives, the Archives of Bosnia and Herzegovina, Archives of Yugoslavia in Belgrade, University Libraries in Zagreb, Belgrade and Sarajevo, as well as the National Library of Serbia. At the Sarajevo Historical Archives, I met Aida Ličina Ramić who through conversations and suggestions offered many valuable research advices. The same applies to Robert Donia, who during my stay in Ann Arbor selflessly shared his great insights and knowledge about Sarajevo and Bosnia.

This book itself has benefited tremendously from generous readings made by different colleagues at different phases in writing. Radina Vučetić, Bojan Aleksov and the mentioned colleagues at the Many Roads in Modernity provided valuable insights, criticism and suggestions, especially at earlier stages of writing. The book manuscript has been enormously enriched by astute comments and suggestions made by Nicolas Moll and Richard Mills—both of whom I remain deeply indebted. Finally, I am immensely grateful to Marie-Louise Karttunen for proofreading the manuscript.

Even though I was lucky to receive help from all these sides (off which some in fact came completely unexpectedly), all errors are exclusively mine.

On a more personal note, I would also like to thank all those who enriched my trips to Sarajevo, Belgrade and Zagreb, as well as my residency at the University of Michigan: Ajna, Amra and Nedo, as well as Sanela, Haris and čika Asim in Sarajevo, Saša and Irena in Belgrade, Ivan and Josipa in Zagreb and John Fine in Ann Arbor.

Finally, I thank my friends and family whose daily support and love helped me maintain a sense of perspective even in hard times: my sisters Spomenka and Mima, my nephews Marko and Petar and my niece Selma, as well as Niho, Mirna, Borko, Jonathan, Samia, Barbara, Jimmy, and ultimately my soulmate Gilbert.

# CONTENTS

xii    CONTENTS

# LIST OF IMAGES

# CHAPTER 1

# Introduction: Sarajevo's Olympic Spirit

Early in 2018, new signposts marking the city limits were placed in several locations around the city of Sarajevo, on which, along with the inscription 'Welcome to Sarajevo', the Cantonal Ministry of Traffic decided to include the five Olympic rings. This choice was directly related to Sarajevo's role as the host city for the 2019 European Youth Olympic Winter Festival (EYOF). However, the logic behind the option arguably rested less on the newly won bid for the EYOF than on the city's historic position as the host city for the 1984 Winter Olympic Games. In fact, the whole idea of nomination for the 2019 EYOF was related to the trope of *Olympic Sarajevo* that emerged while the city was preparing and hosting the 1984 Winter Olympics. Accordingly, when now the two administratively divided cities of Sarajevo and Istočno ('East') Sarajevo decided to submit their collective bid for the 2019 EYOF in the early 2010s, this was envisaged as a part of *the revival of Sarajevo's Olympic spirit*, a project proposed and pursued by different local institutions and organisations, and strongly supported by the Olympic Committee of Bosnia and Herzegovina. In consequence thereof, when in 2012, now Sarajevo and Istočno Sarajevo won their nomination for the EYOF, this view was voiced by mayors of both Sarajevo and Istočno Sarajevo, claiming that with the Olympic Winter Festival 'the city's Olympic spirit' would return to Sarajevo (Tina Jelin-Dizdar, Radio Slobodna Evropa, 10.12.2012).

© The Author(s), under exclusive license to Springer Nature Switzerland AG 2021
Z. Jovanovic, *A Cultural History of the 1984 Winter Olympics, Modernity, Memory and Identity in South-East Europe,*
https://doi.org/10.1007/978-3-030-76598-9_1

Thenceforth, while reporting from the 2019 EYOF, several media out-lets—including Radio Sarajevo (10.2.2019)—repeatedly argued how 'the Olympic spirit' now in fact had returned to Sarajevo, thence implicitly referring to the city's position as the host city for the 1984 Winter Olympics. Meanwhile, Jure Franko, a Slovenian-Yugoslav former alpine skier, who won a silver medal at the 1984 Sarajevo Winter Olympics, went even further, suggesting that 'the Olympic spirit' actually had never left the capital city of Bosnia and Herzegovina (Tanović 6.2.2019). The same claim had also been made some nine years earlier in 2010, when in relation to an exhibition about the Sarajevo Olympics, the then Mayor of Sarajevo, Alija Behmen, similarly argued that 'the spirit of Olympism' had never left the city (Grad Sarajevo/Agencija FENA, 3.6.2010).

This development—manifest in Franko's and the mayor Behmen's claims, as well as media reportage from the EYOF—becomes particularly interesting when seen against a statement offered by Sarajevo's youth peri-odical *Naši dani* on the second-last day of the 1984 Sarajevo Winter Olympic Games in February 1984. Back then the periodical's journalist Zoran Milanović argued: 'It is not important why this or that competitor did or did not win a medal. Because we all won a medal. And that [medal] will shine out, now and forever, from the top of the city of Sarajevo, show-ing the people of the world our soul. And the Olympics will live with it, and we will, for centuries.'[1] As prophesised by Milanović, several decades after the Sarajevo Winter Olympic Games finished the Olympics nonethe-less continue to play the role of one of the central markers in the self-perception and self-image of Sarajevo and its political leadership.

Put differently, Sarajevo has become impossible to imagine without its Olympic 'identity', a view shared by many locals, who see their city insepa-rably interlaced with and unimaginable without the 1984 Winter Olympics. It is therefore quite noteworthy that although Sarajevo, during the recent years, has attracted much attention among the scholars, there has not yet been published a book about the making of Olympic Sarajevo, telling the story of the extensive infrastructural and socio-political transformation of the city in relation to hosting the 1984 Winter Olympic Games. This has been the premise for the research project behind this book—a goal-specific case study exploring cultural implications of the Sarajevo Olympics and the change in representations of the city of Sarajevo from the mid-1960s

---

[1] Zoran O. Milanović, 'Olimpijada iz ugla jednog vojnika. "Zašto volim Sarajevo"', *Naši dani* 804, 18 February 1984, 10.

to the mid- to late 1980s. The dynamics of this change lies at the centre of analysis, in which my ultimate goal is to explain agency, origin and causality behind the emergence of the trope of Olympic Sarajevo. The title of the book, *A Cultural History of the 1984 Winter Olympics: The Making of Olympic Sarajevo*, should be seen from the perspective of a cultural historian interested in explaining the change in the image of the city generated by the conjuncture of infrastructural and socio-political transformation of it in relation to hosting a major sporting event.

## 1.1   The 1984 Sarajevo Olympics and the Cultural History of Sport in Socialist Yugoslavia

Focusing on the changing image of the city of Sarajevo in relation to hosting of the 1984 Winter Olympic Games, this research project is placed within the emergent but still under-explored field of the social history of sport in the Socialist Federal Republic of Yugoslavia (hereafter the SFRY, Socialist Yugoslavia or merely Yugoslavia). As such this book contributes to a field of academic literature that, until very recently, has been rather limited. Regarded as trivial and unimportant, as well as impossible to pigeonhole in a single scholarly discipline, the subject of sport in Yugoslavia was largely ignored by scholars until a few years ago, most commonly only touched on in passing. Hence, even the most important sporting events were only mentioned as anecdotal introduction to other, presumably more important, issues. There were nevertheless several notable exceptions, such as sociologist Srđan Vrcan (1990, 2002; Vrcan and Lalic 1999) and anthropologist Ivan Čolović (1996), who in their respective works focused on the relationship between football fandom and violence in the context of rise of ethnonationalism in Yugoslavia's constituent republics in the 1980s and early 1990s, or historian Vjekoslav Perica (2001), who explored the pan-Yugoslav, supranational sense of unity engendered by Yugoslav basketball success. Meanwhile Allen L. Sack and Zeljan Suster (2000) and Richard Mills (2009) had looked at respectively Croatian and Serbian football in relation to the disintegration of Yugoslavia, while changing meanings of football in relation to the ethnic cleavages in Slovenian society have received Peter Stankovič's attention (2005). Besides football and basketball, skiing had also attracted some attention, particularly from Gregor Starc (2002) and Vlado Kotnik (2007) who both analysed the sport discipline in relation to the construction of the Slovenian national identity in the 1990s. These works paved the way for the emergence of a new loosely defined research field addressing an array of research questions and different topics. What these topics all have in common is an emphasis on sport's position as a major twentieth-century cultural phenomenon and its placement at the centre of analysis.

The relationship between football and national identity—including that of fandom and nationalism as well as the wars of Yugoslav succession—still remains one of the largest research subfields and focus in works of scholars such as Dario Brentin (e.g., 2013, 2016; Brentin and Hodges 2018), Richard Mills (e.g., 2010, 2016b, 2018), Andrew Hodges (2018; Brentin and Hodges 2018), Andrew Gilbert (2017) and Martin Blasius (2017), as well as in an edited volume by John Hughson and Fiona Skillen (2014). Yet question of diplomacy and Yugoslavia's specific geopolitical position during the Cold War period has also been addressed over the past decade by, for instance, Richard Mills (2016a), Hrvoje Klasić (2016) and Nicola Sbetti (2017), while the ideological uses of sport and physical culture in the construction of either the new socialist sporting policies (and 'new socialist man') or pan-Yugoslav identity has received the attention of, among others, Dejan Zec and Miloš Paunović (2015) and Ana Petrov (2017). Different aspects of sport in its capacity as a popular-cultural genre relate to the topic of consumption, including sports' professionalisation in socialist countries, which has for instance been studied by Marko Miljković (2017) and Hrvoje Klasić (2017) and published in a recent special issue on history and social history of sport in Socialist Yugoslavia, edited by Dario Brentin and Dejan Zec (*Sport in Socialist Yugoslavia* 2018). Sporting architecture and infrastructure have been explored by Richard Mills (2017), while the large sporting events hosted by Socialist Yugoslavia have, among others, been studied by Jasenko Zekić, who has proposed in his work on the 1979 Split Mediterranean Games (2016) and the 1987 Zagreb Universiade (2007) that, as mega-events, these were not only sporting competitions but also political episodes. Taking this a step further, in my previous work on the Sarajevo Olympics (Jovanovic 2017) I have argued against reducing the study of the Olympics to its sporting, political and economic aspects, and called for a cultural-historical analysis of the Games.

While almost all of these studies (not least my own) have exclusively focused on sport in the specific context of Socialist Yugoslavia, in this volume I place a strong emphasis on the global context of the Sarajevo Olympics. Thus, despite this volume's origins in a goal-specific case study examining different cultural representations of its host city, in my analysis

I approach the Sarajevo Winter Games from the perspective of their location within global Olympic culture. Approaching the Sarajevo Olympics by placing the event in line with general trends in global Olympic culture makes the analysis relevant for general studies of mega-events in the twentieth and twenty-first centuries. Placed in the global context, academic discussion of the 1984 Winter Olympics in Sarajevo contributes to discussions of the role sport plays in national and international politics and those concerning the urban impact of international mega-events. It further contributes to broader debates concerning the cultural and tourism-related impacts of the Olympics on their host cities.

In terms of the role Olympics play in national and international politics two works with an analytical focus on the Sarajevo Olympics should be mentioned here. The first is an article by Kate Meehan Pedrotty: 'Yugoslav unity and Olympic ideology at the 1984 Sarajevo Winter Olympic Games' (2010). It focuses on the political debate over the financing of the Olympics and discusses the international image of peace-loving Yugoslavia that emerged during the Olympic period in relation to the ideological axiom that Yugoslavia's people lived harmoniously in brotherhood and unity in the early to mid-1980s. The second work, Jason Vuic's *The Sarajevo Olympics. A History of the 1984 Winter Olympic Games* (2015) places the Sarajevo Olympics in the context of Cold War geopolitics. This book offers a skilfully written interpretation of the Games' political, economic and sporting results and debates, providing many valuable insights, both from the Yugoslav and from the international (primarily American) perspective. What is missing in both these works is the cultural aspect of the Olympics. As Philip A. D'Agati observes in the introduction to his book *Nationalism on the World Stage. Cultural Performance and the Olympic Games*, (2011, 5) the very nature of the Olympics as a cultural festival implies that the Olympics always have cultural connotations and, therefore, produce important cultural ramifications. Consequently, D'Agati argues, consideration of the Olympics should extend beyond their sporting competitions and the narrow political and economic results of the Games.

An interesting cultural aspect of the Sarajevo Olympics is presented in the article 'An Integrative Symbol for a Divided Country? Commemorating the 1984 Sarajevo winter Olympics in Bosnia and Herzegovina from the 1992–1995 War until Today' by Nicolas Moll (2015). Studying memory of the event in contemporary Bosnia and Herzegovina, Moll places his analytical focus on the Olympics' integrative potential in this deeply divided post-Yugoslav state. Yet, while focusing on the present-day Bosnia and Herzegovina, Moll nevertheless provides a valuable, even if only short, analysis of the discourses around the Sarajevo Olympics when they took the place in 1984. On this basis, he outlines the main Olympic discourse as one according to which 'Sarajevo and its Olympics [were] bringing all of Yugoslavia together, and Sarajevo and Yugoslavia [were] bringing the whole world together'. As a result, the author suggests, proving themselves as an enormous success for Yugoslavia, even before the Games event actually took place, the Sarajevo Olympics quickly became a largely positively connoted memory site and symbol, and have remained one of the few integrative symbols in today's Bosnia and Herzegovina.

In relation to the urban impact of the Sarajevo Olympics the chapter 'The Construction of Sarajevo's "Olympic Hotel"' in Kenneth Morrison's *Sarajevo's Holiday Inn on the frontline of politics and war* (2016, 47–69) provides an interesting angle on the Sarajevo Olympics from the perspective of the city's prestigious hotel project for the Olympics, the Holiday Inn. The chapter offers some valuable insights; most notably those concerning the infrastructural work on the hotel and the political context in which the Sarajevo Games took place. However, while broadening our horizon on the Olympics, the chapter's primary purpose seems to be to serve as a kind of an overture to the book's main topic, namely the period after the Olympics, during the 1992–1995 war in Bosnia and Herzegovina and the three-and-a-half-year siege of Sarajevo. A somewhat similar impression of an Olympic prelude to Yugoslavia's breakup and the siege of Sarajevo is left by yet another important work in relation to the urban development of Sarajevo: the arguably most prominent monograph on Sarajevo's long durée history, *Sarajevo: A Biography* by Robert J. Donia (2006). Depicting how the city drew immediate benefits not only from the event itself but also from the preparation for it, Donia lists a number of important infrastructural projects built in relation to the Games. While skilfully mapping urban development of the city throughout the centuries, and accordingly placing the Olympics in this larger context, this book nonetheless pays relatively little attention to the event itself. While sharing Morrison's and Donia's (as well as Moll's) arguments and drawing on their valuable insights, my focus in the present book is exclusively concerned with the urban re-making and re-imaginings during the Olympic period itself.

In this regard, a recent article by Aida Ličina Ramić (2017) should be mentioned in relation to the urban impact of the 1984 Winter Olympics.

Titled 'From an Ecological Catastrophe to the Olympic city—Sarajevo 1971–1984' ('Od ekološke katastrofe do olimpijskog grada—Sarajevo 1971–1984') this article deals with the urban pollution in Sarajevo, and the implementation of the so-called Project for protection of the human environment (Projekat za zaštitu čovjekove sredine) that was conceived as a remedy for the air, water and soil pollution in the city. Not really dealing with the Olympic event as such, Ličina Ramić nonetheless offers an important argument that without this basically infrastructural project and the betterment of Sarajevo's urban environment, the 1984 Winter Olympics would never happen.

In regard to the Olympic events' impact on the host cities, and in accordance with the general literature on the topic, the Olympic Games have always served as a catalyst of urban change (Essex and Chalkley 1998). However, whilst the main impact of hosting the event up until 1960s was in terms of building sport facilities, since the 1960 the Games have become a major stimulus for transformation of built environment in the broadest sense (Essex and Chalkley 1998, 195). Sharing this view on the chronology of the urban impact of the Olympics in their discussion on the topic, Hanwen Liao and Adrian Pitts (2006, 1238–1239) have called the post-1960 Olympic period 'The Age of Urban Transformation'. Meanwhile, zooming in on the Winter Games alone, Stephen Essex and Brian Chalkley (2004, 217–223) have localised four phases of urban transformation relating to the event in the period 1924–2002. The earliest phase, 1924–1932, was characterised by *minimal infrastructural transformations.* The following mid-century phase, 1936–1960, is associated with the *emerging infrastructural demands* and was followed by a phase in which the winter Olympic event was seen as a tool of *regional development,* lasting from 1964 to 1980. The final phase, starting in fact with the Sarajevo Games, brought *large-scale (urban) transformations* and was characterised by the growing challenge to provide accommodation to the increasing number of both athletes and support staff participating in the event and the media personnel covering it (Essex and Chalkley 2004, 222–223). One of the results thereof has been that after the 1980 Lake Placid Olympics most Winter Games have been staged in centres with larger population, while smaller Olympic host centres typical of the early Winter Games have become rather uncommon (Essex and Chalkley 2004, 213). In accordance with this trend towards larger urban centres, the Winter Games attained a role of securing major infrastructural change and intensifying modernisation of the host cities. Accordingly, the 1984

Sarajevo Games also became an opportunity to modernise the city, argue Essex and Chalkley (2004, 222).

Meanwhile, urban impacts of the Olympic Games have always been closely linked to the economic issues. Colossal Olympic investments boost the host city's visibility on the international scene and stimulate the tourist industry. Most researchers agree that the Games stimulate the local economic development of the host cities, sometimes helping to upgrade, modernise, restructure and diversify the local economy of these cities, thereby contributing to the growing competitiveness between them on a global scale (Gaudette et al. 2017, 304–305). Hence, as some researchers have pointed out, bidding for and eventually winning Olympic nomination can be seen as a kind of global intercity competition and comparison (Short 2012, 256; Roche 2000, 10). Winning the Olympic nomination provides host cities with an extraordinary opportunity to produce and transmit a positive image to a global audience. Yet, in order to retain the positive image, the host city must host a thoroughly successful Games (Short 2012, 255–256). Fundamentally, success or failure is determined by the Games' 'legacy'—a measuring-stick concept involving long-term planned and unplanned economic, social, cultural, infrastructural and environmental impacts on a host city. Urban renewal, increased tourism and employment, an enhanced city image and reputation and a renewed sense of community are some of the most commonly coveted positive legacies. It is as a result of assessing the possibility of attaining such outcomes that cities from around the globe choose to bid for the opportunity to host the Olympic Games.

## 1.2    SARAJEVO'S 'OLYMPIC IDENTITY'

As among others Jason Vuic (2015) has shown in his aforementioned book about the topic, the Sarajevo Olympics were generally regarded as being successful in all these parameters. Yet the most prominent impact of the 1984 Winter Olympic Games concerns what the US bi-weekly newspaper, the *Christian Science Monitor*, referred to as the emergence of a 'fresh new identity' for the city. In his immediate post-Olympics report from Sarajevo the newspaper's journalist Ross Atkin told the readers that Sarajevo might not necessarily become a major global tourist destination, as the organisers of the event had hoped. Nonetheless, hosting the Games had other huge impacts on the city, resulting in new roads, buildings and sports facilities. Based on the enormous infrastructural development that

Sarajevo had undergone, the report argued, the city had attained nothing less than a completely new 'identity' (Atkin 1984).

This *Christian Science Monitor*'s commentary effectively encapsulated several key ideas behind the 1984 Sarajevo Winter Olympic Games. As we will see in the subsequent chapters, by hosting the Olympics event, the organisers hoped to turn Sarajevo into a winter tourism centre with global status—one of the primary reasons why cities around the world choose to become Olympic candidates in the first place. Then, whether or not they eventually become global tourist centres, host cities commonly undergo massive infrastructural makeovers in order to meet the requirements for hosting the Games. This was also the case in Sarajevo, which underwent enormous infrastructural transformation during the preparation period prior to the Olympics, a process that actually started before winning the bid, as improvement in several fields was viewed as a prerequisite for consideration as a serious Olympic candidate. With this infrastructural metamorphosis, Sarajevo attained its new physical identity, its true 'Olympic' look.

Yet, besides the impact on the development of tourism and improvement in the sphere of urban infrastructure, the Olympics also have the capacity to affect how the host city is viewed, both nationally and internationally. As Maurice Roche (2000, 6) puts it, the Olympics are key occasions on which host cities and nations can construct and present images of themselves to other nations and 'in the eyes of the world'. This is where the concept of *representation* becomes interesting because, as Stuart Hall argues (2005, 6), representation means 'to present', 'to image', 'to depict', and carries with it the notion that something is already there to be represented. However, as it is impossible to represent all aspects of the Olympic host city, and as not everything is equally important or sufficiently desirable to be included in a representation, the process of depiction and image-construction is one of collating specific elements and leaving others out. Studying representations is, thus, an important analytical task that reveals a great deal about the society producing them. Hence, although dealing with Sarajevo as an actual locality, this book concomitantly approaches *Olympic* Sarajevo also as a microhistorical unit, telling a story of a larger macrohistorical Yugoslav, and even global, transformation occurring in the studied period. Put differently, mapping the changing dynamics in cultural representations of the city in relation to the hosting of the Games also offers important insights into Yugoslav society during the period of late socialism (1960–1980s), including those relating to the country's unique geopolitical position.

Against these theoretical considerations, the present book is conceived as comprising a series of representation analyses wherein I examine transformations in Sarajevo's image. In these representation analyses I have been methodologically guided by the theoretical assumption of *intertextuality*, stressing that a text can only communicate its meanings when placed in relation to other texts and the larger issues. This is so because a text's meaning arises between texts and is often relating to issues larger than those directly addressed (Gracyk 2001, 56). Having said that, it is necessary to point out that although there frequently exists a preferred reading of a text, this is not necessarily true for the audience as a whole (Shuker 2008 [1994], 94). It is therefore possible that some people have read and interpreted the sources used in this study differently than I do, bringing to attention issues I have left out, while not noticing the messages I bring attention to. Relating to this, I want to underscore that I do not try to give one for all interpretation of the sources; my goal has been to point at general trends.

With these goals in mind, I have examined a broad range of empirical material, beginning with a range of newspapers, magazines and relevant official publications including monographs and reports. These have been used, firstly, to provide factual historical information on the Olympics and related fields; secondly, as my main sources of textual representations of Sarajevo in the period from the mid-1960s to the mid- to late 1980s; and, thirdly, as valuable records of the various debates concerning the Olympics. With regard to the latter, the youth-targeted media used in analysis—periodicals and other popular-cultural sources, notably song lyrics—provided important primary data on debates about popular culture, and were also central to mapping popular-cultural representations of *Olympic Sarajevo*. In addition, I have consulted a number of letters sent from both Yugoslavs and foreigners to the city mayor after the Games, as well as official reactions to the event in the international press. I have furthermore compiled relevant statistical data, like those on population and tourism. Finally, I have also collected a range of visual and audio-visual material including Olympic posters and videos. Along with images in the press and publications, these were a valuable source for analysing visual representations from and of the XIV Olympic Winter Games and their host city, Sarajevo.[2]

## 1.3    A PREVIEW: A MULTI-DIMENSIONAL READING OF THE SARAJEVO OLYMPICS

Drawing on the existing literature and the presented source material, this book offers a multi-dimensional reading of the cultural implications of the Sarajevo Olympics. In accordance with this multi-dimensionality, the book is organised into three parts: the first a single chapter and the following two comprising two chapters each. The inspiration for this organisation comes from Maurice Roche's book *Mega-events and Modernity: Olympics, Expos and the Growth of Global Culture* (2000), in which the author argues that, from a sociological perspective, the Olympics can be fruitfully analysed as complexes of three sets of characteristics that each contains an axis and/or oppositional poles: the modern/non-modern dimension, the national/non-national dimension and the local/non-local dimension.

To explain the first dimension, the modern/non-modern, Roche argues (2000, 8–9) that, as modern cultural events, the Olympics involve ideologies and principles of 'Western civilisation'. As modern sport events, the Olympic culture has been increasingly globalised since the late nineteenth century. This process is according to Roche (2000, 168) driven by, among other factors, the ideological agendas of European empires, the internationalist mission of the Olympic movement, the globalisation of consumer markets and the global reach of television. Hence, it makes sense to argue that the development of the Olympics parallels the growth and spread of 'modernity'. Consequently, as the Olympics at times contribute to social change and because modernity necessarily contain and/or refer to some non-modern, the periods preceding the Olympics become commonly seen as pre-modern and 'traditional' (Roche 2000, 8–9).

When it comes to the national/non-national dimension of the Olympics, Roche emphasises (2000, 9–10) that the Olympics are nationally based as national power-elites in the host nation and the official 'invented traditions' of host-state nationalism are involved in their

[2]While I used conventional archive research to locate copies of official Olympic posters, I used media archaeology methodology—a process of searching for relevant popular cultural material on the internet—to researching video material like TV commercials, music videos and broadcasted sequences from the Olympic event itself.

organisation. At the same time, as the host nation plays a significantly more powerful role than guest nations, its power-elites often use the Olympics to emphasise their claim to the host nation having a mission or a destiny in the world's international order and world history. Finally, dealing with the local/non-local dimension of the Olympics, Roche insists (2000, 10) that the Olympics are urban events, having important and distinctive 'urban'-level characteristics that provide a model of host cities in terms of their architecture, habitation areas, public functions, services and so on. As such, they are usually intended to physically transform some strategically important area(s) and project the image and status of the local power-elites, while at the same time also projecting the city to the world and re-positioning it in the world of global intercity comparison and economic competition.

Accommodating Roche's inspiring multi-dimensional approach to Olympics in general to my own case study of the 1984 Sarajevo Winter Olympics, I have borrowed, used and somewhat transformed Roche's three-dimensional apparatus and its conceptual framework. Thence, the book's three parts deal with respectively the locality, the modernity and the nationality dimensions of the Sarajevo Olympics. In the first part, 'Sarajevo, "The Place"', dealing with the global/local dimension of the Sarajevo Olympics in relation to promoting the city into a global tourist destination, I examine how the Olympics emerged as an important temporal reference for local elites, including the city's political regime, which saw the Games event as a turning point and a milestone in the city's development. Members of the local political and economic elites chose to support the Olympic nomination because they hoped that the Olympics would bring more foreign tourists to the city and therethrough strengthen the city's economy. Yet, as we will see in the chapter, despite the elite's strictly economic logic and strategy, the Olympics soon proved also to carry several important cultural ramifications. These firstly concerned the idea that the Olympics meant the beginning of a new, qualitatively different, post-Olympics future. In the chapter, I argue that this idea had more to do with the inherent ability of the Olympic Games to strengthen the sense of a break with the past than about the break itself. Second, crafting the city's global image paradoxically made Sarajevans more aware of their city's particularity. Following the same line of argument, I also argue that for the city's youth, the Olympics emerged as a prism through which they regarded the world around them. In this respect, the Olympics became a tool that they could use when positioning themselves in the popular-cultural space of Yugoslavia and the world, stressing Sarajevo's particularity as a place.

In relation to the modernity dimension of the Sarajevo Olympics, which is addressed in Part II, 'Sarajevo, Modern', I suggest that the 1984 Games set the pace and direction in the further development of the city. Most notably, as we will see in Chap. 3, the first of Part II's chapters, the Olympics pointed the city in the directions of greater environmental consciousness and more disciplined social conduct. Yet, despite the general assumption that the Olympics initiated this development, I argue in the chapter that the hosting of the event only made different already existing urban imaginaries possible. Out of this new situation and the fulfilment of these imaginaries, there then emerged a sense of urgency for environmental betterment and social disciplining of the local population. The ultimate goal was to modernise the city in every possible aspect. Approaching modernity from a somewhat different perspective, the second chapter in Part II, 'Catching Up with the West' (Chap. 4), places Olympic Sarajevo in the context of the emerging research field on socialist consumption and everyday life. From this position, I discuss the cultural implications of the Olympics in relation to Yugoslavia's socialist ideology, Sarajevo's Ottoman past and the contemporaneous global economic developments.

Part III, 'Sarajevo, "An Oasis"', discusses the national/non-national dimension of the Sarajevo Olympics. Its first chapter, Chap. 5, deals with the international element of this axis, placing Yugoslavia's unique geopolitical position in the Cold War period at the centre of analysis. Exploring how in the period of rising East-West tensions in the late 1970s and early 1980s, a mode of representation emerged suggesting that the non-aligned Yugoslavia was 'the best possible Olympic host'. Linking this emerging mode of representation to the image of Sarajevo as a city in which the shooting of Archduke Ferdinand in 1914 allegedly initiated World War I, I then examine how this global image of the city changed with the Olympics, when it appeared as an exception—an 'oasis of peace and international cooperation'—in the troubled Cold War world. The following, sixth, chapter explores how hosting the Olympics affected the (self)-representations and (self)-perception of Sarajevans by boosting their pride in being Yugoslavs. Placing the Olympics in the context of economic crisis and rising ethnonationalism in 1980s' Yugoslavia, the chapter, titled 'Framing Olympic Sarajevo as a Truly Yugoslav City', stresses the complexity of Yugoslav nationality policies and discusses different—and at times contradictory—development patterns in national identity-formation in the last decade of Yugoslavia's existence. Also in this regard, Sarajevo was often depicted as an oasis; more precisely, 'a leftover oasis' of Yugoslavia from some better times than those of the crisis and nationalism-ridden 1980s.

## BIBLIOGRAPHY

### INTERNET PORTALS REFERENCED

Tanović, Muamer. 2019. Jure Franko: Život dijelim na onaj prije i onaj poslije Sarajeva '84. *AlJazeera*, February 6, 2019. Accessed February 1, 2021. http://balkans.aljazeera.net/vijesti/jure-franko-zivot-dijelim-na-onaj-prije-i-onaj-poslije-sarajeva-84.

### BOOKS, ARTICLES, REPORTS, BLOGS AND WEBSITES

Atkin, Ross. 1984. Olympics Had Moments of Brilliance Plus a Good Host in Sarajevo. *Christian Science Monitor*, February 21, 1984. https://www.csmonitor.com/1984/0221/022107.html.
Blasius, Martin. 2017. FC Red Star Belgrade and the Multiplicity of Social Identifications in Socialist Yugoslavia: Representative Dimensions of the 'Big Four' Football Clubs. *The International Journal of the History of Sport* 34 (9): 783–799.
Brentin, Dario. 2013. 'A Lofty Battle for the Nation': The Social Roles of Sport in Tudjman's Croatia. *Sport in Society* 16 (8): 993–1008.
———. 2016. Ready for the Homeland? Ritual, Remembrance, and Political Extremism in Croatian Football. *Nationalities Papers* 44 (6): 860–876.
Brentin, Dario, and Andrew Hodges. 2018. Fan Protest and Activism: Football from Below in South-Eastern Europe. *Soccer and Society* 19 (3): 329–336.
Čolović, Ivan. 1996. Football, Hooligans and War. In *The Road to War in Serbia: Trauma and Catharsis*, ed. Nebojša Popov, 373–396. Budapest: Central European University Press.
D'Agati, Philip A. 2011. *Nationalism on the World Stage. Cultural Performance and the Olympic Games*. Lanham, MD: University Press of America.
Donia, Robert J. 2006. *Sarajevo. A Biography*. Ann Arbour: University of Michigan Press.
Essex, Stephen, and Brian Chalkley. 1998. Olympic Games: Catalyst of Urban Change. *Leisure Studies* 17 (3): 187–206.

———. 2004. Mega-Sporting Events in Urban and Regional Policy: A History of the Winter Olympics. *Planning Perspectives* 19 (2): 201–232.

Gaudette, Marilyne, Romain Roult, and Sylvain Lefebvre. 2017. Winter Olympic Games, Cities, and Tourism: A Systematic Literature Review in This Domain. *Journal of Sport & Tourism* 21 (4): 287–313.

Gilbert, Andrew. 2017. Tri vjere, jedna nacija, država Tuzla! Football Fans, Political Protest and the Right to the City in Postsocialist Bosnia–Herzegovina. *Soccer & Society* 19: 1–27.

Gracyk, Theodore. 2001. *I Wanna be Me: Rock Music and the Politics of Identity*. Philadelphia: Temple University Press.

Hall, Stuart. 2005. Representation and Media, 6. https://www.mediaed.org.

Hodges, Andrew. 2018. *Fan Activism, Protest and Politics. Ultras in Post-Socialist Croatia*. London: Routledge.

Hughson, John, and Fiona Skillen, eds. 2014. *Football in Southeastern Europe: From Ethnic Homogenization to Reconciliation*. London: Routledge.

Jovanovic, Zlatko. 2017. The 1984 Sarajevo Winter Olympics and Identity-Formation in Late Socialist Sarajevo. *The International Journal of the History of Sport* 34 (9): 767–782.

Klasić, Hrvoje. 2016. The Tito-Stalin Football War. *RADOVI—Zavod za hrvatsku povijest* 48: 387–404.

———. 2017. How Falcons Became Partizans. *The International Journal of the History of Sport* 34 (9): 832–847.

Kotnik, Vlado. 2007. Sport, Landscape, and the National Identity: Representations of an Idealized Vision of Nationhood in Slovenian Skiing Telecasts. *Journal of the Society for the Anthropology of Europe* 7: 19–35.

Liao, Hanwen, and Adrian Pitts. 2006. A Brief Historical Review of Olympic Urbanization. *The International Journal of the History of Sport* 23 (7): 1232–1252.

Ličina Ramić, Aida. 2017. Od ekološke katastrofe do olimpijskog grada—Sarajevo 1971–1984. In *Poplava, zemljotres, smog: prilozi ekohistoriji Bosne i Hercegovine u 20. stoljeću: zbornik radova*, ed. Amir Duranović, 115–147. Sarajevo: Udruženje za modernu historiju/Udruga za modernu povijest (Edicija Zbornici; knj. 3).

Miljković, Marko. 2017. Blind-Alleys on the Road to Communism: 'Isms' of the Automobile Sport in Socialist Yugoslavia, 1945–1992. *The International Journal of the History of Sport* 34 (9): 815–831.

Mills, Richard. 2009. 'It All Ended in an Unsporting Way': Serbian Football and the Disintegration of Yugoslavia, 1989–2006. *International Journal of the History of Sport* 26: 1187–1217.

———. 2010. Velež Mostar Football Club and the Demise of 'Brotherhood and Unity' in Yugoslavia, 1922–2009. *Europe-Asia Studies* 62 (7): 1107–1133.

———. 2016a. Cold War Football: Soviet Defence and Yugoslav Attack following the Tito– Stalin Split of 1948. *Europe-Asia Studies* 68 (10): 1737–1741.

———. 2016b. The Pitch Itself Was No Man's Land': Siege, Željezničar Sarajevo Football Club and the Grbavica Stadium. *Nationalities Papers* 44 (6): 877–903.

———. 2017. Laying the Foundations of Physical Culture: The Stadium Revolution in Socialist Yugoslavia. *The International Journal of the History of Sport* 34 (9): 729–752.

———. 2018. *The Politics of Football in Yugoslavia: Sport, Nationalism and the State*. London: IB Tauris.

Moll, Nicolas. 2015. An Integrative Symbol for a Divided Country? Commemorating the 1984 Sarajevo Winter Olympics in Bosnia and Herzegovina from the 1992–1995 War Until Today. *Croatian Political Science Review* 51 (5): 127–156.

Morrison, Kenneth. 2016. *Sarajevo's Holiday Inn on the Frontline of Politics and War*. Palgrave Macmillan.

Pedrotty, Kate Meehan. 2010. Yugoslav Unity and Olympic Ideology at the 1984 Sarajevo Winter Olympic Games. In *Yugoslavia's Sunny Side: A History of Tourism in Socialism (1950s–1980s)*, ed. Hannes Grandits and Karin Taylor, 333–363. Budapest and New York: CEU Press.

Perica, Vjekoslav. 2001. United They Stood, Divided They Fell: Nationalism and the Yugoslav School of Basketball, 1968–2000. *Nationalities Papers: The Journal of Nationalism and Ethnicity* 29 (2): 267–291.

Petrov, Ana. 2017. How Doing Sport Became a Culture: Producing the Concept of Physical Cultivation of the Yugoslavs. *The International Journal of the History of Sport* 34 (9): 753–766.

Roche, Maurice. 2000. *Mega-events and Modernity: Olympics, Expos and the Growth of Global Culture*. London: Routledge.

Sack, Allen L., and Zeljan Suster. 2000. Soccer and Croatian Nationalism: A Prelude to War. *Journal of Sport and Social Issues* 24: 305–320.

Sbetti, Nicola. 2017. Like a Bridge Over Troubled Adriatic Water: The Complex Relationship between Italian and Yugoslavian Sporting Diplomacy (1945–1954). *The International Journal of the History of Sport* 34 (9): 800–814.

Short, John R. 2012. Globalization, Cities, and the Summer Olympics. In *The Making of Olympic Cities: Critical Concepts in Urban Studies, Volume I: Contexts and Overviews*, ed. John R. Gold and Margaret M. Gold, 235–262. London and New York: Routledge.

Shuker, Roy. 2008 [1994]. *Understanding Popular Music Culture*. London and New York: Routledge.

*Sport in Socialist Yugoslavia*. 2018. Ed. Dario Brentin and Dejan Zec. London: Routledge.

Stankovič, Peter. 2005. Soccer and Nationalism in Slovenia. *Ethnologia Balkanica* 9: 305–320.

Starc, Gregor. 2002. Skiing Memories in the Slovenian National Mnemonic Scheme: An Anthropological Perspective. *Anthropological Notebooks* 12: 5–22.

Vrcan, Srđan. 1990. *Sport i nasilije danas u nas i druge studije iz sociologije sporta.* Zagreb: Naprijed.

―――. 2002. The Curious Drama of the President of a Republic versus a Football Fan Tribe. *International Review for the Sociology of Sport* 37: 59–77.

Vrcan, Srdjan, and Drazen Lalic. 1999. From Ends to Trenches, and Back: Football in the Former Yugoslavia. In *Football Cultures and Identities*, eds. Gary Armstrong and Richard Giulianotti, 176–185. New York: Palgrave Macmillan.

Vuic, Jason. 2015. *The Sarajevo Olympics: A History of the 1984 Winter Olympic Games*. Amherst and Boston: University of Massachusetts Press.

Zec, Dejan, and Miloš Paunović. 2015. Football's Positive Influence on Integration in Diverse Societies: The Case Study of Yugoslavia. *Soccer & Society* 16 (2–3): 236–237.

Zekić, Jasenko. 2007. Univerzijada '87.—drugi ilirski preporod. *Časopis za suvremenu povijest* 39 (2): 299–318.

―――. 2016. Mediteranske igre u Splitu—odrazi političke dimenzije u tiskanim medijima. *Časopis za suvremenu povijest* 48 (1): 97–117.

# PART I

# Sarajevo, 'The Place' (Local/Non-local Dimension of the Sarajevo Olympics)

# CHAPTER 2

# Putting Sarajevo on the World Tourist Map

The 1984 Sarajevo Winter Olympic Games were an unmitigated success in more ways than one: breaking all previous records for the number of participants,[1] they also became the first Olympic Games at which fully integrated Information Technology (IT) solutions, according to today's criteria, were implemented (Sakac 2008).[2] For the first time ever, animations and special graphics were possible, which could show, among other things, the course layouts of downhill races (Beattie 1984, 36). Furthermore, the Games' opening and closing ceremonies, transmitted to a global TV audience, were also considered highly successful, as evidenced by the numerous appreciative letters sent to the Mayor of Sarajevo in the immediate post-Olympics' period from all over the world. Sarajevo was also widely complimented for its Olympic village. According to Dan Miller, the then executive director of the US Olympic Committee, this was 'by far the best Olympic Village' built up until then (Schaap 1984,

[1] There were 49 participating countries in Sarajevo compared with 37 at the Games in Grenoble 1968, Innsbruck 1976 and Lake Placid 1980. The record in terms of number of the athletes was also broken, with the Sarajevo Games easily surpassing the previous record held by the Grenoble 1968 Games with 1290 participants (1280 in Lake Placid and 1260 in Innsbruck 1976). In Sarajevo 1490 athletes competed.

[2] It is less known, but in no way less interesting, that the winter events for the physically handicapped were also organised for the first time at the Sarajevo Games (J.-L. Chappelet 2012, 78).

© The Author(s), under exclusive license to Springer Nature
Switzerland AG 2021
Z. Jovanovic, *A Cultural History of the 1984 Winter Olympics,
Modernity, Memory and Identity in South-East Europe*,
https://doi.org/10.1007/978-3-030-76598-9_2

14). In addition, everybody praised the Yugoslav Olympic Committee and the citizens of Sarajevo for the organisation and coordination of their activities and how well they coped with the troublesome weather conditions, the latter mostly affected alpine skiing, which had to be postponed on several occasions (Beattie 1984, 36). It is possible to argue, therefore, that with the weather appearing to be the biggest problem in Sarajevo, other aspects of the Games looked even brighter.

Finally, as Jason Vuic's recent book on the topic excellently demonstrates, the Olympic success contributed greatly to producing a positive image of Socialist Yugoslavia in the eyes of the world (Vuic 2015). It can be advanced that Sarajevo's Olympic success was, in fact, greatest in its capacity of creating the immensely positive image of Yugoslavia and Sarajevo. It goes without saying that boosting the global profile of candidate cities and their nations is inherent to the very idea of bidding for Olympics. This is so not least because the development of post-Olympic tourism has, from the start of the modern Olympics, been one of the major motives for hosting them. The research in the field shows us that throughout the twentieth century the idea of hosting the Olympic Games has become inseparably interlaced with the global tourist culture. In this respect, bidding for and hosting the Games has provided host cities with an opportunity to promote positive images of themselves globally. As John R. Short (2012, 256) explains in his work on the global city imaginary of Olympic host cities, local residents are most often encouraged to support Olympic bids with the rhetoric of 'putting the[ir] city on the world map'. The ultimate ambition is to make and reaffirm the global city status of candidates. Hosting the Olympics, argues Maurice Roche (2000, 10), provides cities with the opportunity to project themselves onto the world screen and to re-position themselves in terms of global intercity comparison and economic competition, ultimately attracting tourists and inward investments. Thus, as Short (2012, 256) puts it, hosting the Games can be seen as 'winning the gold medal of global inter-city competition'.

Given this background, this chapter begins by looking behind Sarajevo's candidacy for the 1984 Winter Olympics. On the one hand, this is meant to provide necessary historical context; on the other, it is not only important because it provides a background against which the story is told, but even more so because such contextualisation contributes substantially to explaining the cultural connotations and ramifications of the Sarajevo Winter Olympics. In the interests of further exploring their cultural implications, I then proceed to analysing how hosting the XIV Olympic Winter Games influenced cultural representations of the city of Sarajevo. I first investigate changes in official representations of Sarajevo in relation to the Olympic goal of turning the city into a global winter sports centre. An analysis of the relationship between the desired economic goals and the cultural ramifications of the Olympics follows. Pursuing the same analytical direction, I then turn to examination of how the Olympics influenced Sarajevans' perceptions of their city, in particular their awareness of the city's peculiarities and uniqueness. To frame this more hypothetically, while the Olympics are international or even global events, they are at the same time also localised in space and time. As such, they unavoidably influence local self-perceptions through the processes of constructing and projecting the host city's 'place' image. Building further on this argument, in the final section of the chapter, I discuss how 'the Olympics' became an important temporal and cultural reference point among the city's youth, depicting how members of these subcultures appropriated the universal Olympic phenomenon and turned it into a local identity marker.

## 2.1   THE MOST UNLIKELY OLYMPIC CANDIDATE CITY

The idea of Sarajevo as a winter tourist centre that could potentially bid for the Winter Olympics was first introduced in 1968 in a paper entitled, 'Analysis of the Possibilities and Problems of Developing Winter Tourism in Yugoslavia', produced as a report by the Organisation for Economic Cooperation and Development (OECD). This is a Paris-based transnational economic organisation that originally administered the Marshall Plan but has, since the 1950s, refocused its activities and objectives to promote business practices and trade and tax policies that would, in the organisation's view, stimulate economic growth in different parts of Europe. The paper argued that Sarajevo and its surroundings had all the necessary conditions to become a winter tourist centre and that, for the same reason, Sarajevo should consider a Winter Olympic bid.[3]

At first the idea did not receive much response (Vuic 2015, 29), probably because it seemed almost unattainable, much easier said than done.

---

[3] Pripremni komitet za kandidaturu grada Sarajeva za organizovanje zimskih olimpijskih igara 1984. g., 'Prijedlog mogućnosti grada Sarajeva za zimske olimpijske igre 1984.g.', Sarajevo 30.9.1977, 3–5, JOK—832/F-11. Arhiv Jugoslavije [The Archives of Yugoslavia], Belgrade, Serbia.

At that time Sarajevo lacked most of the necessary infrastructure and had rather limited winter sports traditions. Certainly, there was Jahorina, a mountain situated less than 30 km south-east of the city centre, which had a tradition of alpine skiing going back at least to the beginning of the twentieth century and, according to the 1958 *Tourist Encyclopaedia of Yugoslavia*, 'the best and the most complete skiing centre in the whole of Yugoslavia'. However, as the encyclopaedia also pointed out, as a destination the mountain had the grave defect of poor traffic connections with the city (*TEJ* 1958, 130). Furthermore, at the time the OECD paper was published, the city had only just started building its first ice rink, within the Skenderija cultural and sports centre, and it did not even have an active ice-hockey or skating club. In fact, as indicated by an official English translation of the city's tourist guide from 1966 (discussed below), winter sports were not particularly popular in Sarajevo when the Olympic idea was first envisaged.

Thus, while the mountains surrounding Sarajevo had the potential to become international ski resorts of quality, and a certain tradition of alpine skiing existed in the city, when the idea of Sarajevo's bidding for the Olympics was first conceived, very few people, including highly positioned members of the International Ski Federation (FIS), associated Sarajevo with winter sports. Illustrating this is a comment made by Günter Reissner, one of the FIS's experts in alpine skiing, during his inspection visit to Sarajevo a couple of weeks after it won the Olympic nomination in May 1978. Reissner told Sarajevo's major daily, *Oslobodenje* (Liberation), that he was sceptical about the city's ability to host a Winter Olympics, not least because, while he had been to Jahorina twenty years earlier, he had received little information about the current state and development of alpine skiing infrastructure in Sarajevo since his visit.[4] Although Reissner was ultimately very positive in his comments on the current developments in Jahorina and other ski resorts around the city, the fact that, despite his expert position, he did not know much about the situation in Sarajevo says a lot about how peripheral and isolated Sarajevo was in the world of alpine skiing and winter sports in general.

The winter sports centre of Yugoslavia was in the northernmost republic, Slovenia. Commonly referred to as 'Yugoslavia's Alpine republic', Slovenia had a relatively strong tradition of winter sports, most notably

---

[4] Alija Resulović, 'Atinski dnevnik (3): Kako je Sarajevo postalo domaćin Zimske olimpijade '84. Invazija inspektora', *Oslobodenje* 2.6.1978, 10.

alpine skiing and ski jumping. The republic had internationally acclaimed winter sport centres in Kranjska Gora (alpine skiing) and Planica (ski jumping), two centres situated near each other and in close proximity to both the Austrian and Italian borders. Moreover, the industrial town of Jesenice, one of the leading centres for Yugoslav ice hockey, was also situated here. Thus, if Yugoslavia were to host the Winter Olympics, it would arguably be most logical to do so in Slovenia, preferably in this northwestern corner of the republic. This said, Slovenia was also rather marginal and isolated in terms of the major winter sport centres. Even in alpine skiing and despite the somewhat widespread assumption that Slovenes were the first alpine nation in the world (Masia 1984, 48), Slovenia was actually far behind the leading alpine skiing nations regularly winning medals in World Cup Championships and Olympic competitions. In fact, prior to the Sarajevo Olympics, Yugoslavia—and thus Slovenia—had not won a single medal in any of the winter sports. Yugoslavia was more of a Summer Olympics sports nation, gaining medals in team sports like basketball, volleyball, handball and water polo, but also in a number of individual or double disciplines, including athletics, kayaking, boxing and table tennis.

All this made the world sceptical about Yugoslavia's ability to prepare for and host the Games in Sarajevo. Hence, when, in the end, both country and city proved themselves ready, it came as a surprise. ABC's Bob Beattie expressed this very aptly in the Olympic issue of the American magazine *Ski* in February 1984 when he wrote that he had 'visited Sarajevo with ABC-TV each of the past three years, and [...] [was] amazed at the progress that [had] been made'. Beattie argued that this was a 'testimony to the hard-working and very proud people of Sarajevo' and that '[it all] had been made even more difficult when one [considered] not only how isolated Yugoslavia [was] as an alpine ski nation, but how geographically isolated Sarajevo [was] from the rest of Yugoslavia itself' (Beattie 1984, 36).

As Beattie pointed out, Sarajevo's isolation did not only come to the fore because of its marginality in alpine skiing (and other winter sports, for that matter), but also its geographical position and poor traffic connections with the rest of the country and the world. As a Yugoslav journalist put it in 1982, when interviewing the director of the 1984 Sarajevo Winter Olympic Press and Information Office, Pavle Lukač, 'Not only did Sarajevo not have a winter sports tradition, it could not, due to its geographical and climatic conditions, develop into a winter sports centre'.[5] Its position in the geographical centre of the country, surrounded by mountain massifs and isolated from all major rail and road traffic routes, meant that the city, as an Olympic host or a potential winter tourism centre, could best be reached by air. That said, even flying into Sarajevo airport was not without problems as its location in a valley sandwiched between high mountains resulted in a microclimate that made winter fog very common, causing frequent flight cancellations during the winter months.

This geographic-climatic and sports-historical context inevitably leads one to ask why anyone would propose Sarajevo as a host city for the Winter Olympics in the first place. In order to answer that question properly we need to look more closely at the political and economic context in which the nomination of Sarajevo occurred. The political economy of Socialist Yugoslavia was complex. Prior to World War II (WWII), the Kingdom of Yugoslavia had been one of the poorest countries in Europe and it emerged from the war badly devastated. In addition, already large before the war, the economic gap between the individual regions of the country further widened in the post-war period. Meanwhile, at the end of the war, Sarajevo became the capital of the Socialist Republic of Bosnia and Herzegovina, one of Socialist Yugoslavia's six federal units. However, despite formally being a federation, Socialist Yugoslavia in fact remained a rather central-ised state in the immediate post-WWII period (Woodward 1995, 63–70, 88pp). Only in the early 1960s did it become de facto increasingly decen-tralised, politically, economically and culturally. This development led to largely independent economic policies in each federal unit and, although all experienced dramatic economic growth and improvement in standards of living throughout the 1950s and 1960s, economic differences between the individual federal units did not decrease, as the Federal Government had hoped; quite the contrary. Bosnia and Herzegovina, which had only been slightly below the Yugoslav average in the immediate post-war years, fell more and more behind, despite making marked progress in some areas, especially mining and heavy industry. In fact, it is possible to argue that Bosnia and Herzegovina suffered most in terms of the widening gap between the federal units of Yugoslavia.[6] Falling increasingly further below

---

[5] 'Intervju: Pavle Lukač, direktor sektora za štampu i informiranje 'ZOI 84. Vučko pada na nos', *Polet* 206, 6.10.1982, 6–7.

[6] According to *The Great Geographic Atlas of Yugoslavia*, in the period between 1955 and 1984 Bosnia and Herzegovina's GDP per capita fell from 83% to 69% of the Yugoslav aver-age (*VGAJ* 1987, 60).

the Yugoslav average, the republic continued to be an underdeveloped region, depending on federal funds for capital investment.

Yugoslavia's economic decentralisation coincided with the Yugoslav government's serious investments in tourism. In this situation, Bosnian officials reacted by investing in tourism too, seeking to attract increased federal funds. As in the rest of the country, the main target was to attract more Western tourists.[7] However, Bosnia could not compete with Croatia and Montenegro, which both had long coastlines catering to summer tourism, or with Slovenia that profited by having the best infrastructure and being geographically closest to the West. Nor could Bosnia compete with Serbia or Macedonia which both had much more developed traffic infrastructure and were on the main road route between Western Europe and Greece and Turkey. It was in this situation that the Bosnian officials read and discussed implementing the 1968 report by the OECD—a report that, as noted, claimed that Sarajevo and its vicinity had all necessary conditions and should therefore seriously consider an Olympic bid (Vuic 2015, 29).

As also noted, the paper did not gain currency immediately after being commissioned. Instead, it was largely ignored for a few years, until, according to Jason Vuic (2015, 30), some sport enthusiasts in the city council picked up on the idea of Sarajevo's candidacy in 1973. It was then presented to Artur Takač, a Yugoslav-born technical director at the International Olympic Committee (IOC) in Lausanne, and to Boris Bakrač, a high-ranking federal politician and a former Mayor of the Croatian capital, Zagreb. The former, Takač, would later become a central personality in lobbying for Sarajevo, while the latter, Bakrač, would be remembered for making a joke to the effect that 'Sarajevo should go ahead and submit the bid, but pray to God not to get it'.[8]

The idea was then discussed back and forth—both on the level of the Sarajevo City Council and the Government of Bosnia and Herzegovina— before it was turned down based on the widespread view that it was too early for the city to pose its Olympic bid. The logic behind this decision was, that in 1973 Sarajevo was a mess, as Jason Vuic (2015, 31) puts it in his depiction of the development. He was referring to Sarajevo's problem

---

[7] As Kate Meehan Pedrotty (2010, 336) puts it, the foreign tourists had been 'Yugoslavia's bread and butter since the mid-1960s'.

[8] 'Dobro nam došla olimpijado', *Nedeljna Borba* (Specijalni dodatak povodom 14. zimskih olimpijskih igara), 4–5.2.1984, 1.

with water and air pollution and the fact that much of the city's infrastructure was in rather poor shape. According to the official figures, presented by Vuic (2015, 31), a full 30% of Sarajevo's residents still got their water from backyard wells rather than pipelines. Waste from the sewer system flowed directly into the Miljacka River,[9] while the larger part of residents still used coal-consuming stoves in their everyday lives. In addition to several large air-polluting factories in the city and its close surroundings, some 400 furnaces provided the city with heating during the winter months (Vuic 2015, 31). The geographical position of the city was the final straw. Sandwiched between mountains, Sarajevo lacked the air circulation to shift the polluted air. As a result, heavy smog would form in the city during winter months, often lasting for several days in a row. Hence, in order for its bid for the Olympics to be seriously considered, the city had at least to start working on solutions to some of these problems.

On the positive side, and independently of the Olympic idea, city officials had already recognised these environmental issues by the early 1960s. They launched a massive $72-million public initiative called the Project for the Protection of [Sarajevo's] Human Environment, founded by a loan from the World Bank and maintained through so-called voluntary financial contributions from the citizens of Sarajevo. The loan from the World Bank was the largest Yugoslavia had received up until then, and the 'voluntary contributions'—according to Vuic (2015, 30) equalling 1.19–2.5% of the pay cheques of employed Sarajevans—were carried out in four separate increments, usually lasting for a year, in the period between 1962 and 1982. However, as discussed in the next chapter, contemporaries viewed the Project for the Protection of the Human Environment and those relating to preparations for the 1984 Winter Olympics as constituting a single terribly needed project to improve and modernise the city.

As results of the Project's initiatives became increasingly visible in the early 1970s, the idea of bidding for the Olympics became more realistic. In consequence, almost precisely a year before the decision on the venue for the 1984 Olympics was supposed to be made in Athens, the Preparation Committee, Sarajevo's bid committee, came into being in May 1977. It is

---

[9] According to Aida Ličina Ramić (2017, 129), a test of the quality of water in the Miljacka in the early 1970s showed that at times up to 71% of the water in the river originated in the city's sewers.

noteworthy that throughout this time Sarajevo's City Council, the Yugoslav Olympic Committee and the Union of the Organisations for Physical Culture of Yugoslavia were all quiet about the idea. In fact, the sources show how careful these organisations were about keeping a lid on the Sarajevo candidacy. They even warned journalists from the public service media covering their meetings not to bring the story about the Olympic nomination idea to the wider public. At the Yugoslav Olympic Committee meeting in May 1977, Ljubiša Zečević, a professor of Physical Fitness and Sport at the University of Sarajevo, told those assembled that this was a 'semi state secret' not to be leaked out to the public.[10] Half a year later the country's Olympic Committee still requested from the press members participating in the meeting not to rush and report on the story, before there was some more concrete response from the IOC.[11] Hence, only after the first positive international reactions to Sarajevo's bid surfaced, and when the chances of winning the bid substantially increased, did the first articles on the topic appear in the Yugoslav media.

Meanwhile, in October 1977, the Preparation Committee wrote and submitted the proposal for Olympic candidacy. It did so, in accordance with the custom, in both English and French. At the time, several other cities were announcing their candidacies. However, in the end only two other cities applied: Japan's Sapporo, which had already hosted the 1972 Winter Olympics and Sweden's second largest city, Gothenburg. After registering their candidacy, Artur Takač, 'the Yugoslav man' in Lausanne, took over, doing the hard-lobbying work. According to Jason Vuic, Takač's main strategy was to disqualify Sapporo. Among the leaders of the IOC, the Japanese bid was the preferred one, due to Sapporo's already having all the necessary facilities. This was not an unimportant issue, as the American city of Denver, Colorado, had recently withdrawn from hosting the 1976 Winter Olympics, mostly due to disagreement on how to finance the Games and their potential environmental impact on nearby rivers.[12] In this situation, the IOC chose to award the Games event to the Austrian city of Innsbruck, because it had all necessary infrastructure due to having hosted the 1964 winter Olympics. In response to these circumstances,

---

[10] Jugoslovenski Olimpijski Komitet, 'Stenografske beleške sa sednice Predsedništva Jugoslovenskog Olimpijskog Komiteta', 26.5.1977, 48, JOK—832/F-10. Arhiv Jugoslavije [The Archives of Yugoslavia], Belgrade, Serbia.

[11] Jugoslovenski Olimpijski Komitet, 'Stenografske beleške sa Prve sednice Predsedništva Jugoslovenskog Olimpijskog Komiteta', 15.10.1977, 66, JOK—832/F-11. Arhiv Jugoslavije [The Archives of Yugoslavia], Belgrade, Serbia.

[12] For more on this topic see (Berg 2016).

Takač argued that if the IOC held the Games twice in Innsbruck (which hosted the 1976 Olympics due to Denver's withdrawal) and twice in Sapporo, it would be giving 'the impression that there [was] something of a crisis in winter sports' (Vuic 2015, 34).

Compared to Sapporo, the Gothenburg bid was somewhat less 'dangerous' for Sarajevo. The logistics were probably too radical for the times, as non-stadium activities were scheduled to take place in resorts hundreds of kilometres away from the city.[13] In contrast, all the activities in Sarajevo were scheduled to take place within a radius of 25 kilometres. For all that, the international press still did not have much faith in Sarajevo's bid at the beginning of the selection process (Vuic 2015, 35). Even the Yugoslav media were rather circumspect and modest in their reporting on the topic, not daring to suggest that Sarajevo had a real chance of winning. Instead they either pointed nervously that Sarajevo came second best at the beginning of the selection process, as for instance the country's largest sports daily, Belgrade's *Sport*, claimed;[14] or almost resignedly hypothesised whether Sarajevo was going to be 'the eternal second', as the high-circulating Belgrade daily *Politika* phrased it.[15] Nevertheless, the hard-lobbying work by the Yugoslav Olympic Committee proved to be surprisingly effective and, at the IOC meeting in Athens on 18 May 1978, Sarajevo was chosen as the host city for the 14th Winter Olympics. Naturally, Sarajevan and Yugoslav press were congratulatory, not least *Oslobođenje*, which had previously written cautiously about Sarajevo's chances, stressing the confidence of Sapporo and Gothenburg during the selection process.[16] Now the Sarajevo daily became rather bold, writing about 'the debacle of the Swedish idea!' and arguing that Sarajevo was almost a natural choice for the Olympics.[17]

Than, a couple of weeks after the city's bid was accepted, in late May and early June 1978, *Oslobođenje* ran a serial about Sarajevo's Olympic candidacy with the idea of presenting the background story to the wider

---

[13] Falun, the proposed venue for the Nordic events, was almost 500 km away, while Hammarstrand (luge) and Åre (alpine disciplines) were both over 800 km away from the city of Gothenburg.

[14] Milan Nikolić, 'Na startu Sarajevo drugo', *Sport* 18.5.1978, 23.

[15] P. Lukač & M. Radojčić, 'Ili prvi ili "večiti drugi"', *Politika* 18.5.1978, 22.

[16] For example Ml. T., 'Realne šanse Sarajeva', *Oslobođenje* 18.4.1978, 13.

[17] Z. Čolić, 'Debakl švedske ideje' & Alija Resulović, 'Čestitke koje nose obavezu', *Oslobođenje* 19.5.1978, 16.

populace.[18] Interestingly, neither the OECD paper nor the lobbying work of the members of the Yugoslav Olympic Committee was mentioned. Instead, the focus was placed on Sarajevo's 'sports enthusiasts' who, according to the daily, had 'worked hard and persistently' for 'ten years' to bring the Winter Olympics to Sarajevo. The serial left an impression of Sarajevo as a predestined winter sports centre and an apparent Winter Olympics host city. Not surprisingly, the daily placed Jahorina's ski resort at the centre of its story, stressing that it had always had the necessary qualities to become a world-class, quality winter sports hub. According to the serial, the world had simply not been noticing these qualities, despite the hard work done by 'Sarajevo's sports enthusiasts' to make it aware of them—until now, that is.

## 2.2    OLYMPIC SARAJEVO AS AN EMERGING WINTER TOURISM CENTRE

After winning the bid, Sarajevo's local government and urban elites began to prepare the city for the Olympics, assembling the Olympic Organising Committee and drafting the so-called Olympic Spatial Plan and the Social Agreement on Organising and Financing the XIV Olympic Winter Games.[19] Once established, the members of the Organising Committee rolled up their sleeves and got down to the hard work of promoting the future Olympic city around the country and the world. The first major milestone in this project was the 1980 Winter Olympics in Lake Placid in the USA. It was here that Sarajevo was going to be 'officially promoted to [the position of] Olympic city', as *Oslobođenje* put it on 14 January 1980, precisely a month before the opening of the Lake Placid Games.[20] However, in accordance with the central argument of this chapter, attaining this position was still only a part of a bigger project of putting Sarajevo on the world map, that is, of turning it into a global winter tourism centre. It is therefore quite interesting that *Oslobođenje*, when reporting from Lake Placid during the Games, titled one of its articles, 'The Name on the

---

[18] Alija Resulović, 'Atinski dnevnik: Kako je Sarajevo postalo domaćin zimske olimpijade '84', *Oslobođenje* 31.5.–8.6.1978.

[19] Izvršno vijeće Skupštine Socijalističke Republike Bosne i Hercegovine, 'Društveni dogovor o organizovanju i finansiranju XIV zimskih olimpijskih igara 1984. godina u Sarajevu'. Historijski Arhiv Sarajevo [Sarajevo Historical Archives], Sarajevo, Bosnia and Herzegovina.

[20] H. Arifagić, '"Srebrna vidra" olimpijskom gradu', *Oslobođenje* 14.1.1980, 9.

World Map'. The article argued that the 1980 Winter Olympics provided an occasion for the promotion of Yugoslavia's winter tourism and of Sarajevo as a winter sports centre. From this perspective, the title of the article clearly implied that, helped by its position as a future Olympic host city, by 1980 Sarajevo had emerged as a winter tourist centre with a place on the world map.[21]

This was a rather big step because, less than fifteen years earlier, nothing was pointing to Sarajevo's becoming a winter sports centre. In fact, in the 1966 *Tourist Guide Through Sarajevo*, the English-language Sarajevo tourist guide mentioned above, no winter sport was mentioned among the most popular recreational activities of Sarajevans. Correspondingly, skiing was not mentioned in relation to the mountains in the city's vicinity, which were assumed to be mostly interesting to mountaineering visitors (Tihić 1966, 31–33). Given that this was the official city tourist guide targeting international tourists, it can be asserted that in 1966—that is, not long before the idea of Sarajevo's Winter Olympics nomination was born—the city's cultural and political elites did not see the city as a touristic winter sports destination at all.

This apparent discrepancy between 1966 and 1980 indicates a substantial shift in representations of Sarajevo as a winter sports and tourist centre. To understand this, its dynamics and course, two sources comparable to the 1966 *Tourist Guide Through Sarajevo* can help map this shift. These are the two editions of the official, illustrated, English-language Sarajevo monograph, published in 1975 and 1983 respectively. Simply called *Sarajevo*, the two editions (Prohić and Balić 1975 and 1983), combined with the 1966 guide, present an interesting chronological frame for analysis of the influence of the Olympics on representations of the city as a winter tourism centre. Just as the *Tourist Guide Through Sarajevo* was published approximately two years before the idea that Sarajevo could host the Winter Olympics was first conceived, the earlier edition of *Sarajevo* came out a couple of years prior to the city's actually submitting its Olympic bid, while the second edition was published in 1983, that is, in the last year of the city's preparation for the Games. Thus, we have three official publications projecting the official image(s) of the city onto the world screen shortly before three central moments for the Sarajevo Olympics. Given this chronological coincidence, these three books can be regarded as mirrors in which to read official representations of the city shortly before the birth of the Olympic

[21] 'Olimpijski dnevnik: Ime na karti svijeta', *Oslobođenje* 19.2.1980, 15.

idea, before entering the Olympic candidature process and just before the Games themselves. In what follows, I use these three publications to inform discussion of how Sarajevo's sudden appearance as a candidate and, eventually, host city for the Winter Olympics influenced its self-representation as a global winter tourism centre between 1968, when the idea for the Sarajevo Winter Olympics was first mooted, and 1984, when the city hosted the XIV Olympic Winter Games.

While I argue that bidding for and hosting the Olympics strongly influenced representations of Sarajevo, I can hardly stress enough that these transformations were in no way solely a result of this. The Olympics did not occur in a vacuum, but in a symbiotic interrelation with both the development of the global tourist culture and internal Yugoslav socio-politico-historical development. For this reason, when mapping changes in representations in (pre-) Olympic Sarajevo we must pay very close attention to the broader socio-political context, Yugoslav and global alike.

The 1966 *Tourist Guide*, a book in a small, rather modest format with black-and-white illustrations, gave an impression of a city and a country that had only just begun opening its doors to international tourism. While the text certainly indicates that the authors were well aware of Sarajevo's tourist potential, it was presented in a rather vapid way, even shyly. It had compulsory sections covering topics such as nature, history, sport, the ethnic composition of the population, the economy and culture. It is also noteworthy that WWII and the so-called People's Liberation Struggle— the resistance fighting that occurred during the war—were given considerable space. This was hardly surprising, given that the narrative of the People's Liberation Struggle served as the founding myth of Socialist Yugoslavia. Having said that, I nevertheless argue that while the degree of focus on the war might have been specific to Yugoslavia, it must be remembered that this was the pre-1968 period when WWII was still a current theme across the European continent.

It is therefore more striking that this focus was still very much present in the first edition of *Sarajevo*, in 1975, when the idea of nominating the city for a Winter Olympics was starting to gain ground among local elites and the political regime, and Yugoslavia had begun seriously investing in tourism.

On a more general level, this is a fairly typical city monograph aimed at international tourists. The book's design is much more modern and visibly of a higher standard than the 1966 guide, comprising colour photographs accompanied by interesting captions, unlike the 1966 guidebook, in which the black-and-white photographs served exclusively as illustrations for the general texts. However, there are several other elements that make this book interesting in the context of Sarajevo's becoming an international winter tourism centre—most notably its focus on the city's modernity. While paying due attention to its history and historical heritage, *Sarajevo*'s 1975 edition places the city's modernity in the foreground, not least in respect to the different leisure activities available in its modern urban society. This is an aspect almost completely missing in the 1966 guide. To understand this change we have to take into account socio-cultural development in Yugoslav society more broadly.

Daniel J. Goulding (2002 [1985], 111), the historian of Yugoslav film, argues that in the quarter of a century from the end of WWII to the early 1970s, Yugoslavia had accomplished a remarkable transition from a predominantly rural and small-town-based society based on an agrarian economy to an increasingly modern, urbanised and industrial state. This transition accelerated throughout the course of the 1960s, after the necessary level of material prosperity was attained (Bojičić 1996, 30–31). Thus, when the idea for Sarajevo's Olympic nomination was gaining momentum in the mid-1970s, Yugoslavs were already accustomed to modern urban living and the leisure activities that increasingly characterised such a lifestyle. I return to this issue in Part Two, where I deal in more detail with the modernity dimension of the Sarajevo Olympics. For now, I want to stress that this socio-cultural shift was explicitly formulated in the 1975 edition of *Sarajevo*.

To this end, the monograph stressed the modern urban character of the city, placing physical and cultural modernisation at the centre of its narrative. Nonetheless, compulsory sections on history, the economy and ethnic composition are still included in the traditional manner, and WWII also features. With the Olympic nomination still only an idea circulating among local elites and the political regime, and lacking profile in the broader population, it does not come as a surprise that the 1975 edition of *Sarajevo* still placed mountaineering above skiing. This said, winter sports had nevertheless now gained a place in the presentation of the mountains around the city. Jahorina merited several pages of illustrations, while the monograph's authors claimed that 'few towns [had] in their immediate vicinity as beautiful a mountain as Sarajevo's Jahorina'. Described as being 'amongst the most attractive winter sports centres in Yugoslavia', this 'snowy beauty' was already an internationally established ski centre which 'starting in 1974 became one of the venues for the

European Alpine Skiing Cup Championships'. In addition, in the textual follow-up section under 'Excursions', Jahorina was described as 'becoming an ever more famous winter sports centre'.

This indicates that even before and without the Olympics, Sarajevo had started slowly developing into an international ski centre. However, what the monograph did not tell readers is that Jahorina only became a Euro-Cup venue because the original location, Maribor's Pohorje Ski Resort in Slovenia, did not have enough snow to host it that year.[22] Leaving this information out, the book nonetheless went on claiming that in 'the winter of 1974/75 Jahorina was practically the only mountain in Europe on which it was possible to hold a big international skiing competition'. It is equally noteworthy that also some of the other future Olympic venues were mentioned and described as sites where there were 'beautiful slopes suitable for skiing, tobogganing and other winter pleasures'.[23] However, the monograph did not yet dare to ascribe any international significance to these venues. Finally, Sarajevo's Skenderija cultural and sports centre, opened in 1969, was given its own short section in which the authors awarded it special attention as it represented 'a symbol and a sight of modern Sarajevo'.

It should also be noted that the monograph spoke of Sarajevo as 'a town'. This would change by 1983 when the second edition of the monograph was published wherein the opening sentence was altered from 'Sarajevo is a *town* which, today, has before it increasingly certain, new and modern prospects' to 'Sarajevo is a *city* which today stands face to face with its increasingly specific, new and modern prospects'. This change indicates an increased self-confidence that could easily be the result of winning the bid for the Olympics and many subsequent positive reactions from around the world, which meant that things had changed considerably by the time the second edition of *Sarajevo* came out. To explain this change, I will draw attention to the intertextual context of the second edition of *Sarajevo* and to that end bring in a 1982 serial in the city's main daily, *Oslobođenje*.

It was published in December 1982 under the title 'The Sarajevo Olympic Time Machine' (*Sarajevski olimpijski vremeplov*). By this time, several planned Olympic venues had already received initial recognition from international experts and sportsmen. Hence, the serial's first series told readers that internationally acclaimed ski jump architect, Slovenian Janez Gorišek, had explained to the daily back in April 1980 that Sarajevo's

---

[22] B. Radosavljević, 'Sarajevski olimpijski vremeplov (5): Jahorina—Kolijevka igara' 18.12.1982, 9.

[23] The mentioned mountains were *Bjelašnica* and *Trebević*.

Igman Mountain provided superb conditions for future ski jumps, of a quality rarely seen anywhere in the world.[24] A couple of days later, the daily repeated positive comments on the Trebević Bobsleigh and Luge Track offered by Heinz Deering, Austrian president of the International Luge Federation Committee. *Oslobođenje* used the occasion to explain how the track was innovative, extraordinary and unique as it was the first to combine bobsleigh and luge.[25] A few days later, it was the turn of down-hill bronze medal winner at the Alpine World Ski Championship 1982, Austrian Anton Steiner, who was quoted as praising the organisers and the facilities on the newly built Bjelašnica Mountain Olympic Ski Centre. Notably, this article in the serial was named 'Bjelašnica. From Wilderness to World Centre',[26] appearing the day after an article that had been named Jahorina 'the cradle of the Olympics'. Claiming that Jahorina's skiing tra-dition was 'the germ' from which the idea for Sarajevo's Olympic nomina-tion was born, the newspaper explained that as a ski resort which, even prior to the Olympics, already had most of the necessary facilities, the least construction work had been done there of any of the resorts during prepa-rations for the Olympics.[27] Jahorina's position as 'the cradle' of the Sarajevo Olympics was also affirmed when the mascot of the Sarajevo Olympics, later globally known as Wolfie (Vučko, the Little Wolf), was initially named Jahorinko (Image 2.1).[28]

With the intertextual context in which the second edition of *Sarajevo* was published being established, some important disparities between the two editions become apparent. Not surprisingly, one of the things that immediately stands out is that the 1983 edition covered all the Olympic venues individually. Naturally, as they were only a year away, the textual section of the monograph also discussed the Olympics, noting that 'Mounts Jahorina, Bjelašnica, Igman and Trebević [had] become excep-tionally attractive places for winter sports'. Nonetheless, the People's Liberation Struggle was still there, albeit more implicitly: 'On what were

[24] B. Radosavljević, 'Sarajevski olimpijski vremeplov (1): Ljepotice Malog polja', *Oslobođenje* 13.12.1982, 8.

[25] B. Radosavljević, 'Sarajevski olimpijski vremeplov (3): Trebevićke inovacije', *Oslobođenje* 15.12.1982, 11.

[26] B. Radosavljević, 'Sarajevski olimpijski vremeplov (6): Bjelašnica—Od bespuća do svjetskog centra', *Oslobođenje* 19.12.1982, 11.

[27] B. Radosavljević, 'Sarajevski olimpijski vremeplov (5): Jahorina—Kolijevka igara', *Oslobođenje* 18.12.1982, 9.

[28] V. Spahović, 'Tri nagrade čekaju prvu', *Oslobođenje* 12.2.1981, 12.

**Image 2.1**  An early image of the Sarajevo Olympics mascot, originally named Jahorinko. (V. Spahović, 'Tri nagrade čekaju prvu', *Oslobođenje* 12.2.1981, 12)

once the sites of legendary battles in the long struggle for freedom ski-runs now intertwine and there are many attractive sporting terrains and facilities'. We see here how the Olympics mediated the direction of change in the representations of the city, shifting the focus on the Struggles during WWII towards leisure and recreational activities in the present time.

Furthermore, urban sport venues are now being discussed in terms of their Olympic function—both those built earlier and refurbished and those built exclusively for the Games. The monograph offered a noteworthy caption accompanying the two images from Skenderija cultural and sports centre, one of female basketball and one of an ice-hockey game:

> The splendid conditions that have been created with the construction of 'Skenderija' and ZETRA [the new Olympic Ice Hall] facility have given impetus to certain sports which formerly were less well known in this city. Among them a special place is occupied by basketball; Sarajevo is now one of the leading centres for basketball in Yugoslavia. Besides several national trophies, the team 'Bosna' [Bosnia] triumphed in the European Championship. Ice-hockey has received a similar impetus, especially with

the organisation of the Winter Olympic Games, and attracts increasing interest among the young.

Posterity would, in fact, prove this prediction right. Although Sarajevo got its first ice-hockey club in 1953, it no longer had one when the city's officials decided to bid for the Olympics in the mid-1970s. History had it that only a few years after its instigation, enthusiasm for the club disappeared, not least due to the lack of an arena where games could be played. The club was disbanded, leaving the city without ice hockey until 1980, when, in the spirit of hosting the Winter Olympics, the idea was resurrected, and the city got its new ice-hockey club. Named Bosna (Bosnia), just like its basketball counterpart, the ice-hockey club moved rapidly upwards to the Yugoslav First Ice-Hockey League. As a novelty in Yugoslavia, with previously no foreign nationals playing in the Yugoslav ice-hockey clubs, Bosna signed a Czechoslovakian coach along with several Canadian and Czechoslovakian players. In addition, the Sarajevo club also signed several already recognised Yugoslav players, accelerating Bosna's success, now also in the Yugoslav First Ice-Hockey League. In turn, the team's success made the sport increasingly popular in the city, culminating in the 1986–1987 season, when Bosna made it to fifth place in the Yugoslav Championship. This occurred only a few years after the second edition of *Sarajevo* was published, which had featured a picture of Zetra still under construction.

While Ice-Hockey Club Bosna started by playing in Skenderija, where it remained until it moved to Zetra upon its completion in February 1982, the opening of the speed skating rink at the Zetra Olympic Complex meant the emergence of a completely new sport in the city. In March 1983, when *Sarajevo* (2nd ed.) was probably already in publication, Zetra's first major event, the 1983 World Junior Speed Skating Championship, was held at the skating rink. In its final reportage immediately before the opening of the event, *Oslobođenje* had it that speed skating was 'A New Sport Discipline in the Hearts of Sarajevans'.[29]

As already argued, the second, 1983, edition of the monograph showed a sense of self-confidence, and even boldness, not present in the 1975 edition, the reason for which should be sought in the success of the Olympic nomination strategy of stressing the proximity of the sporting sites to the city. Accordingly, the 1983 edition of the monograph translated this

[29] O. Đoković, 'Novi sport u srcima sarajlija', *Oslobođenje* 5.3.1983, 12.

success into a story of Sarajevo's uniqueness, arguing that the city was a perfect winter sports centre even beyond the Olympics:

> The world of nature and urban amenities are in unique proximity here. The Olympics terrains and installations are situated within a radius of 22.5 km, which is considered one of the most ideal concentrations in the world. Facilities for all winter sports are scattered within this narrow radius, which enables devotees of various winter-sport disciplines to very quickly reach the skiing terrains, the bobsled and sledging runs, the ice-skating rinks, the ski-jumping installations, the biathlon stadium etc., and afterwards return to enjoy the city, which offers many historical, cultural and artistic attractions and wide variety of entertainment.

With the second edition now covering—with illustrations and thorough descriptions—all the Olympic mountains, the first edition's single-minded focus on Jahorina had vanished. Yet, although the coverage of the Olympic mountains was now more dispersed, there was no doubt that Jahorina, 'the white beauty', still occupied a special position and was celebrated for 'its excellent skiing terrains [...] renown as a first-class winter-sports centre long before the Olympics'. In fact, the Olympics, claimed the 1983 edition of the monograph, 'have merely accelerated the development of this resort'. Furthermore, in contrast to the 1975 edition, in which some of the other smaller and non-Olympic mountain ski resorts were only mentioned in passing, the 1983 edition also brought illustrations with accompanying captions of such places.[30] This clearly indicates that Sarajevo now saw itself as a winter sports centre offering more than just Olympic venues and installations.

That said, the monograph still emphasised that the Olympics marked a 'historic step' in the development and affirmation of winter sports in the city and its vicinity, as well as the whole of Yugoslavia. One of the emerging Olympic and winter sport centres to which the monograph now paid attention was Mount Bjelašnica, stressing that prior to the Olympics this ski resort had commonly been viewed as isolated and inaccessible, until the Olympics had altered all that. This wording describing how Bjelašnica evolved from 'isolated wilderness' into a world ski centre resembled that in *Oslobođenje*'s serial, 'The Sarajevo Olympic Time Machine', and also the 1958 *Tourist Encyclopaedia of Yugoslavia* descriptions of Jahorina (*TEJ*

---

[30] This was most notably the case with Pale and Koran.

1958, 130) as isolated and only connected with the city of Sarajevo. While by the mid-1970s Jahorina was commonly considered an affirmed world-class ski resort, and was in the early 1980s defined as 'the cradle of the Sarajevo Olympics', by the fall of 1983 it became a common practice to call Bjelašnica 'the most attractive Olympic site'.[31]

It is also interesting that in 1983 mountaineering is only mentioned after skiing and other winter sports, now appearing as a secondary, or even lower-grade attraction. Nonetheless, the monograph still claimed that 'mountain-climbing and mountain-walking [were] sports which [had] been highly regarded and loved in Sarajevo since long ago'. Finally, yet another novelty in the 1983 edition was the way in which it embraced Sarajevo's newly won position in the world electronic media:

> Thanks to the TV camera Sarajevo and its environs, and in particular the Olympic terrains, have become accessible to the whole world. Throughout the participation of all the world's RTV companies in direct broadcasts of the XIV Olympic Winter Games, the beauties of Sarajevo and of mounts Jahorina, Trebević, Igman and Bjelašnica become, in a way, the 'property' of the entire world—intimate and accessible landscapes in all meridians of the world.

In a very similar manner, *Borba* (Struggle or Combat), a Belgrade-based organ of the Yugoslav Federal Government, wrote how 'the times are such that there is no sporting competition without television'. 'The cameras are making it possible for the whole world to watch the Games', emphasised the Belgrade daily, while adding that providing high-quality TV coverage is sometimes more complicated than organising the sporting events themselves. Given these observations, it does not come as a surprise that *Borba* chose to title this January 1984 article, 'The Olympics for the Whole World'.[32] This appeared only a couple days after another article on the topic, called, very interestingly in the context of this book, 'The World Journalism Centre'.[33]

The latter title, as well as the 1983 monograph's captions, clearly exposes the local/global dimension of the Olympics that is at the centre of this part of the book. While being localised in space and time—in a particular city and period—the Olympics are also national and, importantly,

[31] B. R. 'Točkić', *Oslobođenje* 16.10.1983, 7.
[32] Dragan Nikitović, 'ZOI za ceo svet', *Nedeljna Borba* 21–22.1.1984, 16.
[33] R. Mučibabić, 'Novinarski centar sveta', *Borba* 19.1.1984, 10.

international and global. This international and global aspect of the Olympics is closely related to the idea that the event is—from the point of nomination to the final closing ceremonies—always mediated. In other words, the Olympics provide the opportunity for host cities to project themselves onto the world screen. As such, the Olympics are, as Maurice Roche (2000, 10) puts it, at the very least 'news'. Yet, in the late twentieth century they became increasingly also 'more than news'. Olympic Games events have unavoidably also become *media events* with the 'participation' of a global audience. It is noteworthy, in this context, that the Olympics developed from the late nineteenth century parallel to, and as Roche phrases it, 'in a kind of symbiotic interaction with', the development of different forms of mass media. For this reason, event organisers were always extremely interested in connecting up with the latest mass communication technologies in order to promote and disseminate their event. This was almost certainly the main reason why Sarajevo and Yugoslavia put so much effort into developing the new integrated IT solutions mentioned in the introduction to this chapter. These IT solutions supported almost all the areas that are supported by today's systems. The results system integrated in the solutions processed results in real time and was directly interfaced with timing and judges' devices (Sakac 2008, 106). In line with this, *Borba* wrote about new 'analytical' cameras, providing the previously unavailable opportunity to analyse every detail of the sporting competitions.[34]

The system also provided TV output graphics at all venues, so TV commentators were, for the first time ever, able to broadcast from all venues, as well as the International Broadcasting Centre, at the same time. Furthermore, INFO system terminals allowed retrieval of Games databases and were installed at all venues and at the Olympic village. The result was that the international news press agencies could now easily receive online-like results data feeds, and all the Games' participants were accredited through the system as well (Sakac 2008, 106). In the final sections of this chapter I examine more closely how this global aspect of the Olympics affected self-representations of Sarajevo by leading to an increasing awareness among the local population of their city's uniqueness. Before that, however, the following section examines the economic aspect of the Olympics.

[34] Dragan Nikitović, 'ZOI za ceo svet', *Nedeljna Borba* 21–22.1.1984, 16.

## 2.3    THE CULTURAL AND THE TEMPORAL IMPLICATIONS
## OF THE OLYMPIC ECONOMICS

Marking the 37th annual liberation day of the city on 6 April 1982, *Oslobođenje* published a special supplement about the present state of things in the city. Entitled 'On the Day of Liberation—Sarajevo', it included an article dealing with the upcoming Olympics. The article, titled 'Towards the 14th Winter Olympic Games "Sarajevo '84". Honour and Duty', discussed preparations for the Games. The story told in the article had it that from the very beginning the Olympics were welcomed in the city as a 'unique opportunity for economic development of not only Sarajevo, but also its broader region, the republic [of Bosnia and Herzegovina], and even the whole country'. For this reason, it was argued, investments related to the hosting of the Olympics should not be viewed as only concerning 'those approximately fifteen days' that the Olympic competitions were set to last. They also pertained to 'the post-Olympic period' and the development of what the daily called the 'white industry' which would, according to the article, lead to foreign currency 'snowing' on the city. This was so, the daily argued, because with the Olympics Sarajevo was set to become an international winter sports centre which, due to its hosting such an important winter sports competition as the Olympics, would soon 'find its way into brochures and tourist maps, all around the world'.[35]

As we will shortly see, this type of writing was in many ways typical of the Olympic preparation period. In its references it did not only inscribe itself in the dominant discourse of the time. It also accurately summed up the central elements of the discourse concerning the economic aspect of the Sarajevo Olympics. First, in talking about Olympic investments as contributing to general economic development, *Oslobođenje* embraced the idea that the Olympics would boost the economy in the city and beyond. Second, it placed the emphasis on the post-Olympic period, arguing, as was common at the time, that the economic impact of the Games reached far beyond the short-term sporting event. Third, in employing the notion of 'white industry'—which referred to the development of tourism based on the city's newly won position as a winter sports centre—*Oslobođenje* also defined the direction of this potential and desired economic development. Finally, and in relation to this position, by talking metaphorically of

---

[35] 'U susret XIV ZOI "Sarajevo '84". Čast i obaveza', *Oslobođenje (specijalni dodatak 'Uz dan oslobođenja—Sarajevo')* 6.4.1982, 3.

'snowing' foreign currency, the newspaper implied that the city specifically aimed to attract more foreign tourists.

The potential economic impact of the Olympics was at the centre of Sarajevo's Olympic idea from the beginning. As we saw earlier, this idea was first conceived by the OECD, an intergovernmental economic organisation focusing its work on stimulating economic development. The organisation's 1968 paper on Sarajevo's possibilities for hosting the Winter Olympics would in subsequent years become a central document to which all the relevant decisive bodies would refer. This was also the case with the proposal for the city's Olympic candidacy, drafted by the Preparation Committee for the Sarajevo Olympics on the last day of September 1977. In the proposal the Committee linked the OECD's 1968 paper and a 1971 paper 'Possibilities for the Development of Skiing in Bosnia and Herzegovina' produced by the Sarajevo Institute for Physical Culture. The proposal explained that the latter paper had been adopted as a guideline for the development of winter sports in Bosnia and Herzegovina by the Executive Council of the republic. According to the Committee, in reaching this decision the Council was particularly convinced by the economic aspect of developing Sarajevo and its vicinity into a winter sports centre and potential host for the Winter Olympics. This aspect was then connected to the 'recent rapid development of winter sports in the whole country, which was in particular happening in Bosnia and Herzegovina', as the Committee put it. Finally, against this background, the Committee argued for Sarajevo's Olympic nomination.[36]

We know the rest of the story. The Yugoslav Olympic Committee accepted the proposal and offered its support before it was sent to the IOC. As already noted, after winning the Olympic bid, the Olympic Organising Committee was constituted in the city. Not surprisingly, at its constitutive meeting in October 1978, the Committee stressed the economic aspect of the Olympics repeatedly. It is also noteworthy that the Committee likewise talked about developing 'the so-called white industry', thereby referring to the development of tourism, or the tourist industry, based on winter sports and recreational activities.[37] From this point of

---

[36] Pripremni komitet za kandidaturu grada Sarajeva za organizovanje zimskih olimpijskih igara 1984. g., 'Prijedlog mogućnosti grada Sarajeva za Zimske Olimpijske igre 1984.g.', Sarajevo 30.9.1977, 3–5, JOK—832/F-11. Arhiv Jugoslavije [The Archives of Yugoslavia], Belgrade, Serbia.

[37] Organizacioni Komitet XIV Zimskih Olimpijskih Igara '84, 'Stenografske bilješke Prve sjednice Organizacionog Komiteta XIV Zimskih Olimpijskih igara 1984', 3.10.1978. Historijski Arhiv Sarajevo [Sarajevo Historical Archives], Sarajevo, Bosnia and Herzegovina.

departure the preparations for the 1984 Sarajevo Winter Olympics began. Among other things, this meant that when the Organising Committee produced the Draft for the Spatial Plan of the Sarajevo Olympics in 1979, its members spent considerable time talking about the economic impact that the Games presumably would have on the city in 'the post-Olympic period'. Resembling the ideas conceived in the OECD paper, the Committee insisted that the Plan's most important long-term goal was the creation of a whole new touristic region with all accompanying services. According to the Plan this would be attained by 'putting "the white industry" into operation'.[38]

Applying the same logic, Ante Sučić, the city's mayor at the time and later the president of the Olympic Organising Committee, argued in an interview for *Oslobođenje*'s new year edition 1979/1980: 'The Olympics are not a parade, nor only a sports event, but a true growth and progress investment'. In the interview, Sučić and Ahmed Karabegović, the general secretary of the Olympic Organising Committee, talked about the cost of the Olympic Games and how a certain part of it went to the infrastructural investments that would have been necessary even if the city did not win its Olympic bid. On this basis they argued that the Olympics were above all an 'economic undertaking' and, as such, would be of benefit for the future generations.[39] A year later, at the December 1980 meeting of the Committee, Sučić once again stressed that the Olympics were an extraordinary 'chance for [economic] development'.[40]

Raif Dizdarević, who was chairman of the Presidency of the Socialist Republic of Bosnia and Herzegovina at the time, also spoke of the Olympics as an 'investment in further [economic] development'. In an early-January 1981 interview for *Naši dani* (Our Days), the official journal of the League of the Socialist Youth of Bosnia and Herzegovina, Dizdarević insisted: 'For us, the Olympics were never solely a big and expensive sporting event. … For us, the Olympics have, from the very beginning when we were deciding whether to place our bid, been a chance for [economic] development.'[41] Dizdarević's wording strikingly resembled that of Sučić and Karabegović, supporting the argument that this was

[38] Organizacioni Komitet XIV Zimskih Olimpijskih Igara '84, 'Nacrt osnove prostornog plana ZOI '84', 1979, 22. Historijski Arhiv Sarajevo [Sarajevo Historical Archives], Sarajevo, Bosnia and Herzegovina.
[39] Kemal Kurspahić, 'Sarajevski koraci u susret 1984. godini. Olimpijske igre—razvojni poduhvat', *Oslobođenje* 31.12.1979, 1.&2.1.1980, 5.
[40] 'Olimpijada—izuzetna razvojna šansa', *Oslobođenje* 25.12.1980, 7.
[41] 'Iz intervjua Raifa Dizdarevića RTS', *Naši dani* 699, 26.12.1980–2.1.1981, 3.

the general view of the Olympics among members of the political estab-lishment. Yet, Dizdarević went even further to specify that the Olympics would provide a big boost for the development of tourism in Yugoslavia and, through tourism, also commerce and the whole service sector.[42]

A few months later, during the spring of 1981, another central figure on the Olympic Committee, the aforementioned Pavle Lukač, now the director of Olympic Press and Information, offered a similar argument. Lukač insisted that the Olympics were a clear incitement for further devel-opment of the city of Sarajevo, asserting that the infrastructure built for the Olympics also served the more general development of tourism and sport in the city. This was not least the case in regard to the modern roads which were built for the needs of the Olympics from the city to the moun-tains of Jahorina and Bjelašnica.[43]

As we see in these examples, when talking about the economic impact of the Olympics, the members of Bosnia's political elite and of the Olympic Organising Committee all placed tourism, implicitly or explicitly, at the centre of economic development. *Oslobođenje*'s cartoonist caught this excellently in February 1982 in a cartoon showing an inscription in which the five Olympic rings were inserted in the place of the letter 'o', to read 'Razv-*o*-j turizma', that is, 'tourism development'. Presented this way, the Olympic rings did not only serve as a substitution for the letter 'o', but also evidently implied that the Olympics were an important element in tourism development plans in Sarajevo. It is also interesting that the per-son depicted as writing this inscription was evidently Branko Mikulić, the President of the Socialist Republic of Bosnia and Herzegovina at that time, and soon to become the President of the Olympic Organising Committee as well (Image 2.2).[44]

Arguably, this was because during the Olympic preparation period, Mikulić had repeatedly stressed the economic impact of the Olympics. On one such occasion, in November 1983, just a few months before they began, he argued that the Olympics were 'a giant development step', meaning an incentive for further economic development. He then explained that the broader populace might not yet be fully aware of this but would certainly very soon be able to see and feel the impact, which

[42] Ibid.
[43] 'Sarajevo među najljepšima', *Oslobođenje Žurnal* 17.5.1981, 6.
[44] Đoko Ninković, 'Bez riječi', *Oslobođenje* 18.2.1982, 3.

**Image 2.2** An *Oslobođenje* cartoon reading 'Tourism development', implying how closely the Olympics were seen in relation to the development of tourism in Sarajevo, its vicinity, Bosnia and Herzegovina, and even the whole of Yugoslavia. (Đoko Ninković, 'Bez riječi', *Oslobođenje* 18.2.1982, 3)

would first fully materialise with the increased inflow of international tourists in the post-Olympic period.[45]

The same idea was expressed, in greater length and detail, a couple of days later in relation to the Day of the Republic, Socialist Yugoslavia's largest public holiday. On this occasion, *Oslobođenje* devoted a whole page, containing two articles, to explaining the short- and long-term impact of the Sarajevo Games on the development of tourism and the city itself. Describing the Olympic venues individually one by one, one of the articles contained similar references to the future as the interview with Sučić and Karabegović. Thus, reflecting Sučić and Karabegović, who talked about the Olympics as an investment and as a benefit for future generations, *Oslobođenje*'s Boro Radosavljević called his article 'The Olympic Investment

---

[45] B. Romano, 'Predolimpijski dani. Igre bez sjenke', *Oslobođenje* 27.11.1983, 2.

in Tomorrow',[46] thereby referring to the post-Olympic future in a manner typical of the time. It is interesting that, a couple of years earlier, while still with the youth periodical *Naši dani*, Radosavljević wrote an article on the Olympics titled 'Sarajevo's Step into the Future'. In the article he noted the connection between the Olympics and an increased inflow of foreign hard currency and claimed that the Olympics were a cost-effective investment. He based his argument on the growing interest in Sarajevo shown by international travel agencies and different sport teams and competitors.[47]

The second article also dealt with the future—the future of tourism in Bosnia and Herzegovina—under the heading, 'The Future Begins in February', referring symbolically to February 1984, when the Olympics would begin. Discussing future developments in tourism in the city with tourism planners from the official Olympic tourist organisation, the newly established Zoitours,[48] the author insisted that 'this was only the beginning'. In continuation of this argument, the article quoted the president of Zoitours, Nedo Mahić. Explaining the organisation's tourist strategies for the immediate post-Olympic period, Mahić insisted that by that time Sarajevo would have built up its global Olympic 'image'. Within the rising global tourism industry, in the post-Olympic future, this image would serve to attract further tourism to the city and its surroundings, claimed Zoitours' president.[49] Similar view was voiced by *Politika* journalist Muharem Durić, who invoked the Yugoslav novelist and the Nobel Prize winner, Ivo Andrić, in his Olympic coverage:

> It is a city—wrote Andrić.
> Yes. Sarajevo has become a big city. Olympic one. With this, its historic, winter it enters into its new development spheres. It is aiming to become a new global winter tourism centre.[50]

[46] Boro Radosavljević, 'Od borilišta do borilišta. Olimpijski ulog za sutra', *Oslobođenje* 28, 29 & 30.11.1983, 5.

[47] Boro Radosavljević, 'Pripreme za 14. zimske olimpijske igre. Sarajevski korak u budućnost', *Naši dani* 699, 26.12.1980–2.1.1981, 22.

[48] Zoi-tours is a compound word referring to the Serbo-Croatian name for the Winter Olympic Games—Zimske Olimpijske Igre, commonly shortened to ZOI.

[49] Boro Radosavljević, 'Bosanskohercegovačke turističke perspektive. Budućnost počinje u februaru', *Oslobođenje* 28, 29 & 30.11.1983, 5.

[50] Muharem Durić, 'Sarajevska olimpijska razglednica: Nadmetanja, radovanja, drugovanja', *Politika* 17.2.1984, 9.

These examples illustrate how the Olympics had become a kind of a benchmark in the city's history and a temporal reference announcing a post-Olympic future. However, this was not an empty temporal signifier, but one impregnated with cultural connotations and meaning. Hence, both the press and the Olympic Organising Committee spoke of the 'Olympics for the twenty-first century',[51] implying that the city's post-Olympic future would be qualitatively substantially different from its pre-Olympic period. At the time, the twenty-first century was synonymous with progress and the desired direction of development. All this was made possible by the Olympics, as it was the Games that 'completely changed the city, by laying foundations for its future', as one of its early post-Olympic publications wrote, referring to the quote taken from the French press (Knežević-Čečez et al. 1984, 91). The Olympics were thus both a temporal and cultural reference which reached far beyond their narrow economic impact, becoming, in fact, an important socio-economic and cultural marker in the city.

Similarly, the Olympics were also believed to be 'the turning point' for tourism in the city, as the secretary of the Sarajevo Tourist Association observed in an August 1983 interview for *Oslobođenje*. Insisting that the Olympics were enriching the tourist offerings in the city, the secretary argued that hosting the Olympics would result in a new, more diverse and a better-quality base for the development of tourism in the city.[52] This idea was not novel. The year before, the city's section of the Socialist Alliance of Working People (SSRN) of Bosnia and Herzegovina, the Bosnian republican branch of the SSRN of Yugoslavia, which was the largest and the most influential mass organisation in the Socialist Federative Republic of Yugoslavia, had argued that the 1984 Winter Olympics provided important motivation and encouragement for development of not only winter tourism, but *continental* tourism in general.[53]

The 1983 edition of *Sarajevo* discussed in the previous section also suggested that the Olympics, and the different facilities built for their purpose, marked a turning point in the development of *continental* tourism in the broader Sarajevo region. Woven into the term 'continental tourism'

---

[51] Ekrem Avdić, 'Intervju "Nedelje": S Olimpijadom u 21. vijek', *Oslobođenje—Nedelja* 28.1.1984, 6.

[52] Darjan Zadravec, 'Ljudi su svjetlost grada', *Oslobođenje* 25.8.1983, 4.

[53] Ekrem Avdić, 'Intervju "Nedelje": S Olimpijadom u 21. vijek', *Oslobođenje—Nedelja* 28.1.1984, 6.

was a strategy that acknowledged the difference between tourism in the hinterland and along the Adriatic coast. Implicated in the idea of the development of 'continental' tourism was the fact that the Adriatic coast, Yugoslavia's major tourist region, held an unassailable position in the country's tourism industry. Stretching from Montenegro through Croatia to Slovenia, and blessed by the Mediterranean climate, it was the favoured destination for tourists, domestic and foreign alike. The Adriatic was, indeed, the epitome of Yugoslavia's tourism, and according to Ljubo Kojoj, the President of the Tourism Board of Bosnia and Herzegovina, 'what the world knew Yugoslavia for before the Olympics'.[54]

Locally, tourism planners and the political leadership of the city of Sarajevo hoped that the Olympics would help transform the character of tourism in the city from 'transit tourism into receptive tourism'.[55] The city had previously been largely a transit point on the route to final holiday destinations—usually on the Adriatic coast—where tourists would, at most, spend a couple of days. The tourist planners and the city's political regime hoped, however, that the Olympics would provide an opportunity to turn the city into a 'receptive' tourist spot—that is, the final destination for tourists and a leading centre for the country's continental tourism—meaning that visitors would stay longer and therefore spend more time and money there. This view was expressed in an *Oslobođenje* article in May 1983 which suggested that, with the Olympics, Stari Grad—the historic, central, Old Town of Sarajevo—would become the number one destination in Yugoslavia's continental tourism.[56] Expressed somewhat less seriously, and very much in line with its general style in writing, the youth periodical, *Naši dani*, jokingly referred to (post-)Olympic Sarajevo as 'Winter Hawaii', where there would be a serious shortage of beds for tourists.[57]

A further perceived tourism opportunity for post-Olympics Sarajevo lay in hosting international conferences and seminars, another idea often mentioned during the Olympic period. For instance, in October 1981, the Olympic Organising Committee, the University of Sarajevo's Faculty for

---

[54] Enver Demirović, 'Poslije Olimpijade: Vrata ostaju otvorena', *Borba* 18–19.2.1984, 4.

[55] This is how the leaders of the new-established 'Olimpik-turs' (Olympic Tours) expressed it on the occasion of 1982 celebration of the city's liberation day. 'Sarajevo: Uz dan oslobodenja: Olimpik Turs. Savremena i renomirana turistička organizacija'. *Oslobođenje* 6.4.1982, 19.

[56] J. Karaga, 'Od suvenira do kreditne kartice', *Oslobođenje* 6.5.1983, 8.

[57] Miroslav Arapovich, 'Olimpijada jeeeeeeeeee!!!—Interview: Vučko (glavom i bez brade) "Auuuu!"', *Naši dani* 803, 10.1.1984, 11.

Sport and Physical Culture, and Tomas Rosandić, president of the Alabama Sport Academy and an American of Yugoslav descent, discussed the possibilities of developing Sarajevo into a global centre for educating sports experts. They proposed organising an international seminar for sports doctors and ski instructors on Mount Jahorina in April 1982 and following that annual summer schools for students and researchers from the US Sport Academies.[58] Although these ideas never materialised, they exemplify how Sarajevo, a city that only a decade or two prior to the 1984 Winter Olympics was not considered an important sports centre—let alone a winter sports centre—could now re-imagine itself as a locus for the education of sports scientists. Furthermore, it demonstrates that ideas about the economic impacts of the Olympics also indirectly influenced the cultural understandings of the city's political leadership and urban elites. In other words, while the economic aspect of the Olympics was at the centre of the Olympic idea and discourse, they also enabled certain cultural imaginaries unthinkable before.

In the remainder of this chapter, I examine some of the imaginaries that emerged with the Olympics but, before that, and in order to conclude the discussion concerning the economic features of the Olympics, I want to stress that hosting the Olympics was not only seen as a chance to change the character of tourism in Sarajevo. As Ahmed Ćatić from the Socialist Alliance of Working People explained at a meeting of the organisation (mentioned above), the Olympics also provided an opportunity to change the general strategy of economic development in Sarajevo, which had previously focused on industrial production (Ličina Ramić 2017, 122). With the Olympics, the possibility emerged of placing more emphasis on development of the service sector.[59] The Socialist Alliance of Working People was not alone in arguing for this change. It was an opportunity also recognised by the City Assembly. Thus, a couple of years later, in September 1983, at a meeting discussing the approaching Games, the City Assembly held that the Olympics presented 'a new direction in the [economic] development' of the city, thereby acknowledging the innovation. Interviewed members of the Assembly explained that the new direction was structured by the natural, material and human resources of the city, while the president of the Assembly's Executive Board, Ešref Korijenić,

---

[58] B. Radosavljević, 'Sarajevo—svjetski centar za obrazovanje sportskih stručnjaka', *Oslobođenje* 22.10.1981, 12.
[59] S. Rakočević, 'Jugoslovenska turistička šansa', *Oslobođenje* 27.10.1981, 7.

suggested that utilisation of these resources in the forthcoming post-Olympic period should enable a significant increase in services and 'have a high net impact in the foreign currency'.[60] Hence, it can be concluded that the tourism planners in Sarajevo looked on the Olympics as a catalyst in the development of a tourist industry targeting foreign tourists in particular (Pedrotty 2010, 336).

## 2.4   THE OLYMPICS AND SARAJEVO'S *OTHERNESS* (IMAGE 2.3)

When, in October 1977, the Preparation Committee submitted Sarajevo's candidacy for the 14th Winter Olympics, it also, in accordance with standard policy, submitted a nomination poster. The poster was a rather simple picture of the city, accompanied by the standard text in English and French, 'Candidate Host for XIV Olympic Winter Games/Candidat Pour les Jeux Olympiques D'Hiver'. The picture, easily recognisable to any Sarajevan was, nevertheless, impregnated with references. It is, in fact, hard to exaggerate the number of possible, yet clear, connotations, or overanalyse its meanings. It showed a panoramic view over the city, taken from the perspective of Trebević Mountain looking downwards over the old part of the city. There are no big modern buildings visible, only old houses and a few smaller buildings with snow-covered roofs. The picture leaves no doubt that the city, its climate and its geographical position have the necessary potential to host the Winter Olympics. It is also interesting that this universalist representation—of an alpine winter city—functions as the picture's background.

In the foreground of the picture we see an old mosque or, more precisely, the white and green wooden minaret of the Havadže Zade Ahmed-Podtakiša mosque, built in 1565. Most Bosnians and Yugoslavs would certainly define it as an 'old Bosnian-style' mosque, easily recognisable for its design and style. Next to it we see a ropeway cable car structure, with two cars passing each other in different directions. Every Sarajevan would recognise this as the Trebević ropeway cable car, one of the landmarks of Sarajevo. Built in 1959—almost 400 years later than the mosque next to it—the ropeway quickly became a symbol of modern urban life in Sarajevo during the late socialist era. This was the period, in which, as noted in the

[60] N.L. 'Zasijedala skupština grada. Olimpijada—novi pravac razvoja', *Oslobođenje* 28.10.1983, 9.

HOST FOR XIV OLYMPIC WINTER GAMES
POUR LES JEUX OLYMPIQUES D' HIVER

CANDIDATE
CANDIDAT

**Image 2.3** A nomination poster for the Sarajevo Winter Olympic Games (Courtesy: Sarajevo Historical Archives)

previous section, Yugoslavia was transforming from a predominantly rural and small-town-based society into a modern industrial state defined increasingly by the way of life characteristic of large cities. By the late 1950s, post-WWII reconstruction was complete and the standard of living substantially improved. Everyday life, especially in the larger urban centres, was increasingly defined by the citizenry's consumption patterns and leisure activities. It was in this period that the Trebević ropeway was built in Sarajevo to take city dwellers on excursions and picnics, away from urban noise and bustle. Fast becoming one of their favourite leisure activities, the ropeway ride took Sarajevans to one of the iconic viewing points over the city. From here, they could see the old part of their city, the popular Čaršija, a view very similar to the one that the Preparation Committee chose for the nomination poster: a poster that embraced, simultaneously, the city's antiquity and modernity, emphasising both the universalism of the Winter Olympics and the uniqueness of Sarajevo's urban character.

The choice of image for the nomination poster indicates how well the Olympics Preparation Committee understood the logic of global intercity competition, which is, according to the arguments proposed by John R. Short and Maurice Roche, integral to the modern Olympics. In describing this competition, Short has gone to some lengths to explain the increasing global media coverage of the Games event and how it provides an opportunity for the marketing of positive images of a potential host city. Hence, the Olympic Games are situated between the global (Olympic) stage and the local (host) city, something aptly summarised by Short in his heading, 'Global stage/local city' (2012, 255–256). Roche (2000, 10) frames it similarly, insisting that despite the Olympics being performed on the global stage, they are always also localised in space and time. According to this argument, the localism of the Olympics consists in the fact that they are as much about concrete embodied participation and spectatorship as about the particularity of place, that is, a host city's 'place' image. What these arguments implicitly tell us is that bidding for and hosting the Olympic Games supplies the potential to foster and strengthen the candidate and host cities' awareness of their peculiarities and uniqueness.

In arguing the above, I do not mean to suggest that Sarajevans were not aware of their city's distinctiveness and the uniqueness of its urban character prior to the Olympics. Sources, including the 1966 *Tourist Guide Through Sarajevo* and the 1975 edition of *Sarajevo*, show that even before they placed their Olympic bid, local elites emphasised that Sarajevo was a unique city in that it was a place where East meets West, or where 'East and West came to a halt', as *Sarajevo*'s 1975 edition put it (Prohić and Balić 1975). What seems to have changed with the Olympics is that the city's exposure to the world brought international (even global) recognition of the city's peculiarity, uniqueness and otherness. As Jason Vuic (2015, 32) shows in his work on the Sarajevo Olympics, before Sarajevo won its Olympic bid, the city was *terra incognita* to most North American tourists, seen, perhaps, as a nameless city 'somewhere in the central boondocks of Yugoslavia', or, due to the industrial pollution, as the 'Pittsburgh of Yugoslavia'. Similarly, prior to the Olympics, Stewart Powell of the *US News & World Report* described Sarajevo merely as a 'grimy industrial city' (Powell 1984, 35).

As the world began to recognise Sarajevo's special qualities during the preparation period, local media responded by diligently transmitting the now mostly positive comments and reactions of the surrounding world. In particular, *Oslobođenje*, the largest and the most influential media outlet in Bosnia and Herzegovina, reported on a daily basis on how the world press was reacting to the future Olympic host city. This had the effect of emphasising the significance of Sarajevo's otherness and particularities in the context of global intercity competition, and strengthening the sense of the uniqueness of the city. Put differently, the result was that while the city increasingly 'turned to the world'[61] and its 'contact with the world' became 'tighter and stronger',[62] as *Oslobođenje* often stressed in its writings of the time, a raised level of contact also made the residents increasingly proud of their city and its peculiarities.

In one of its reports, *Oslobođenje* explained to its readers that, to the world, Sarajevo appeared exotic, quoting American UPI Press in support of this: 'Never before were the Olympics—either summer or winter—held in such an exotic place'.[63] Sources from the period made it very clear that the idea of Sarajevo's exoticism was closely related to the city's Ottoman past, and in particular to the old bazaar, Baščaršija, which is not only the historical and cultural centre of Sarajevo, but also the trademark of the city. Consequently, the restoration of Baščaršija during the Olympic preparation period was valued highly by the local political regime and cultural elites. The five-year plan for the period 1980–1985 proposed by the Tourism Association of Sarajevo and presented in *Oslobođenje* in September 1980 also promoted greater investment in the city's cultural-historical

---

[61] D. Švarc, 'Sarajevo okrenuto svijetu', *Oslobođenje* 8.3.1983, 10.

[62] The president of the Central Committee of the League of Communists of Bosnia and Herzegovina, Hamdija Pozderac, argued that the Olympics provided the city with an opportunity 'to open itself to the world'. In B. Radosavljević 'Olimpijada—još čvršća veza sa svijetom', *Oslobođenje* 27.8.1982, 1.

[63] 'Olimpijska hronika. Strana štampa o ZOI. Egzotičan grad', *Oslobođenje* 23.12.1983, 10.

heritage and in the restoration of old bridges, fountains and the most valuable old house, while calling for the complete renovation of 'the old
Čaršija', that is, Baščaršija. Without such restoration, claimed the planners, Sarajevo
could never develop into a global tourist centre.[64]

Over the next three years, in accordance with the plan, Baščaršija
underwent substantial modernisation, resulting in 'the new glow of
Baščaršija', as an October 1983 issue of *Oslobođenje* had it.[65] However,
opinions about this development were mixed. For instance, in July 1983,
an *Oslobođenje* journalist called for even more to be done, insisting that in
its capacity as city trademark, further necessary means should be found for
a complete restoration to help 'the old *čaršija* become prettier than ever'
for the Olympics.[66] On the other hand, some visitors to the city were
openly critical of too much modernisation of its old sections. Among these
was a Yugoslav family from the town of Pančevo in Vojvodina, who told
an *Oslobođenje* journalist in August of the same year that way too much
modernisation had been carried out. The family disliked the development
which, they thought, had made the old Sarajevo, which they always liked
best, almost disappear.[67]

Undeniably, even if sources often stressed Sarajevo's allegedly distinctive combination of old and new, it was the old, particularly the Ottoman,
Sarajevo that was unique. This was clearly expressed in an August 1983
issue of *Oslobođenje*, which described Sarajevo as 'a mosaic of old and
new'. However, the author's wording clearly indicated that the great age
of the city was the more important element. Hence, according to the
author, visitors staying in 'a modern hotel, could, within few minutes by a
car or tram, reach [...] Baščaršija, a unique old urban complex filled with
numerous handcraft and service outlets and shops, most commonly the
ultimate destination of any tourist'. Moreover, the newspaper's choice of
illustration for the article and its caption made it equally clear that it was
the old Sarajevo that was most interesting: a picture from the old town
accompanied by the text, 'Sarajevo [is] a mosaic of the preserved traces of
various cultures and epochs'.[68]

[64] R. Kolar, 'Hoteli uz stare česme', *Oslobođenje* 10.9.1980, 11.
[65] Lj. Đ., 'Novi sjaj Baščaršije', *Oslobođenje* 16.10.1983, 14.
[66] J.V. 'Uređenje Baščaršije za olimpijadu', *Oslobođenje* 10.7.1983, 6.
[67] El. Ka. 'Gosti grada. Sarajevo je svake godine bogatije', *Oslobođenje*, 13.8.1983, 12.
[68] Darjan Zadravec 'Ljudi su svjetlost grada', *Oslobođenje* 25.8.1983, 4.

The same impression came to the fore in a special Olympic supplement in the Belgrade daily, *Borba*, on 5 February 1984. In an article titled 'Sarajevo, the Olympic City', it was explained that anyone coming to the capital city of Bosnia and Herzegovina for the Olympics 'would experience "more than just sport" because Sarajevo, through its history and its present, represents a real challenge to every single visitor'.[69] *Borba*'s choice of illustrations and accompanying captions was also quite revealing, resembling those of *Oslobođenje*. Thus, next to each other, *Borba* placed a street motif from 'the famous Baščaršija', as the daily put it, and an image of the post-modernist department store, Sarajka,[70] built in the city centre in the mid-1970s[71]; Sarajka was not even named, however, implying a hierarchy wherein the old bazar area was clearly superior to the modern yet left unnamed department store.

Most foreigners were enchanted by Baščaršija. Among them were two young Spaniards who told *Oslobođenje* that 'Sarajevo [was] an exceptionally interesting city—in particular Baščaršija'. There was something 'romantic' about it, they insisted. 'Those small compact shops, mosques, all that [made] the atmosphere great', they explained.[72] Similarly, according to *Oslobođenje*'s January 1984 summary of the international coverage of Olympic Sarajevo, international reporters found Baščaršija's atmosphere and bazaars provided an extraordinary and unique experience. Others stressed 'the authentic smell of Baščaršija' emanating from *ćevapčići*, a grilled minced meat dish typical of the Balkans.[73] In another January 1984 issue the daily invited ESPN journalist Edward G. Pickett to write an article on the city and its Olympics. Pickett stressed:

> In a way, considering the past, I get the feeling that Sarajevo has been preparing for these Games for centuries. There is no athlete who will walk the streets of Baščaršija and not sense the past centuries' atmosphere.[74]

---

[69] 'Sarajevo, olimpijski grad', *Nedeljna Borba* (Specijalni dodatak povodom 14. zimskih olimpijskih igara), 4–5.2.1984, 2.

[70] Sarajevo's (f) Department Store.

[71] 'Sarajevo, olimpijski grad', *Nedeljna Borba* (Specijalni dodatak povodom 14. zimskih olimpijskih igara), 5.2.1984, 2.

[72] El. Ka. 'Gosti grada. Sarajevo je svake godine bogatije', *Oslobođenje*, 13.8.1983, 12.

[73] Melita Karalić, 'Drugi o Olimpijadi. Duga između svjetova i vjekova', *Oslobođenje* 14.1.1984, 5.

[74] Edvard Piket, 'Igre sa stilom i duhom', *Oslobođenje* 8.1.1984, 13.

Thus, experiencing Baščaršija had become inseparable from the Olympics and an important ingredient for the future global winter tourism centre.

Not everyone was equally enthusiastic, however, as exemplified by a journalist from the Austrian daily, *Kurier*, who was, according to *Oslobođenje*'s summary, the only international correspondent critical in his coverage of the future Olympic city. Conveying how 'not even the Olympics [could] erase 500 years under the Turks', the Austrian daily criticised the haggling in the shops of Baščaršija. This said, *Kurier*'s journalist still praised *ćevapčići* and the local cuisine, as well as the hospitality of his hosts and, despite his initial criticism, ultimately concluded that the haggling was a unique Sarajevan attraction that was far from being only about getting the most money possible out of customers.[75] This criticism, as well as the response offered by *Oslobođenje*'s journalist, is in fact very interesting when seen from a broader cultural-historical perspective. There had been a practice among the national elites of the emergent independent Balkan states since the nineteenth century of blaming the Ottoman rule for everything backward in their countries. The trope of 'the centuries-old Ottoman yoke' served throughout the twentieth century (and serves even today) as an easy explanation for the presumed economic and cultural backwardness of the Balkan states. According to this trope, in order to catch up with Western Europe, the Balkans had to shed the Ottoman past and cultural heritage, to which end political and cultural elites in the Balkans constantly emphasised, and even exaggerated, the *European-ness* of their countries.

Consequently, political and cultural elites in Socialist Yugoslavia put considerable effort into raising the salience of the country's Mediterranean and Central-European cultural and architectural heritage. As Dean Vuletić (2008, 861–879) shows in his work on the Eurovision Song Contest, from the 1950s onwards, when presenting the country to a Western-European audience, Yugoslav elites deliberately, and in accordance with the country's cultural policies, chose to use material showing towns and cities situated along the Adriatic coast. It was in this same context that several members of the City's Committee of the League of Communists in 1983 argued that the Olympics were not only providing the city with an

[75] Melita Karalić, 'Duga između svijetova i vjekova', *Oslobođenje* 14.1.1984, 5.

opportunity to become a winter sports centre, but also to 'become a European city'.[76]

For all that, not everyone shared this obsession with becoming 'European'. For instance, a few months earlier, renowned Yugoslav novelist and short story writer, Ćamil Sijarić, locally well-known at the time for his position as a literary commentator on Radio Sarajevo, wrote a somewhat provocative opinion piece called 'Do We Love Sarajevo?' In it, he stressed the importance of restoration and what he called the 'beautification' of the old buildings and streets of Sarajevo. 'Like a little child that we want to "send out into the world", Olympic Sarajevo had to be "washed", "dressed" and "well-behaved", before appearing in front of the world', argued the novelist. Yet, in order to make Sarajevo known around the globe, Sarajevans had to show their city to the world in all its particularities and uniqueness, because, according to the author, Sarajevo was different from any other European city, unlike Berlin, Prague or Vienna, which 'all look[ed] like peas in the pod'. In contrast to these cities, argued Sijarić, Sarajevo was the 'Orient in Europe' and therefore there was no need for Westerners to go any further east, as they 'would not find anything more different, more strange or prettier than what they already had seen in Sarajevo'.[77]

Here we can see how Sijarić turned the presumed disadvantage of Sarajevo's 'Ottoman yoke' into an asset. The 'Orient' was no longer something to be hidden and erased, but, rather, the brand of the city, which should be flaunted and emphasised. It was in this same manner that *Oslobođenje* brushed off *Kurier*'s criticism, by emphasising that 'the Austrians' were the only ones not liking the old Ottoman Baščaršija. This comment was then followed by a section entitled 'Rainbow between the Two Worlds', opening with the sentence, 'But for all other journalists that [had] visited Sarajevo, [and] Baščaršija, its atmosphere and the bazaars were a unique and extraordinary experience'.[78] It is also interesting that the city's uniqueness was represented in the metaphor of a rainbow connecting 'worlds and centuries', as the title of the summary article indicated. A rainbow is a symbol of peaceful coexistence. In Sarajevo's case, this was the presumed peaceful coexistence of the different 'worlds', as well as of the old and new. It was also in this context that the aforementioned article

---

[76] Sl. D. 'Svaki dom olimpijski', *Oslobođenje* 12.10.1983, 9.
[77] Ćamil Sijarić 'Volimo li Sarajevo? *Oslobođenje* 18.6.1983, 9.
[78] Melita Karalić, 'Duga između svijetova i vjekova', *Oslobođenje* 14.1.1984, 5.

claimed that Sarajevo was 'a mosaic of the preserved traces of various cultures and epochs'.[79] Sarajevo was thus not unique only because it possessed a variety of cultural heritages, unlike Vienna, Prague or Berlin, which all only had their European heritage. Sarajevo was even more unique because these different cultural legacies were in harmony with each other.

## 2.5 THE SARAJEVO OLYMPICS AS A MARKER OF THE CITY'S YOUTH'S LOCAL IDENTITY

A couple of weeks after Sarajevo won the Olympic bid, *Start*, the leading lifestyle magazine in Yugoslavia, published a lengthy article discussing the ideas behind the nomination and the forthcoming preparations. The article also included an interview with Ante Sučić, who was mayor of the city at that time. Describing his expectations and hopes in relation to the city's position as the Olympic host city, Sučić proposed the interesting notion that the Games had already started, as they began on the very day that Sarajevo won its bid.[80] Building upon this claim, I want to draw attention to another, more theoretical, argument concerning the Olympics proposed by Maurice Roche. Roche asserts that the Olympics often attain the function of an important temporal and cultural reference point, in relation to which people in the Olympic host cities orient their 'identity work'. In developing this argument, Roche (2000, 5) insists that people in all societies reflect on and periodise their biographies in relation to the readily identifiable and memorable public events that affect them during the course of their lives. This does not only apply to people's responses to major wars and revolutions, but, as Roche points out, also to cultural events of various kinds, including the Olympics. People use these events as temporal and cultural markers of their identity, meaning that the Olympics, despite being short-term sporting events, function as important points of references with long-term cultural perspectives.

Said more concisely, the Olympics have an inherent identity-building function as important temporal and cultural identity markers which are not restricted merely to the event of the Games but span the whole process of preparing and hosting them. This leads me back to Sučić's statement that Sarajevo's Olympic period started already in May 1978, when the city was chosen as the host for the 1984 Winter Olympics. The same

[79] Darjan Zadravec 'Ljudi su svjetlost grada', *Oslobođenje* 25.8.1983, 4.
[80] Željko Žutelija, 'Olimpia na Jahorini,' *Start 244*, 31.5.1978, 18–20.

view was repeated by Sučić some two-and-a-half years later in an *Oslobođenje* article published on the occasion of the mentioned celebration of the 37th annual Sarajevo liberation day in April 1982. As we saw previously, on this occasion, the Sarajevo Olympic Organising Committee opened an exhibition featuring the city of Sarajevo and its preparation for the fast-approaching 1984 Winter Olympics. Along with several other cultural programmes, the exhibition was conceived as part of the cultural festival named 'The Pre-Olympic Days in Sarajevo'. The following day, on 7 April 1982, *Oslobođenje* covered the vernissage and the opening event and published an interview with Sučić—now the president of the Executive Committee of the Olympic Organising Committee. In the interview, Sučić remarked that, despite its name, the festival was not to be seen as a part of the promotional work that the Olympic Organising Committee was performing at the time in the capital cities of Yugoslavia and around the world. In Sarajevo, Sučić insisted, this had already taken place in the days immediately after 18 May 1978, when the city won its Olympic bid. Since then, Sarajevo and Sarajevans had been living with the Olympics, added Sučić. Advancing its argument from Sučić's statement, the daily suggested that, by April 1982, Sarajevans had 'already been living the pre-Olympic days for four years'.[81]

Seen in relation to Roche's argument, Sučić's statements in *Start* and *Oslobođenje*, clearly indicate that the Sarajevo Olympics were viewed as lasting from 1978 to 1984. However, the Olympics did not only emerge as a temporal reference, but also offered themselves as a reference point around which the city's inhabitants structured their cultural identities. Belgrade's bi-weekly magazine *Duga* (Rainbow) paid attention to this in its Olympic issue, noting that 'the Olympics have been an enchanting and magical word in Sarajevo for several years'. In Sarajevo, everything was about the Olympics, wrote the magazine in its reportage from the Olympic city.[82] And indeed, a year earlier, in January 1983, Sarajevo's own *Oslobođenje* published an article claiming that the Olympics had become *the* theme—that is the major reference point—in Sarajevans' everyday lives.[83]

---

[81] E.I., 'Pet prstenova da ih svako nosi', *Oslobođenje* 7.4.1982, 6.

[82] Milomir Marić, 'Sve o zimskoj olimpijadi: Pred početak Olimpijade. Sneško Belić u bosanskom loncu', *Duga* 259, 28.1.1984, 22–23.

[83] F. Arifagić, 'Pahuljica koja se ne topi', *Oslobođenje* 16.1.1983, 5.

In light of these examples, it makes sense to argue that by 1982 or 1983 at the latest the Olympics had become an important marker in Sarajevans' cultural identity and one of the central images associated with the city. This was expressed rather explicitly eleven days after the aforementioned 1982 interview with Sučić, when *Oslobođenje*, reporting on 'The Pre-Olympic Days' festival, now over, claimed that the event showed how much the Olympics had become 'an indispensable trait' in Sarajevans' lives. Moreover, as the title for the article pointed out, the Olympics had resulted in the emergence of '[*n*]*ovi duh grada*'—a new city spirit.[84] It is as well important to point out that *Oslobođenje* was far from the only newspaper suggesting this. This view was also voiced by the official Bosnian youth periodical, *Naši dani*, which claimed that by 1980 or 1981 'the new emergent Olympic spirit was [now] omnipresent and sensed all over the city'.[85] It was also in this spirit that a new trendy café that opened in the spring of 1981 in the basement of the aforementioned department store, Sarajka, was named *Ski 84*,[86] while the city's leading discotheque *Kaktus* situated within the Skenderija sports and culture centre was popularly renamed *Vučko* ('Dom mladih', Skenderija-website).

This development is probably also the reason why it made sense to the periodical's journalist, Miroslav Palameta, to term the city's emerging (post-)new wave music scene, 'The Olympic Wave' in 1982. Describing it, Palameta wrote that its ideas were 'determined by local mythologemes, [which were] refracted through the upcoming global popularity of the city'.[87] What we see here is the renaming of a universal musical genre—new wave—to fit it to the local Sarajevo context, with the choice of name indicating the extent to which the Olympics had become an indelible part of Sarajevans' world-view. In fact, even the metaphor of 'refracting' used by Palameta implies that the Olympics had become a prism through which Sarajevans—at least the younger generation—saw and organised the world around them.

[84] R. Ćerimagić, 'Predolimpijski dani. Da dodamo. Novi duh grada', *Oslobođenje* 18.4.1982, 11.

[85] M. A. (Miroslav Arapovich), 'Olimpijada jeeeeeeeeee!!!—Mali Vremeplov', *Naši dani* 803, 10.1.1984, 10.

[86] E.L., 'Otvoren "Ski 84"', *Oslobođenje* 4.3.1981, 13.

[87] M. Palameta, 'Oni se bude. Sarajevski rokeri sezona jesen/zima 1982', *Naši dani* 765, 10.12.1982, 8–9.

With this in mind, in the following I discuss the bands mentioned in this *Naši dani* article: Bonton Baya,[88] Elvis J. Kurtovich & his Meteors[89] and Zabranjeno pušenje (No Smoking). These three bands comprised the core of an alternative rock scene in Sarajevo in the early 1980s—a scene which would soon produce a subcultural movement known as *Nju primitivizam* (New Primitivism). The movement expressed itself primarily in musical and radio/television form, and in film and video. It came to light as a subcultural way of life in the central Sarajevo neighbourhood of Koševo[90]—in close proximity to several Olympic venues, including Zetra, and swiftly developed as an artistic movement. It remains best remembered for the music of Elvis J. Kurtovich (& his Meteors) and Zabranjeno pušenje, and for its radio and later television comedy show, Top List of Surrealists (*Top lista nadrealista*), a sort of Yugoslav Monty Python show, often ridiculing the political situation in 1980s' Yugoslavia. Towards the end of the decade, what had initially been a small alternative scene would become a central paradigm in Bosnian popular culture, closely associated with the widely popular Youth Programme on Radio Sarajevo and the increasingly self-confident youth press in the Bosnian capital city.

More recently, Pavle Levi (2007, 63) has argued that New Primitivism was all about the exploration of identity; an assertion already made by analysts contemporaneous with the movement. *Naši dani*'s Zlatko Hadžidedić, for instance, drew attention to the close relation between the emergence of New Primitivism and the awakening of a new socio-cultural self-consciousness among young Sarajevans in September 1984. Hadžidedić related this awakening to the appearance of Emir Kusturica's film debut in 1981, the internationally acclaimed *Sjećaš li se, Dolly Bell* (Do You Remember, Dolly Bell?). A coming of age story set in the summer of 1963 in Sarajevo, *Sjećaš li se, Dolly Bell* was a novelty in the way that it embraced Sarajevo's cultural distinctiveness, which also triggered awareness of a unique local Sarajevan identity among young Sarajevans. It was heavily peppered with easily recognisable local cultural references, not least from popular culture. According to Hadžidedić, all New Primitive

---

[88] A pun counterposing the words Bonton (Etiquette) and Baya (pronunciation version of the word 'baja' meaning 'uncultured' or 'having bad manners').

[89] Pronounced as Elvis G. Kurtović (cf. pronunciation 'tj').

[90] Vlado Pandža, 'Zabranjeno pušenje. Primitives long live now', *Džuboks* 181, 10.1984, 12–13.

bands, in one way or another, reacted to this film.[91] What is particularly interesting here is that *Sjećaš li se, Dolly Bell* appeared in the period 1980–1981, described by *Naši dani* as when the Olympic spirit of Sarajevo reached fruition. Moreover, the film's embrace of the city's cultural distinctiveness greatly resembled the general trend in the city in those years described in the previous section.

Appearing in this socio-cultural context at a time when Sarajevo was being inseparably associated with its position as an Olympic host city, the New Primitives appropriated this position to the extent that the Olympics became a bearer of their subcultural identity. To understand this process fully, New Primitivism must be situated in the specific popular-cultural context of Yugoslav rock music culture. In this respect, I want to stress that in Yugoslavia of the early and mid-1980s, New Primitivism was often described by the youth press as being a part of Yugoslav new wave.[92] However, unlike new wave, which was considered a Yugoslav-wide (and even universal) phenomenon, New Primitivism was limited to Sarajevo. As such, and despite some important musical similarities, New Primitivism distinguished itself from new wave by its pronounced focus, in its style and aesthetics, on the local. The poetics of New Primitivism were poetics of the local, as the historian of Yugoslav new wave, Dalibor Mišina, puts it (2010, 266–267). Drawing upon the Sarajevan socio-cultural milieu for its philosophy and praxis, New Primitivism manifested itself in an alleged anti-intellectualism and the use of local icons and lexical properties, observed a contemporaneous source in the major Croatian youth periodical of the time.[93]

It does not, therefore, come as a surprise that New Primitives were sensitive to their city's uniqueness, both physical and cultural. Thus, for instance, both Elvis J. Kurtovich and Zabranjeno pušenje wrote songs titled with reference to the city's trademark, Baščaršija. Elvis J. Kurtovich's 'Baščaršy[94] hanumen' (Baščaršija Lady) is probably the earliest New

---

[91] Zlatko Hadžidedić, 'Ponovo o primitivcima. Kako se babo Atif vratio kući' *Naši dani* 820, 14.9.1984, 12; It should also be noted that besides being a film director, Emir Kusturica was also bass-guitarist of Zabranjeno pušenje, what makes the connection even closer.

[92] Among others by *Mladina, Polet, Naši dani*, and *Mladost* (For more on this see Jovanovic 2014).

[93] Stanko Brezarić, 'Tko sam ja, dr. Nelle Karajlić? (2): Shockirash me, majke mi', *Polet* 315, 31.5.1985, 27.

[94] Baščaršy is a pun and a typical pseudo-Anglicisation of Baščaršija created by ending the existing word (similarly to Bonton Baya) with the letter 'y', which does not exist in Serbo-Croatian.

Primitive song as its demo was first recorded in 1982 (EJK 1984).[95] This was also one of the songs that later the same year prompted the *Naši dani* article on Sarajevo's emerging (post-)new wave scene to dub this scene 'the Olympic wave', although the song did not mention the Olympics in any way, rather playing strongly on Sarajevo's cultural distinctiveness. This was done very much in the spirit of the time, notably recalling the motifs and style of Emir Kusturica's *Sjećaš li se, Dolly Bell*. Zabranjeno pušenje, on the other hand, chose the song 'Anarhija All Over Baščaršija' (Anarchy All Over Baščaršija) as the opening song for their 1984 debut LP (ZP 1984b). Although this song is naturally not mentioned in the *Naši dani* article—as it only appeared later—the way it connected punk rock and Sarajevo's cultural uniqueness made this song an anthem of New Primitivism. It is also most likely due to this song that the Croatian journalist and cultural critic, Ante Perković (2011, 98), has recently argued that in the early to mid-1980s, Sarajevo emerged as 'probably the only city in the world where punk aesthetics had introduced lyrics based on storytelling, like short film stories, instead of the brief, slogan-like, lyrics typical of punk'.

Given this background and the fact that New Primitivism made the scene precisely at the moment when the Olympics became 'the theme' in Sarajevo, it is possible to argue that the movement and the Sarajevo Olympics were closely interconnected. The fact that New Primitivism reached its heyday in 1984, when the movement's two central bands, Elvis J. Kurtovich and Zabranjeno pušenje, released their respective debut albums, further supports this argument. In fact, the former not only released an album but also gave a promotional concert during the Games themselves, at which a number of upcoming Yugoslav rock bands appeared as guests. *Naši dani* covered the event in an article published during the Games. The periodical had it that 'this musical raid on Olympic Sarajevo will not only be remembered as the band's desire to pay homage to their fans, but also as a kind of rockers' salute to the event that in its importance had far surpassed its predestined sporting character'.[96] Implied in this comment is the assertion that the Olympics were more than just a sports event. Hence, it also leaves an impression that the Olympics and Elvis J. Kurtovich were closely interconnected.

---

[95] It was later released on the band's demo LP *Mitovi i legende o kralju Elvisu* (EJK 1984).

[96] Krešo Palameta, 'Na Elvisovoj promociji. Mitovi i legende o kralju Elvisu', *Naši dani* 804, 18.2.1984, 14.

Due to unexpected delays in recording their material, Zabranjeno pušenje only released their debut album one-and-a-half months after the Olympics. However, the band referred directly to the Olympics in two of their major hits. One was the song called 'Šeki's on the road again' (ZP 1984c). This song opened with the line, 'When night falls on the Olympic city', implying that Sarajevo was *the* Olympic city. This equation of Sarajevo with its position as Olympic host city was not restricted to the band or even the youth culture in Olympic Sarajevo, but was common at the time. One notable example that can serve to inform the point is the illustrated tourist map of Yugoslavia produced for the Olympics where major cities and other interesting spots around the country were marked by the pictures of their most easily recognisable attractions. Interestingly, yet not surprisingly, Sarajevo received three symbols: the Olympic rings, its specific Olympic symbol known as 'snowflake' and a motif from Baščaršija. Implied in this representation was an assertion that the Olympics had become a trademark of the city, in the same fashion as the old Baščaršija had always been.

The second Zabranjeno pušenje song that directly referred to the Olympics was 'Abid' (ZP 1984a), the band's first major hit, already well known to local audiences before it was recorded (the song is discussed in greater detail in the following chapter). This was one of the songs that contributed to Miroslav Palameta's speaking of Sarajevo's 'Olympic (new) wave' in *Naši dani* in December 1982. Including the line, 'Sarajevo my dearest city, we fixed you for the Olympics', the song showed clearly and explicitly the extent to which the Olympics had become a temporal and cultural identity marker in the early 1980s in Sarajevo.

The third and last song (along Elvis J. Kurtovich's 'Baščaršy hanumen' and Zabranjeno pušenje's 'Abid') that provoked Palameta to invent the term 'Olympic wave' and connect the universal musical genre of new wave to Sarajevo's 'global popularity' in relation to hosting the 1984 Winter Olympics was entitled 'Sarajevo, Texas, Nashville, Tennessee' by Bonton Baya (BB 1983). Bonton Baya never attained the same popularity as Elvis J. Kurtovich and Zabranjeno pušenje, and was not always considered a New Primitive band. In terms of popular music genres, Bonton Baya was, in its style and poetics, much closer to (conventional) new wave than Elvis J. Kurtovich and Zabranjeno pušenje or other New Primitive bands— although Bonton Baya unquestionably belonged to the same scene and often played concerts with New Primitive bands. Moreover, several of Bonton Baya's songs certainly qualify in style and poetics as New

Primitivism and 'Sarajevo, Texas, Nashville, Tennessee' was one of these. It was released in 1983 on the band's debut and only record, *Elpi* (LP), several months before Elvis J. Kurtovich's and Zabranjeno pušenje's debuts because the recording company that released *Elpi*, Diskoton, believed that Bonton Baya was the most important new band in the city at that time.[97] Posterity proved this prediction wrong as the band dissolved soon after, which was part of the reason for their not attaining the same popularity as Elvis J. Kurtovich and Zabranjeno pušenje.

In many ways, the country-folk 'Sarajevo, Texas, Nashville, Tennessee' was the ultimate Sarajevo Olympic song, with a chorus that claimed:

> This is not Texas. Nor Nashville, Tennessee.
> But it has everything a famous city needs.
> The Sarajevo Assassination and the Winter Olympics.
> Jahorinko, you mighty wolf. Don't let it beat me.
> The world economic crisis. Let me see heaven, from up close. (BB 1983)

There is no doubt that the song was conceived as a satire, which typified the New Primitivism and Bosnian popular culture that emerged with it. More importantly here, however, is that it also clearly showed the extent to which the city was associated with its position as Olympic host. This was not just any city, but the Olympic one. The references to Texas and Nashville, Tennessee were probably due to the song's being conceived musically as in the country-folk genre, but the implication that Sarajevo was not like any other city is very clear. It was unique, despite having 'what a famous city needs'. Olympic Sarajevo was also a heaven that the band members want to observe up close. This was first expressed in the introductory lines of the song which place the singer standing and observing his city. Finally, the reference to the wolf *Jahorinko* not only helps us date the song to the period prior to the Olympic mascot becoming globally known as *Vučko*, it also indicates the symbolic relationship between the band and the Olympics. With these lyrics, it is not surprising that *Naši dani* speculated in May 1983 whether *Elpi* would get released before the Olympics.[98] It was not surprising, because the band, just like the whole subculture of New Primitivism, sought to appropriate their home city's

---

[97] Krešo Palameta, 'Intervju: Nenad Štrbac, Bonton baya. To je odiseja '83' *Naši dani* 806, 2.3.1984, 14.

[98] K.P., 'Baja ipak bez poreza', *Naši dani* 785, 27.5.1983, 15.

position as an Olympic host to the degree that the Olympics became a
bearer of their subcultural identity.

Not very long after the release of *Elpi, Naši dani* started a serial on
New Primitivism, publishing excerpts from the recently released book on
the movement by G. Đorđević, which ran concurrently with news of the
final stage of the preparations for the Olympics during the winter of
1983/1984. Quite notably, the serial finished precisely when the final
Olympic preparations finished. This temporal coincidence further supports the suggested close linkage of 'the Olympic wave' and Olympic
Sarajevo best understood, as noted above, within the specific popular-
cultural context of Yugoslav rock music culture. According to Gregor
Tomc, a Slovenian sociologist and one of the central personalities of the
Yugoslav youth culture that emerged in the Olympic period of the late
1970s and early 1980s, this culture was defined by a 'healthy competition
between a number of local scenes in the country's most important urban
centres' (Kostelnik 2004, 36). While doubtlessly having the potential to
facilitate musical creativity in these urban centres, this competition did not
take place on neutral terms. Instead, it was structured in accordance with
the dominant centre-periphery logic of Yugoslav popular-cultural space,
according to which Sarajevo's cultural production was often viewed as
being unsophisticated, backward and even primitive. This was most notably the case when the city's cultural production was compared to that in
the country's principal cultural metropoles, Belgrade and Zagreb, and to
a lesser extend Ljubljana. This view seems to be quite widespread in the
Yugoslav youth press and voiced for instance by Tomislav Wruss in his
writing in arguably the most popular official youth periodical, *Polet*
(Enthusiasm) from Zagreb.[99] Moreover, in terms of following global popular-cultural trends, Sarajevo was often seen as lagging behind not only
the major cultural metropoles in the country, but also some middle-sized
cities; yet another view voiced in *Polet*'s writings.[100]

In this situation, New Primitives used Sarajevo's position as Olympic
host to re-imagine and re-arrange their city's ranking in Yugoslav popular-
cultural space, and their engagement with the local should be seen from
this perspective. As Dalibor Mišina argues, New Primitives attacked 'the
dominant culture's hypocrisy of privileging non-local cultural experience

[99] Tomislav Wruss, 'Plavi orkestar: Soldatski bal. Dvosjekli mač', *Polet* 315, 31.5.1985, 29.
[100] Fikret N. Mujičić, 'Sarajevska rock scena. Vjetrovi Miljacke lahori Jahorine', *Polet*
1.4.1981, 20.

as the national cultural foundation' with their focus on local icons and lexical properties. The ultimate goal, writes Mišina (2010, 265), was 'to establish a new socio-cultural relationship to the rest of the country'. In this respect, even the very name of the movement, New Primitivism, served to problematise the core-periphery relationship according to which Sarajevo's culture was unsophisticated, backward and primitive. The idea of Sarajevo lagging behind the other principal cultural metropoles in the country was also turned upside down. The frontman of Zabranjeno pušenje, Dr Nele Karajlić (a.k.a. Nenad Janković), explained in a 1985 interview that it was indeed fortunate for Sarajevo that the city was the last of all the major metropoles in Yugoslavia to be influenced by Western popular-cultural trends. Consequently, argued Karajlić, when these trends finally reached Sarajevo they were already 'purified' from commercial inflows, meaning that Sarajevo did not blindly follow trends like punk or new wave in their Western incarnations, but rather adjusted them to fit Sarajevo's identity. Thus, New Primitivism emerged with its own identity—an identity that was not forced on Sarajevo by popular trends and for the benefit of the music industry and sale multiplication. Based on these arguments, Karajlić insisted that Sarajevo, in fact, was '*sredina*', meaning '*the* place', with the emphasis on 'the'.[101]

While the connection may seem tenuous at first sight, it is possible to argue that Karajlić's views were related to Sarajevo's position as an Olympic host city: first, because more or less everything in Sarajevo at that time was revolving around the city's Olympic 'place' image; second, this was arguably the most important band to emerge in Sarajevo while the city was preparing for the Olympics. As demonstrated in the preceding analysis, a special sensitivity to the city's cultural uniqueness developed in this period among the local populace, a sensitivity apparent throughout the interview with Karajlić. This is hardly surprising, as Zabranjeno pušenje and Karajlić were an integral part of the rock music scene in Sarajevo that Miroslav Palameta had dubbed 'the Olympic wave', a scene determined by local *mythologemes* that were refracted through the city's rising global salience. As we have seen in this chapter, this had led to the rise in awareness of, and pride in, the city's particularities and uniqueness, among its residents, and Zabranjeno pušenje was no exception.

---

[101] Stanko Brezarić, "Tko sam ja, dr. Nelle Karajlić? (2): Shockirash me, majke mi," *Polet* 315, 31.5.1985, 27.

It is quite interesting in this context that shortly after the Olympics, yet another member of the subculture gained country-wide popularity. Originally part of the alternative industrial rock band, SCH, and an aspiring actor, Branko Đurić Đuro joined the New Primitive band Bombaj štampa (The Bombay Post) in 1983. Subsequently, Đurić emerged as one of the most prominent members of the movement, becoming particularly known for his role in the aforementioned television comedy show, *Top List of Surrealists*. Đurić also became familiar across the country for his role in another popular TV comedy, *The Audition* (*Audicija* ASU), which premiered in 1985—not long after the Olympics. The show achieved cult status in Yugoslavia, becoming synonymous—just like the *Top List of Surrealists* and New Primitivism—with Bosnian popular culture of the time.

In 1984, shortly after the Sarajevo Olympics, Đurić appeared in a TV commercial for an entity called the Working Organisation ZOI'84. Working Organisation ZOI'84 was the legal heir to the Sarajevo Olympic Organising Committee. In fact, even before the Sarajevo Games opened, a working group was established in the Committee that was responsible for infrastructural and promotional work during the Olympic preparation period. Once the Games were over, ownership of the Olympic venues was transferred to the newly established ZOI'84, which was entrusted with the mission of carrying on and protecting the Olympic legacy. Along with taking care of the Olympic venues, ZOI'84 emerged as a major enterprise promoting and further developing tourism in Sarajevo, its wider region, and in fact, the whole of Bosnia and Herzegovina.

This was very much a continuation of the tourism development strategy in the republic, carried out in the spirit of the Sarajevo Olympics that emerged even before the Olympic idea materialised. As we have already seen, after its first recommendation by the OECD, developing winter tourism in Sarajevo and Bosnia and Herzegovina became one of the principal goals throughout the Olympic preparation period. The idea was also featured in the Final Report of the Sarajevo Olympics, which was published by the Organising Committee of the Sarajevo Olympic Winter Games shortly after they finished. In the report (TSOOC 1984b, 183), the Olympic Organising Committee took the trouble to explain that '[e]ven though the Organizing Committee was primarily in charge of preparation and staging of the XIV OWG, a larger portion of these funds was in fact returned through investments in 23 winter sports centers in Bosnia and Hercegovina'. Considering that the Games could and should provide impetus to the entire development, the Sarajevo Olympic Organising Committee saw the 14th Winter Olympics as an 'incentive for constructing winter sports centres in Bosnia and Hercegovina'. Consequently, it put considerable effort into helping to build these 23 new ski resorts in Bosnia and Herzegovina, treating them 'as a basis for mass sport and tourism development'.

When the Working Organisation ZOI'84 took over, it pursued the same strategy, a continuation brilliantly illustrated by the above-mentioned TV commercial casting Đurić, which comprised two parts, promoting winter and summer tourism in the resorts respectively. Both winter and summer versions of the commercial were conceived as an invitation or call—'Let's get to the mountains' ('*Hajdemo u planine*')—without specifying the mountains to which the audience was invited. However, there was no doubt that ZOI'84 was drawing on the new-won global popularity of the Olympic mountains close to Sarajevo and using it to promote tourism in Bosnian mountains in general. While the purpose of the commercial was unquestionably economic (as is always the case), it had some interesting cultural connotations that can help us identify some important cultural implications of the Sarajevo Olympics.

Both versions—winter and summer alike—had the same catchy pop melody and drew explicitly on Sarajevo's cultural particularity and the city's image and cultural identity, culminating in Đurić's singing in an easily recognisable Sarajevo dialect, before finishing in the slang typical of the New Primitive subculture. The earliest version, the winter segment, went as follows:

> Let's go girls, let's go boys … students, pupils, policemen/Let's get to the mountains (cause) it's never cold up there/Put on [your] scarfs and colourful caps, warm sweaters and woollen gloves/Let's get to the mountains (cause) it's never cold up there/All of you: postmen, soldiers, tired clerks, skiers, walkers and the fresh air explorers/Let's get to the mountains (cause) it's never cold up there.
> It's quick to master skiing/So don't be crazy hanging around the house.

At the end of the song and the commercial, Đurić—now in the role of policeman—reports on his walkie-talkie. Breathing deeply the fresh mountain air, he closes it up: 'What a difference. Pretty drastic!', in the slang of Sarajevan youth subculture (ZOI 84 1984a).

In the later, summer version of the commercial, Đurić claimed that the mountains were even better in the summertime than during the winter skiing season. Thus, in contrast to the winter video, which focused solely on skiing, it presented more varied activities: while singing and reciting a somewhat altered version of the song, Đurić now bikes, mountain-hikes and plays tennis and football. The original text is also slightly altered: 'It is summer girls and boys/students, pupils, policemen/And in the summer the mountains are even better than during the winter'. This musical part of the commercial is then interrupted by Đurić reciting in Slovenian and the Dalmatian/*čakavian* dialect of Serbo-Croatian. The addressed audience is obviously pan-Yugoslavian, as evidenced by the different languages, dialects and slang Đurić uses, and also in his playing different regional characters dressed in the respective regions' easily recognisable clothes. Đurić's message tells Yugoslavs why they should come to 'the mountains' in their summer vacations, most notably—as Đurić's respectively Dalmatian, Montenegrin and Zagreb characters claim in their respective dialects and slang—for the clean mountain air. It is also interesting that this, later, summer version is introduced by Đurić presenting himself with the words, 'Here comes the little Đuro again', indicating that he is now a widely known face on Yugoslav TV, not least due to the earlier winter version of the commercial. As with the winter version, the summer clip closes with typical New Primitive slang: 'This thing you won't find anywhere else, on the [world] map' (ZOI 84 1984b).

Đurić's character's concluding line effectively sums up the discussion in this chapter and part of the book. The Olympics made Sarajevo into a potential global tourist centre, placing the city on the world map, as scholars of both the Olympics and Sarajevo's youth subculture like to frame it. Emerging from this situation and drawing on their city's planetary popularity, the New Primitives reversed the city's position vis-à-vis other major metropoles in Yugoslavia, stressing Sarajevo's exceptionality. The theme of the commercials, '*Hajdemo u planine*' ('Let's get to the mountains'), further illustrates this departure. It was written by Goran Bregović, the leader of the rock band Bijelo dugme (White Button), a central player in what is often referred to as 'the Sarajevo School of Pop and Rock' and arguably one of the biggest and most important Yugoslav rock bands of all time. As such, the music culture of the Bosnian capital city was unthinkable without it, and Sarajevo was often associated with it in the 1970s and 1980s.

Interestingly, a couple of years after the Winter Olympics, in 1986, Bijelo dugme released the song under the same title. Soon to become a big hit across the country, the song crowned Sarajevo's post-Olympic association with skiing and the Olympic mountains. This could hardly stand in a starker contrast to the Sarajevo of two decades earlier, when not even the authors of the official tourist guidebook of the city thought that it made sense to mention skiing, or even to imagine Sarajevo as a skiing destination.

## BIBLIOGRAPHY

Books, Articles, Reports, Blogs and Websites
Beattie, Bob. 1984. Sarajevo. A TV Olympics. *Ski*, February 1984, 36.
Berg, Adam P. 2016. *Denver '76: The Winter Olympics and the Politics of Growth in Colorado during the Late 1960s and Early 1970s* (Doctor of Philosophy, The Pennsylvania State University).
Bojičić, Vesna. 1996. The Disintegration of Yugoslavia: Causes and Consequences of Dynamic Inefficiency in Semi-command Economies. In *Yugoslavia and After, a Study in Fragmentation, Despair and Rebirth*, ed. David A. Dyker and Ivan Vejvoda, 28–47. London: Longman.
Chappelet, Jean-Loup. 2012. From Lake Placid to Salt Lake City: The Challenging Growth of the Winter Games Since 1980. In *The Making of Olympic Cities. Critical Concepts in Urban Studies, Volume I: Contexts and Overviews*, ed. John R. Gold and Margaret M. Gold, 74–93. London and New York: Routledge.
Goulding, Daniel J. 2002 [1985]. *Liberated Cinema. The Yugoslav Experience, 1945–2001*. Bloomington, IN: Indiana University Press.
Jovanovic, Zlatko. 2014. 'All Yugoslavia Is Dancing Rock and Roll'. *Yugoslavness and the Sense of Community in the 1980s Yu-Rock*. PhD Thesis, Faculty of Humanities, University of Copenhagen.
Kostelnik, Branko. 2004. *Moj život je novi val: Razgovori s prvoborcima i dragovoljcima novog vala*. Zaprešić: Fraktura.
Knežević-Čečez, Gordana, Ljiljana Smajlović and Mirsad Zorabdić. 1984. *Svijet o Sarajevu. Svjetska štampa, televizija i radio o XIV Zimskim Olimpijskim igrama*. Sarajevo: Organizacioni komitet XIV Zimskih Olimpijskih igara Jugoslavija.
Levi, Pavle. 2007. *Disintegration in Frames: Aesthetics and Ideology in the Yugoslav and Post-Yugoslav Cinema*. Stanford, CA: Stanford University Press.
Ličina Ramić, Aida. 2017. Od ekološke katastrofe do olimpijskog grada—Sarajevo 1971–1984. In *Poplava, zemljotres, smog: prilozi ekohistoriji Bosne i Hercegovine u 20. stoljeću: zbornik radova*, ed. Amir Duranović, 115–147. Sarajevo:

Udruženje za modernu historiju/Udruga za modernu povijest (Edicija Zbornici; knj. 3).

Masia, Seth. 1984. Yugoslavia: First Alpine Nation on Skis. *Ski*, February 1984, 48.

Mišina, Dalibor. 2010. 'Spit and Sing, My Yugoslavia': New Partisans, Social Critique and Bosnian Poetics of the Patriotic. *Nationalities Papers* 38 (2): 265–289.

Pedrotty, Kate Meehan. 2010. Yugoslav Unity and Olympic Ideology at the 1984 Sarajevo Winter Olympic Games. In *Yugoslavia's Sunny Side: A History of Tourism in Socialism (1950s–1980s)*, ed. Hannes Grandits and Karin Taylor, 333–363. Budapest and New York: CEU Press.

Perković, Ante. 2011. *Sedma republika. Pop kultura u YU raspadu*. Zagreb-Beograd: Novi liber/Glasnik.

Powell, Stewart. 1984. Winter Olympics' Real Winner Is Sarajevo. *US News & World Report*, February 13, 1984, 35.

Prohić, Kasim, and Sulejman Balić. 1975. *Sarajevo*. Sarajevo: Turistički savez Sarajevo.

———. 1983. *Sarajevo*. Sarajevo: Turistički savez Sarajevo.

Roche, Maurice. 2000. *Mega-events and Modernity: Olympics, Expos and the Growth of Global Culture*. London: Routledge.

Sakac, Boris. 2008. 'From the Mediterranean Games Split 1979 to the Beijing 2008 Olympic Games' in the Report for the IOC and the ORIS (Olympic Result and Information Services), 99–108 (Conference Paper).

Schaap, Dick. 1984. *The 1984 Olympic Games: Sarajevo/Los Angeles* (The Official Book of the US Olympic Committee).

Short, John R. 2012. Globalization, Cities, and the Summer Olympics. In *The Making of Olympic Cities: Critical Concepts in Urban Studies, Volume I: Contexts and Overviews*, ed. John R. Gold and Margaret M. Gold, 235–262. London and New York: Routledge.

*TEJ (Turistička enciklopedija Jugoslavije I)*. 1958. Eds. Ljubica D. Trajković. Beograd: Turistička štampa.

Tihić, Smail. 1966. *Tourist Guide Through Sarajevo*. Beograd: Turistička štampa.

TSOOC: The Sarajevo Organizing Committee of the XIV Olympic Winter Games Yugoslavia. 1984b. *Sarajevo '84. Yugoslavia 8-19.02*. Final Report Published by the Organizing Committee of the XIV Winter Olympic Games 1984 in Sarajevo. Sarajevo: Oslobođenje.

*VGAJ (Veliki geografski atlas Jugoslavije)*. 1987. Ed. Ivan Bertić. Zagreb: Liber.

Vuic, Jason. 2015. *The Sarajevo Olympics: A History of the 1984 Winter Olympic Games*. Amherst and Boston: University of Massachusetts Press.

Vuletić, Dean. 2008. Generation Number One: Politics and Popular Music in Yugoslavia in the 1950s. *Nationalities Papers 36* (5): 861–879.

Woodward, Susan. 1995. *Balkan Tragedy: Chaos and Dissolution after the Cold War*. Washington, DC: The Brookings Institution.

RECORDS (DISCOGRAPHY)

BB (Bonton Baya). 1983. Sarajevo, Texas, Nashville, Tennessee. *Elpi*. Sarajevo: Diskoton.

EJK (Elvis J. Kurtovich). 1984. Baščaršy hanumen. *Mitovi i legende o kralju Elvisu*. Ljubljana: RTV Ljubljana.

ZP (Zabranjeno pušenje). 1984a. Abid. *Das ist Walter*. Zagreb: Jugoton.

———. 1984b. Anarhija All over Baščaršija. *Das ist Walter*. Zagreb: Jugoton.

———. 1984c. Šeki's on the Road Again. *Das ist Walter*. Zagreb: Jugoton.

VIDEOS

ZOI 84. 1984a. *ZOI 84 Promotivni spot 1—Branko Đurić Đuro*. Accessed January 29, 2021. https://youtu.be/p4GgMGTFhjs.

———. 1984b. *ZOI 84 Promotivni spot 2—Branko Đurić Đuro*. Accessed January 29, 2021. https://youtu.be/fs5U1A1h5Js.

# PART II

# Sarajevo, the Modern (Modern/Non-modern Dimension of the Sarajevo Olympics)

# CHAPTER 3

# Fixing Sarajevo for the Olympics

Borrowing the idea for its title from Zabranjeno Pušenje's song, 'Abid', this chapter explores connections between Sarajevo's physical transformation and infrastructural improvement for the Olympics and the aspect of modernity inherent in the Games as an event. As noted in the previous chapter, Zabranjeno Pušenje started performing 'Abid' in 1982 and it became one of the band's most popular songs. However, it was not recorded and released until a couple of months after the Olympics, during the spring of 1984—when it appeared on their debut album—reflecting the inescapable point of reference the Games had become among the city's youngsters. While the band had conceived the song as a satirical commentary on the situation and life of the Yugoslav working class, 'Abid' also offers some perceptive comments on the Olympics and related topics. Of particular interest is how the event is linked to the aforementioned Project for the Protection of Sarajevo's Human Environment as well as the statement that Sarajevo was 'fixed' for the Olympics:

> I skip the street canal/and look to the ground/And I see you, Abid/Abid, tell us, com' on/What is that, your hands are doing?/—Working hard, bro'/So there is gas for everyone/All within the Project for the Protection of Our Environment.
>
> Abid, tell us, com' on/Where the finances are coming from?/—Two percent from every paycheck/Not one of us said 'no' to that.

Z. Jovanovic, *A Cultural History of the 1984 Winter Olympics, Modernity, Memory and Identity in South-East Europe*, https://doi.org/10.1007/978-3-030-76598-9_3

77

Abid, tell us, com' on/Does your kid still collect old papers?/—No, my
bro'/He works in a grocery store near the market.
Abid, tell us, com' on/Is there some plotting going around?/—Sarajevo,
my dearest city/Lots of people work me in here.
Abid, tell us, com' on/Is it getting better in a year or two?/—Sarajevo,
my dearest city/We fixed you for the Olympics! (ZP 1984a)

While evidently localised in space (Sarajevo) and time (the early 1980s)
and thus about Olympic Sarajevo's 'place' image, as emphasised in the previous chapter, the announcement that Sarajevo was 'fixed for the Olympics'
should nonetheless be placed in the global context of the Olympic Games
event. Drawing on examination of a number of the existing case studies,
John R. Short (2012, 256–258) points out that the Olympics provide host
cities with an opportunity to undertake massive urban renewal and restruc-
turing, major environmental remediation and dramatic infrastructural
improvements. In short, he claims that they have historically encouraged
host cities to engage in city-wide, coherent planning that helps turn them
into modern metropoles. In keeping with the model, the 1984 Winter
Olympics led to enormous infrastructural renovations and resulted in huge
environmental betterment in Sarajevo, culminating in an overall impression
that the city had changed to an almost unrecognisable degree, becoming a
completely new, modern, urban metropolis.

This impression draws attention to the close connections between the
development of infrastructure and the idea of modernity which, while self-
evident, are nonetheless analytically fruitful to examine. In his work on
this topic, Paul N. Edwards (2003, 187–188) has argued that the concept
of 'infrastructure' is best defined negatively, that is, as those systems without which modern societies cannot function. As mature technological systems (such as roads, municipal water supplies, sewers, telephones and
railroads), they are not particularly salient most of the time; rather, to
most people, modern society's infrastructure is 'naturalised background',
as ordinary and unremarkable as trees, daylight and dirt (Edwards 2003,
186). This said, as Edwards also argues, over the recent decades, historians, sociologists and anthropologists of technology have increasingly
come to recognise that all infrastructures are in fact *socio*technical in
nature. In other words, infrastructure is not only a question of technology,
but also of organisation, ideology, socially communicated background
knowledge, general acceptance and reliance (Edwards 2003, 188). Thus,
infrastructure is also important in that infrastructural projects create

commitments, foster responsibilities and expectations and, not least, enable certain imaginaries.

Mapping the city-planning ideas relating to the building of 'the Olympic city' in Sarajevo, the present chapter examines how hosting the Winter Olympics helped unleash different urban imaginaries—physical and social alike—in the city. Placing these at the centre of analysis, we can see how the Olympics made it possible for Sarajevo to become a modern city, although it should not be overlooked that some of the directions of improvement had been conceived well before it was decided to nominate the city as host to the 1984 Winter Olympics. The chapter's central discussion concerns the process of cleaning-up and greening the city, which, during the preparation period, became inextricably interconnected with the Olympics. We have already seen in the previous chapter that the cleaning-up of the city and the completion of the Project for the Protection of Sarajevo's Human Environment were commonly seen as a prerequisite for Olympic nomination. However, as this chapter will demonstrate, in the course of helping solve the city's concrete pollution problems the Project for the Protection of Sarajevo's Human Environment emerged as an inseparable component of the preparations for the Olympics. Directly and indirectly, after the completion of the Project, ideas about protecting the environment emerged as the vehicle for a new discourse of greening—not only of the city, but of the Olympics at large.

From this point of departure, in the first two sections of the present chapter I explore this process of cleaning-up the city for the Olympics and the emergence of the discourse of greening, including the logic behind it and its implementation. This is then followed by a discussion concerning some interesting social imaginaries relating to the city's position as the Olympic host. The logic behind this is that although towards the end of its Olympic preparation period Sarajevo emerged as a clean, modern city, there was yet another aspect of it that—according to the local authorities and press—needed to be 'fixed for the Olympics'. In the view of the local authorities and press, solving infrastructural and pollution problems was only part of the necessary prerequisites for the Games' ultimate success. Hence, it was not enough just to make Sarajevo modern for the Olympics, its citizens also had to become modern. With this goal in mind, in the late spring of 1983, the city's leading daily, *Oslobođenje*, helped by the local authorities, launched a media project lasting more than six months that covered ongoing inspections of the services provided by, among others, the city's retailers, restaurants, hotels, banks, taxi companies and public services. Against this socio-political backdrop, the last part of the chapter looks closer into this episode. Using this media project to inform discussion of a range of concerns with Sarajevo's and Sarajevans' modernity—in relation to the city's hosting of the Olympics—the last part of this chapter makes it clear that preparations for hosting the Olympics were never only about developing the infrastructure in and around the city, but also about inculcating certain forms of social conduct in the city's inhabitants or, as I term it, about disciplining them for the Olympics.

## 3.1    'THIS IS SARAJEVO?' MODERNISING SARAJEVO FOR THE OLYMPICS

Even though every individual Olympic Games event is inevitably unique, all Olympic Games are also, equally inevitably, and in many important respects, standardised. In other words, they are as identifiably and uniformly 'Olympic' as each other. This is most notably the case in regard to the standardised 'Olympic city-within-a-city'. As most of the numerous sports comprising the Games event must be sited in the host city, the key elements of such a 'city-within-a-city' are the main athletics stadium or sports arena (which is usually either newly built or extensively refurbished for the Games), the athletes' accommodation or Olympic village, and the media centre. Furthermore, in connection with the sporting events, cultural programmes must be managed both in the Olympic village and also in the city more generally.[1] This effectively makes central areas of the city and its transportation infrastructure into elements of the 'Olympic city', at least for the duration of the event (Roche 2000, 137–138).

In Sarajevo, these three elements were, respectively, Zetra Olympic Hall, Mojmilo and Dobrinja Olympic Villages and Skenderija cultural and sports centre which, besides hosting different sporting competitions, also served as the Games' main media centre. These three elements were situated in the northern (Zetra) and the western (Mojmilo and Dobrinja) edges of the central urban area of the city, and in the very centre of it, on

---

[1] It is noteworthy how this was handled by the country's largest sport daily, *Sport*, which in the days immediately prior to and during the Games did not only narrowly cover sports results, but also different cultural programmes organised for the participants and visitors. For instance, a couple of days before the official opening of the Games, the daily provided lengthy coverage of the cultural and entertainment programmes in the Olympic village. 'U "selu" kao u velegradu', *Sport* 6.2.1984, 8–9.

the southern bank of the Miljacka River (Skenderija). It should also be noted that while Zetra Olympic Hall and the Olympic villages were built exclusively for the 1984 Winter Olympics, Skenderija was only refurbished for it. The city's major stadium, Koševo Stadium, which served as a site for the opening ceremony and was situated immediately next to Zetra, was also extensively refurbished.

The main emphasis of transportation infrastructure improvement was the expansion and modernisation of the tram network for the Olympics. Running north of the Miljacka River in an east-west direction and connecting the heavily populated western suburbs with the old city, the tram network had always been the backbone of Sarajevo's urban transportation. To the west of the old town, the trams run on the city's main traffic axe and, prior to the Olympics, they took up the outer lanes in both directions, leaving a somewhat chaotic impression of the city's streets. To solve this problem, the tracks in both directions were moved to the middle lane, creating a more streamlined, orderly impression of a well-functioning city supplied with modern transportation.[2]

Meanwhile, in the central city neighbourhood of Marijin Dvor—along the tram route from the old town towards the heavily populated western suburbs—a new hotel was built exclusively for the Olympics. This was Sarajevo's 'Olympic hotel', a Holiday Inn. Initially referred to interchangeably as 'Hotel Sarajevo' and 'Hotel Olympic', it quickly became a symbol of modern Sarajevo.[3] As Kenneth Morrison (2016, 60) puts it, upon its construction, the Holiday Inn became 'the benchmark of modernity and luxury' in Sarajevo. In fact, in the local media the hotel was a benchmark of the city's modernity even before its formal opening, with the *Oslobođenje* of 4 September 1983 praising it as 'one of the most modern hotels in Yugoslavia'. Although the daily discussed general changes in 'the Olympic city' and mentioned several other examples, the emphasis was clearly on the Holiday Inn. The choice of images the daily used in the

---

[2] D. Stanojlović, 'Moderan prevoz u olimpijskom gradu', *Oslobođenje* 18.1.1983, 12; Aziz Hadžihasanović, 'Sarajevo: Postolimpijske refleksije (II). Red za ugled', *Oslobođenje* 29.3.1984, 3.

[3] It is interesting that in June 1982 an *Oslobođenje* journalist tried to explain to the daily's readers how the official name of the hotel was '"Olympic" (Olimpik)' and not 'Sarajevo'. E. Isaković, 'Nije "Sarajevo" nego "Olimpik". Hotel na šest stolova', *Oslobođenje* 16.6.1982, 6. Furthermore, as late as the summer of 1983, that is, only a few months before the hotel's completion, *Oslobođenje* still from time to time used the terms 'Hotel Sarajevo' and 'Hotel Olimpic'. But one example is J. Vričko, 'Hotel u oktobru', *Oslobođenje* 28.7.1983, 14.

**Image 3.1**   A photo of the new 'Olympic' hotel Holiday Inn, accompanied by the article title 'This Is Sarajevo?' (J.V. (Vričko), 'Zar je to Sarajevo?', *Oslobođenje* 4.9.1983, 6)

article followed the same logic, with a leading image of the hotel equalling in size three lower images from some of the other city locations mentioned in the article. The article's point was that, in the course of a few years, the whole city had changed so dramatically that those who had been away for some time would be surprised upon their return, most probably asking whether this was still Sarajevo. For this reason the article was entitled 'This Is Sarajevo?', the headline placed immediately under the photo of the Holiday Inn, implicitly presenting the hotel as the symbol of this change (Image 3.1).[4]

That said, the Holiday Inn was only one of several symbols indicating that the Olympics had changed the city drastically, creating a new modern Sarajevo. Other objects built or restored for the Olympics were also used to emphasise this, not least the Zetra Olympic Complex. An *Oslobođenje* article on the completion and opening of the complex, published in

[4] J.V. (Vričko), 'Zar je to Sarajevo?', *Oslobođenje* 4.9.1983, 6.

December 1982, claimed that '[h]ere with this ZETRA and up there in the mountain heights a new Sarajevo is being born'.[5]

The examples of the Holiday Inn and Zetra—and several other Olympic venues and installations mentioned later in the chapter—indicate that the general impression of the time was that, due to hosting the Olympics, Sarajevo had emerged as a new, completely changed and modern city. Thus, the Olympics seemed to constitute a major break in the city's history. Nonetheless, in the following, I draw attention to historical continuities because, despite the omnipresent sense of a rupture with the pre-Olympic past, most of the planning ideas realised during the preparation period predated the idea of nominating Sarajevo as host city. My argument is that the sense of the break with the pre-Olympic period had much to do with an inherent characteristic of the Olympic imaginary to inevitably allude to both 'pre' and 'post' Olympic periods, installing more or less explicitly a sense of dramatic change. Or, as Maurice Roche (2000, 9) suggests, the Olympics contain implicit or explicit references to modernity's changing versions of its past and the future. Hence, being chained to the idea of modernity the Olympics inherently refer to some non-modern—that is, pre-Olympic—dimensions of the host city.

The construction of the Zetra Olympic Complex, which *Oslobođenje* used as a point of departure in its argument that with the Olympics a new Sarajevo was being born, will serve to illustrate the point. Some eight months after the mentioned article, on 7 August 1983, in its serial 'Sarajevo Then and Now', the newspaper counterposed a picture from the Zetra area in August 1981 with one taken two years later. Titled 'The Beauty Emerged from the Gravel', the article's header read, 'Within only two years, the valley of ZETRA experienced a metamorphosis from a decrepit sports site to a sports complex rarely seen anywhere in the world'.[6] Woven into this counterposition is the implication that the Olympics had created *two Sarajevos*: one that existed before the city won the bid for the 1984 Winter Olympics and another that emerged with and after them. Presented in this way, the Olympics appeared to have led to processes of modernisation whose cutting edge of change was seen as beyond and qualitatively different from the pre-Olympic periods. Accordingly, as early as November 1979—just a year-and-a-half after the city won the bid—Yugoslavia's leading lifestyle magazine, Zagreb's aforementioned *Start*, could announce:

---

[5] Branko Tomić, 'Olimpijski podvig Sarajeva', *Oslobođenje* 14.12.1982, 1.
[6] B. Radosavljević, 'Na šljaci nikla ljepotica', *Oslobođenje* 7.8.1983, 7.

'never before has the city been developing so fast and, what is even more important, so systematically'.[7]

In these examples we see that the Olympics were offering Sarajevans something dramatic and extraordinary, something beyond the rationality and routine of their everyday lives. This is, according to Maurice Roche (2000, 7), one of the central characteristics of the relationship between the Olympics and modernity. In addition, through the reflexivity that the modernity of the Olympics implied, a 'systematic development' of the city implicitly referred to the presumed lack of the same in pre-Olympic Sarajevo. Here, Jason Vuic's argument (2015, 31), mentioned in the previous chapter, that Sarajevo was 'a mess' immediately springs to mind. As we saw, this statement was closely related to the city's environmental problems, but defining the environmental situation as a 'mess' was not simply a statement concerning the state-of-things in pre-Olympic Sarajevo. It was largely provoked by the idea of nominating Sarajevo for Olympics. The Olympics—it could therefore be argued—made the already existing need for infrastructural improvement even more visible and urgent. Hence, the very idea of nominating Sarajevo for the Winter Olympics created an important stimulus for the improvement of the city's infrastructure. This is also one of the reasons why the Olympics, from their inception, absorbed the Project for the Protection of the Environment as part of a larger Olympic venture. Thus, both the Project and infrastructural work carried out in preparation for the Olympics appeared as general modernising projects. Nonetheless, technically the Project preceded the Olympics, and comprised the single largest modernising endeavour in the city's history.

This is also how the Project was presented in the 1975 edition of *Sarajevo*—the monograph discussed in the previous chapter. In this earlier version of the monograph the project was mentioned several times. Most notably, it was described in a lengthy caption to an illustration of the recently built Sarajka department store:

> In 1975 Sarajevo is preparing what must be the biggest and most significant communal venture in its history. In order to protect the environment created by nature and by the labour of man, it is necessary above all to reduce air-pollution and to reconstruct the underground installations for water supply and drainage. During the next four years natural gas will be piped to the town and all the larger consumers will transfer from solid or liquid fuels to this much cleaner fuel which is less dangerous to health. In addition to this,

[7] Alija Hafizović, 'Sarajevski svjetski velelslalom,' *Start 283*, 28.11.1979, 36–41.

a big collector will be built into the right bank of the Miljacka, while a special wastewater-purifying plant will be constructed where the River Bosna joins it. Thus, the Miljacka, celebrated in song, will once again become a clean river. This programme also includes the construction of a solid waste disposal plant. A new water supply network is also planned which will be adequate for the needs of the whole town until the end of the century. The International Bank for Reconstruction and Development is a participant in the financing of this enormous communal reconstruction.

The content of the caption and the logic of combining the Project for the Protection of Sarajevo's Human Environment with the modern department store imply that the former was seen as being basically a modernising project. Finally, even though the Project at that time was still not publicly related to Sarajevo's potential Olympic nomination, later reports showed that local elites and Sarajevo's urban political regime were already seeing the Project and the Olympics as closely related.

In fact, sources clearly indicate that the Project was broadly viewed as the ultimate prerequisite for Sarajevo's Olympic bid. There was broad agreement on this issue among the different bodies of the Olympic Committee, including the Preparation Committee. The proposal for the city's Olympic candidacy, which the Preparation Committee drafted in September 1977, claimed that the prospect of the completion of the Project for the Protection of Sarajevo's Human Environment created an opportunity for the Olympic nomination.[8] A couple of years later, Ante Sučić, who at that time had become the president of the Olympic Organising Committee, insisted that Sarajevo had an enormous advantage over previous Olympic host cities because, by realising the Project, it had started preparing for the Olympics even before officially placing its bid.[9] Conversely, the final report on the Olympic Games by the Sarajevo Olympics Organising Committee (1984b, 4) explained in its introduction that nominating Sarajevo as host city had been out of the question for the 1972, 1976 or even 1980 Winter Olympics because some visible improvement and at least partial completion of the Project had to be in place

[8] Pripremni komitet za kandidaturu grada Sarajeva za organizovanje zimskih olimpijskih igara 1984. g., 'Prijedlog mogućnosti grada Sarajeva za Zimske Olimpijske igre 1984.g.', Sarajevo 30.9.1977, 3–5, JOK—832/F-11. Arhiv Jugoslavije [The Archives of Yugoslavia], Belgrade, Serbia.

[9] Kemal Kurspahić, 'Sarajevski koraci u susret 1984. godini. Olimpijske igre – razvojni poduhvat', *Oslobođenje* 31.12.1979, 1.&2.1.1980, 5.

before the city had any realistic chance of winning the bid. Thus, not only the bid's eventual success, but even its mere nomination, possessed the necessary impetus to galvanise successful realisation of the environmental Project. So, as I have argued, the city's potential position as Olympic host city was not only dependent on the Project, but also a stimulus and a chance to promote and, what is even more important, to justify it. The Olympics made it possible to call for public support for the Project and, not least, validate the tax hikes, to which Zabranjeno Pušenje's 'Abid' refers in the line, 'Two percent from every paycheck/Not one of us said "no" to that'. This is further connected in the song with 'working hard to provide gas for everybody within the Project for the Protection of Our Environment'. In this line, the band referred to the project of building of the gas pipeline to and around Sarajevo, which was the Project's largest single subproject (Ličina Ramić 2017, 137), while its final goal was 'to fix Sarajevo for the Olympics' (ZP 1984a). Although, as I have already pointed out, this song was meant as a satire, it also discloses the logic whereby the Project for the Protection of Sarajevo's Human Environment and the preparations for the Olympics were seen as intertwined.

A more official equivalent of the song's message on the popular-cultural level appeared in the pamphlet *Sarajevo—The Olympic City. The People and the Project* (*Sarajevo—Olimpijski grad. Ljudi i akcija*), which was published not long after the Olympics, in December 1984, by the city's section of the aforementioned SSRN—Socialist Alliance of Working People. As already noted, this was the largest and most influential mass organisation in the Socialist Federative Republic of Yugoslavia. In the pamphlet, the Alliance insisted that in the decade preceding its publication, Sarajevans had 'regenerated' their city, 'doing more for it than different previous regimes had done for centuries'. This, according to the pamphlet, was closely related to the Project for the Protection of the Human Environment and the preparations for the XIV Olympic Winter Games (SSRNBiH 1984, 5), giving the unmistakable impression that the Project was inseparable from preparations for the Olympics.

Aida Ličina Ramić's recent work on Sarajevo's environmental history further supports this argument. In an article titled 'From an Ecological Catastrophe to the Olympic City Sarajevo 1972–1984', Ličina Ramić (2017, 123) meticulously analyses developments in the Bosnian capital from the early 1970s, when Sarajevo was widely considered one of the most polluted cities in the Balkans,[10] to the Project's successful realisation which, she argues, was closely related to the promotion and eventual awarding of the XIV Olympic Winter Games. Quoting from an interview in the German weekly *Der Spiegel* with Ante Sučić, the Mayor of Sarajevo at the time when the city won its Olympic bid, she builds on this claim, further capturing how the Project and the Olympics were closely correlated. To *Der Spiegel*'s interviewer, Sučić revealed: 'We have made a giant leap of 30 years in three years. [...] The water-supply system and the road network have been renovated and improved thanks to the Olympics. And in combating harmful smog, the city is switching from coal heating to gas' (Ličina Ramić 2017, 141). Here, one of the leading figures of Olympic Sarajevo linked the infrastructural improvements generated by the Project for Protection of the Human Environment to the Olympics,[11] in much the same way as Zabranjeno Pušenje's 'Abid' spoke of gas, the protection of the environment and the Olympics, as if they were inseparably interlaced.

The local press also wrote about the Project and the Olympics as if they were parts of the same project or development. For instance, *Oslobođenje* published an article in September 1981 on how the city's position as host city for the Olympics was affecting its visual appearance, in which it was claimed that 'each new day, with the realisation of the Project for the Protection of the Human Environment and the XIV Olympic Winter Games approaching, Sarajevo is attaining new tones of *velegrad*' [emphasis added]. In other words, the direction which the upcoming Olympics (and the—at that point—almost finished Project) were taking the city was towards becoming a *velegrad*—a modern metropolis.[12]

The city's youth periodical, *Naši dani*, offered a similar argument in its final pre-Olympic issue. In a timeline for the Olympics, covering the period from conceiving the idea in the late 1960s to the Games in February 1984, the periodical suggested that between 1980 and 1982 'the surgery performed on the city's womb was successfully completed, giving Sarajevo

---

[10] In her work on the environmental history of Sarajevo, Aida Ličina shows that Yugoslavs, due to the air and water pollution in the late 1960s and early 1970s, sometimes referred to the city as 'London of the Balkans'.

[11] It is also interesting that already in 1978—just a few days after Sarajevo won the Olympic bid—Sučić linked the future preparations for the Olympics to the Project for Protection of the Human Environment (Željko Žutelija, 'Olimpia na Jahorini,' *Start 244*, 31.5.1978, 18–20.).

[12] Boro Radosavljević, 'Sarajevo u tonovima velegrada', *Oslobođenje—Žurnal*, 13.9.1981, 8–9.

the new face of a new and modern world-class city', adding that '[t]he Olympic spirit [could] already be sensed in the city'.[13] Given that the majority of the construction work on the Olympic venues, installations and accompanying infrastructure was performed later, between 1981 and 1983, there is no doubt that the periodical was referring to the work of the Project, completed in 1982. The metaphor of 'womb', the interior of the city, likewise affirms this. Also interesting is the marked degree to which this discourse supports the argument proposed by Paul N. Edwards (2003, 187–188) that urban technological systems like water supply, sewers and so on are not always salient to residents; rather, although fundamental to the functioning of the modern city, they are hidden in its 'interior'. It is only once these systems start working properly that results become visible, materialising in the form of a well-functioning modern city. This is also what the 'new face of a new and modern world-class city' implies in the timeline presented in *Naši dani*.[14] Finally, no less interesting is that this emergence of 'a new and modern city' is further connected to the 'Olympic spirit' that had surfaced as a result of the described development.

Biological metaphors—like 'womb'—were typical of contemporaneous Sarajevan language, the central theme of which was environmental remediation and the re-creation of a healthy city organism. This is exemplified in the final report on the Project for the Protection of Sarajevo's Human Environment, which presented the Project as 'the necessary environmental remediation of the city's organism'.[15] Similarly, *Oslobođenje* talked about the 'heart surgery' performed on the city, implying a complicated and very important undertaking.[16] Finally, the very popular 1984 book, *Wonderful Yugoslavia* (*Čudesna Jugoslavija*), a must-have at the time, published by Sarajevo's major publishing house, Svjetlost, talked proudly and self-congratulatorily about the Project as a unique undertaking of its kind anywhere in the world, one resulting in the 'new-washed face of the old city of Sarajevo' (Jokić 1984, 251). The reflexive character of the modernity attributed to the Olympics—one constituting a bridge from the pre-Olympic pre-modern past to the post-Olympic modern future, as described above—stands out very clearly in this last sentence.

[13] M. A. (Miroslav Arapovich), 'Olimpijada jeeeeeeeeee!!!—Mali Vremeplov', *Naši dani* 803, 10.1.1984, 10.
[14] Ibid.
[15] Z. Elez, 'Raport na kraju mandata. Iz akcije ostao trag', *Oslobođenje* 19.3.1982, 10.
[16] 'Uspjela operacija na srcu grada', *Oslobođenje Žurnal* 10.8.1980, 2.

Against this background, and in the context of the two editions of *Sarajevo* (the monograph) discussed in the previous chapter, it is rather interesting that the Project for the Protection of Sarajevo's Human Environment—proudly presented as a 'globaly unprecedented communal project' in the 1975 edition—disappeared completely from the 1983 edition of the monograph, probably because it no longer sounded as impressive as it had before the city won the Olympic bid. Having said that, I nevertheless argue that the Project was not simply put aside. In fact, as I discuss in the next section, it metamorphosed into another environmental project integrated into infrastructural work in preparation for the coming Olympics—that of the greening of the city for the 1984 Winter Olympics.

## 3.2   GREENING SARAJEVO FOR THE OLYMPICS

We saw in the previous chapter that hosting the Olympics provided an opportunity for Sarajevo to re-imagine and re-make itself in light of its emergent position as a global city. In the course of this, as I have argued, the city turned the presumed disadvantage of its Ottoman past and heritage into an asset. Here, I want to propose a similar argument, according to which the Olympics provided the city with an opportunity to re-imagine and re-make itself as an environmentally progressive metropolis. Previously a seriously polluted city, it was now armed with the local pride of sponsoring 'the unprecedented communal environmental project',[17] which was increasingly being perceived as part of the preparation for the Olympics, and it began projecting itself as a city that took environmental issues very seriously.

This new Olympic environmentalism discourse coincided with a more general global imaginary of environmental protection, the result of several decades of historical development. As noted, Sarajevo won its Olympic bid not long after Denver had turned down the role of host city for the 1976 Winter Olympics, partly due to environmental concerns (Berg 2016, Ch. 4; Sarantakes 2010, 41). These were closely related to processes of planetary urban expansion in the second half of the twentieth century which were prompting a radical transformation in the perception of urban and natural environments and a surge in environmental awareness and activism. On the level of city planning the development resulted in a growing

---

[17] This expression was used both in the 1983 edition of *Sarajevo* (Prohić and Balić 1983) and in *Čudesna Jugoslavija* (Jokić 1984, 251).

recognition of the need for the integration and interconnection of natural and urban space that among others David Harvey talks about in his work on the topic (Harvey 1996).

The construction of Sarajevo's Olympic infrastructure occurred in this historical context. Thus, if seen from this perspective, Zetra Olympic Hall, the city's new multipurpose arena (ice hockey, figure and speed skating) exemplified the urban imaginary of integrating and interconnecting natural and urban entities. In fact, its very name presents a reification of this development. Ze-tra is a portmanteau word combining abbreviations of two words: *ze-lena* and ***tra-nsverzala***, meaning 'the green belt'. Behind this name is the idea of allowing the natural environment to penetrate the very centre of Sarajevo city, an idea which originated in the early 1950s when Juraj Neidhardt, arguably Sarajevo's most important modernist architect, proposed it in *Mozaik—the contemporary Yugoslav magazine* (Dabac 1953).

Neidhardt's proposal disclosed a modernist-functionalist approach to society, which he saw as an organism, and hence he spoke of cities as urban organisms (Dabac 1953). He was also strongly in favour of 'opening the vistas' in densely built areas of the old city of Sarajevo (Ottoman and Austro-Hungarian alike) and forging closer connections between the city centre and nature, apparently by allowing and even helping nature to penetrate the city. To this end, Neidhardt discussed several possible penetration points and corresponding corridors, one from the direction of Koševo valley, situated immediately to the north of the city. Neidhardt called this corridor 'the green artery', evoking once again the idea of the city as an organism. This green artery was supposed to start in the valley's 'gymnasium park', where the city's new football stadium, Koševo Stadium, opened in 1947. From here, via Đuro Pucar Stari Street, Neidhardt wanted to see a green belt stretching as far as possible into the city. In fact, in order to achieve the best possible connections with nature and 'open the vistas', he argued that the greenness from outside the city had to be pulled all the way to its core (Dabac 1953).

In pursuing the goal of integrating city and nature, Neidhardt planned several buildings for both sides of Đuro Pucar Stari Street, which would shortly after the publication of the *Mozaik* article change its name to Đure Đakovića Street.[18] According to Vladimir Kulić (2014), a historian of

---

[18] This is today's Alipašina Street.

Yugoslav socialist-modernist architecture, Neidhardt's work was strongly inspired by the 1950s' most influential international modernist, Le Corbusier,[19] and the buildings along the conceived 'green artery' were Corbusian in style. In keeping with the modernist character of Neidhardt's original idea, by the 1970s Đure Đakovića Street had become one of the most important *korzos* (promenades) in the city. Hence, during the Olympic period, a number of the city's popular movie theatres and music clubs were situated along it.[20] Just a short walk from the southern end of the street via its 350-metre-long extension, Hamze Hume Street, and just across from where Koševo Creek runs into the Miljacka River, stood Skenderija, the cultural and sports centre. Opened in 1969, it was host to a youth centre, among other things, which, by the time the city was preparing to host the Olympics, had become famous for its discotheque, still proudly claimed by locals to be one of the most modern of its kind in the whole of Yugoslavia ('Dom mladih', Skenderija-website).

During the Olympic period, the green artery (including the *korzo* part of Đure Đakovića) that Neidhardt outlined in *Mozaik* in 1953 would become what historian Kenneth Morrison (2016, 50–51) recently has called 'a new north-south [Olympic] axis within the city'. This axis, stretching from Skenderija (and its Olympic media centre) on the southern bank of the Miljacka River, to Zetra and Koševo Stadium, both in Koševo Valley, or, more precisely in the former 'gymnasium park'. It is noteworthy that the Games' opening ceremony took place in Koševo Stadium, the medal ceremonies in the square outside Skenderija and the closing ceremony at Zetra Ice Hall. Thus, the 'green artery' imagined by Neidhardt had become the inner city's 'Olympic artery'.

Not surprisingly, Đure Đakovića Street was thoroughly renovated for the Olympics,[21] partly in connection with the introduction of trolleybuses in Sarajevo that also affected many other streets between 1981 and 1984.[22]

[19] In fact, Le Corbusier toured Yugoslavia in 1953 (the same time as the *Mozaik* article appeared), initiating an enthusiastic wave of distinctly Corbusian buildings in most major cities. By this time, writes Kulić (2014), architects like Edvard Ravnikar in Ljubljana and Juraj Neidhardt in Sarajevo were well past replicating Le Corbusier's style and, in the case of the latter, slowly starting to develop a regionalist interpretation of Le Corbusier.

[20] It is noteworthy that the aforementioned youth subculture of New Primitivism emerged precisely in this area.

[21] J.V. (Vričko), 'Zar je to Sarajevo?', *Oslobođenje* 4.9.1983.

[22] A. Ku., 'Izmijenjen režim saobraćaja. Trolejbusi rekonstruišu ulice', *Oslobođenje* 8.9.1983, 8.

The trolleybuses were, as Jan Čihák (2016, 128) put it, a 'child' of Emerik Blum, a highly influential member of the Sarajevo Olympics' Organising Committee and Mayor of Sarajevo from 1981 to 1983, the period in which most of the construction of the Olympic venues and installations was completed. Blum is best known for his position as the founder and director of Sarajevo's largest and most successful company and Yugoslavia's most flourishing socialist conglomerate, Energoinvest, a multifaceted engineering and energy company that had offices in more than thirty countries, including the USA (Levinston 2013, 170). In the early 1970s, under Blum's leadership, Energoinvest was recognised in the West and in particular in the USA as one of the most prosperous conglomerates in the socialist world (Anderson 1972b, 43). Blum used his reputation and contacts in the USA to obtain the loan from the International Bank for Reconstruction and Development for the Project for the Protection of Sarajevo's Human Environment (Ličina Ramić 2017, 135–136). On this basis a recent biography has argued that Blum realised the importance of environmental protection before such issues became a global preoccupation, going on to apply his intellect and reputation to the protection of Sarajevo's environment (Baum 2002, 77). Blum's idea of introducing trolleybuses to Sarajevo should be seen from this perspective. Thus, new trolleybus lines in the city were not only meant to ease increasing traffic congestion. Running on electricity they were also seen as more environmentally friendly than buses. However, as the scope of the preparatory work necessary for the completion of the trolleybus network proved more extensive than anticipated, they did not start running until shortly after the Olympics finished, in September 1984.[23] Yet this was still 'the Olympic year', and as the initiative was indirectly connected to the Project for Protection of the Human Environment, in the collective memory of the city the introduction of trolleybuses was viewed as connected with the 1984 Olympics.[24] Moreover, the trolleybuses connected all the elements comprising Sarajevo's Olympic 'city-within-a-city': Zetra, the Koševo Stadium, Skenderija and the newly built Mojmilo and Dobrinja Olympic villages. Consequently, in Sarajevo's urban imaginary, the trolleybuses

[23] It is nevertheless interesting that in December 1983, the city's planning bureau still expected that trolleybuses would be introduced before the beginning of the Games. J. Vričko, 'Iz zavoda za izgradnju grada: Trolejbusi i prije početka igara', *Oslobodenje* 27.12.1983, 9.

[24] This popular view is also voiced in the Bosnian version of the popular internet encyclopaedia, *Wikipedia* 'GRAS Sarajevo'.

took their place in the Olympic transportation infrastructure along with the streamlined tram service, creating a sense of the emergent metropolis blessed with modern up-to-date public transportation.

Presented in the highly intellectual publication, *Mozaik*, and subsequently discussed by the city's planners and elites, 'the green belt' vision and the logic behind Zetra's naming remained largely unknown to the general public until the 1980s. Then, when the Olympics made it possible to realise the Zetra imaginary during the Olympic preparation period, the new Olympic multipurpose arena was named Zetra. Only then, did the newspapers and other local media start disseminating the ideas of Zetra imaginary to the wider populace. One example of how that worked appears in an early 1983 *Oslobođenje* article answering readers' questions, in which the authors devoted a lengthy paragraph to discussing the 'Ze-tra' portmanteau. Offering an answer to a reader's question about the meaning of the name, the supplement's journalist explained the name's origin, its nature-urban logic and the connection with the city's planning strategies.[25] Similarly, the locally appreciated *Sarajevo '84: All on the Games* (1984b, 38 & 60), the multilingual official guide (French, English, German and Serbo-Croatian), also sought to explain how Zetra connected 'the suburban and city green areas', and its centrality to the urban project of 'the so-called "Green Transverse"'.

As Sarajevo was getting closer to the Games, the Zetra portmanteau and the logic behind the construction of the Olympic complex in Koševo Valley was becoming common knowledge, as demonstrated by two articles by *Oslobođenje* journalist Boro Radosavljević. Covering Zetra for the 'Sarajevo Olympic Time Machine' serial in December 1982, the first article finished with: 'At the end, a short explanation for those asking themselves what ZETRA means. It is short for "green transversal", that is, the name for the area in Koševo Valley.'[26] In an article appearing a year later, however, Radosavljević only mentioned the portmanteau in passing, merely adding 'green transversal' in parentheses after mentioning Zetra.[27] Apparently, he, at least, felt that, by that time, further information was superfluous.

[25] H. Arifagić, E. Isaković, D. Paravac & Z. Kapetanović, 'Vi ste pitali "Oslobođenje" je dobilo odgovor—Pripreme za ZOI '84: Pahuljica koja se ne topi', *Oslobođenje* 16.1.1983, 5.

[26] Boro Radosavljević, 'Sarajevski olimpijski vremeplov (2). Biseri arhitekture na Koševu', *Oslobođenje* 14.12.1982, 9.

[27] Boro Radosavljević 'Od borilišta do borilišta. Olimpijski ulog za sutra', *Oslobođenje* 28, 29 & 30.11.1983, 5.

Built exclusively for the Olympics and intended to represent the key part of the Olympic legacy, Zetra became one of the central symbols of Olympic Sarajevo. In fact, it would not be an exaggeration to call it the trademark of Olympic Sarajevo.[28] It was the object of considerable pride, and reporting on its construction was frequent and extensive—in Sarajevo, Bosnia and Herzegovina and Yugoslavia in general.[29] Once finished and, importantly, after praise from the President of the IOC, Juan Antonio Samaranch, Zetra became a powerful tool in boosting a sense of self-confidence, both in the city and the whole of Yugoslavia. Accordingly, in the period immediately after its completion, the Sarajevan and Yugoslav media spared no words of praise and self-congratulation. 'The world is enchanted by Zetra', *Oslobodenje* told its readers in a report from the opening of the World Junior Speed Skating Championship, held in the outdoor part of the arena on the occasion of its completion in December 1982. Praising the architecture of the complex, the newspaper claimed that Zetra Olympic Hall was 'the pride of Sarajevo and the whole country' (Image 3.2).[30] Other Yugoslav newspapers were equally enthusiastic about it. For instance, Zagreb's sports daily *Sportske novosti* (*Sport News*) claimed, resembling *Oslobodenje*'s 'Then and Now' discussed earlier in the chapter, that Zetra arose from the 'ashes' or 'wasteland' to become an architectural wonder.[31] A couple of weeks after the official opening of the complex, *Oslobodenje* went even further and claimed that Zetra was no less than 'the prettiest sports complex in the whole of Europe!'[32] In sum, national and international recognition triggered a strong sense of self-confidence and self-congratulation in the city, boosting locals' pride both as Olympic hosts, but also as citizens of Sarajevo, with the obvious potential to affect Sarajevans' self-conceptions and self-knowledge. Thus, it

[28] As the December 1982 article put it, Zetra was 'the heart' of the Sarajevo Olympics. Boro Radosavljević 'Sarajevski olimpijski vremeplov (2). Biseri arhitekture na Koševu', *Oslobodenje* 14.12.1982, 9.

[29] In my analysis, I have utilised more than 100 articles on Zetra (excluding those in newspaper serials concerning the Olympic construction sites).

[30] Branko Tomić, 'Olimpijski podvig Sarajeva,' *Oslobodenje*, 14.12.1982, 1.

[31] Here from Organizacioni komitet XIV zimskih olimpijskih igara Jugoslavja-Sarajevo 1984, 'Izgradnja objekata (1981–1983)', *U znaku Sarajeva. Kako su xiv zimske olimpijske igre opisane u jugoslovenskoj štampi i JRT*, 1984, 78.

[32] Z. H., '"Zetra" pod ledom', *Oslobodenje* 27.,28., 29.11.1982, 17.

**Image 3.2**   The front page of *Oslobodenje* covering the opening of the Olympic multipurpose arena Zetra and reading 'Sarajevo's Olympic Triumph'. (Branko Tomić, 'Olimpijski podvig Sarajeva', *Oslobodenje* 14.12.1982, 1)

mattered that Zetra was now called an 'Olympic pearl', a jewel and even 'the first medal for the Olympic host city'.[33]

[33] Branko Tomić, 'Olimpijski podvig Sarajeva', *Oslobodenje* 14.2.1982, 1.

Nonetheless, even if the most obvious, Zetra was still far from the only Olympic venue where ideas concerning the integration and interconnection of natural and urban space were applied. The interpenetration of these ideas was omnipresent in most of the Olympic objects and installations.[34] Much like Zetra, Igman Mountain's ski jumps were referred to in *Oslobođenje* as 'the pearls', with the addition, 'if only the jumps could win medals'. It also stressed that construction of the installations was carried out 'in a common language' shared with nature. What that meant was further explained by the architect behind the ski jumps, Janez Gorišek, who was quoted as saying they were built in accordance with a 'modern approach' that integrated their concrete construction with the surrounding nature.[35]

The integration of an Olympic installation with nature was even more pronounced in the building of the Trebević Bobsleigh and Luge Track. In the interests of protecting the natural environment and minimising the construction taking place in it, only one combined track was built, serving both bobsleigh and luge. Both unique and a global novelty, Trebević represented 'model Sarajevo', according to *Sarajevo '84: All on the Games* (1984b, 39). In the same fashion that Zetra became the inner city's Olympic trademark, Trebević became the trademark for the surrounding mountains: a symbol of the emergent new Olympic Sarajevo.[36] Moreover, and again very similarly to Zetra, Trebević was praised in a range of official publications and newspaper articles which sometimes claimed the integrated Bobsleigh and Luge Track to be the most original contribution to the Olympics.[37] According to *Oslobođenje*, in an article headlined 'The Trebević Innovations' in its serial, 'Sarajevo Olympic Time Machine', it

---

[34] Moreover, one of the most-read popular-culture magazines in the country, Zagreb's *Start*, argued that Sarajevo as a city, in its entirety, was an ideal Olympic host due to its not being too big or too small and its proximity to nature and the surrounding mountains (*U znaku Sarajeva* 1984, 51). In an article on international press views of the city, *Oslobođenje* went even further, calling Sarajevo a 'tourist heaven'. Melita Karalić, 'Drugi o Olimpijadi. Duga između svijetova i vjekova', *Oslobođenje* 14.1.1984, 5.

[35] Henrik Ibelajz, 'Biseri Malog polja. Kad bi se za skakaonice dijelile medalje', *Oslobođenje* 9.2.1983, 13.

[36] It is also interesting that Trebević was one of Neidhardt's 'penetration directions', and, as we saw in the previous chapter, the main excursion and leisure destination for city dwellers.

[37] Boro Radosavljević 'Sarajevski olimpijski vremeplov (3). Trebevićke inovacije', *Oslobođenje* 15.12.1982, 11.

was not only one of the best in the world, it was also 'the most natural'.[38] Along the same lines, the Olympic Organising Committee insisted shortly after the Games that Trebević's innovativeness was not solely due to the combination of bobsleigh and luge tracks. The whole installation was, according to the report, conceived and built to fit 'the magical harmony of a built object and the [surrounding] nature' (*U znaku Sarajeva* 1984, 73). In addition, when reporting on construction of the track in August 1982, the newspaper claimed that, 'in an extraordinarily preserved natural ambience the construction of the bobsleigh and luge track on Mount Trebević is approaching its completion'.[39]

As is evident from the preceding analysis, within just a few years Sarajevo had managed to re-invent itself as an 'environmentally sensitive city', a view also voiced in the later edition of the aforementioned monograph *Sarajevo* (Prohić and Balić 1983). Moving away from its pejorative epithet, 'London of the Balkans', referring to the air pollution, Sarajevo now re-imagined itself as a model city taking its natural environment seriously. We saw that Drago Baum, Blum's biographer, argued provocatively that, when it came to environmental concerns, Blum was ahead of his time. Against that background, it is possible to posit the equally provocative argument that Olympic Sarajevo was also ahead of its time in terms of environmental protection. In discussing such issues in relation to host cities of the Summer Olympics, John R. Short (2012, 257) has argued that the creation of a green city has been among the dominant Olympic narratives since the 2000 Sydney Games when a deliberate greening of the event was instigated, one that coincided with a more general global imaginary of the green city.

Yet Sarajevo was already focusing on greening the Games in 1984. In that fashion, even the geographical advantage of having all the sports venues within a short radius was reinterpreted during the Olympic period as a matter of environmental concern. Thus, according to the second, 1983, edition of the *Sarajevo* monograph, 'The world of nature and urban amenities are in unique proximity here. The Olympics terrains and installations are situated within a radius of 22.5 km, which is considered one of

---

[38] Dodatak 'Izgradnja olimpijskih objekata. Radovi prije roka', *Oslobođenje* 16.12.1982, 4; B. Radosavljević 'Staze za aplauze', *Oslobođenje* 15.10.1981, 13; B. Radosavljević, 'Trebević—Najbolja staza na svijetu', *Oslobođenje* 23.9.1982, 9; Boro Radosavljević 'Sarajevski olimpijski vremeplov (3). Trebevićke inovacije', *Oslobođenje* 15.12.1982, 11.

[39] B. Radosavljević 'Trebevićka ljepotica u planiranom roku', *Oslobođenje* 31.8.1982, 2.

the most ideal concentrations in the world' (Prohić and Balić 1983). It
was also in this context, as mentioned above, that the Project for the
Protection of Sarajevo's Human Environment—previously proudly and
vividly celebrated as, among other things, 'the undertaking of the century'[40] and 'the unprecedented communal project'[41]—disappeared from the
discourse.

However, even if the Project gave up its place to the Olympics as the
largest infrastructural project in the city, it nevertheless left an indelible
mark. As the title of a 1982 *Oslobođenje* article had it, after the Project
ended, a strong imprint of it remained on the city.[42] Yet, in the sense of the
previous argument on the sociotechnical character of infrastructure, and
based on source material, it makes sense to argue that the mark the project
left on the city did not only take the form of physical infrastructure; it was
also imprinted on the attitudes of the city's population and its urban leadership towards the city's urban environment. An issue of *Oslobođenje* (3
May 1978) will serve to illustrate the point. Published in the period when
the city was impatiently waiting for the International Olympic Committee's
decision on its 1984 Winter Olympics bid, the issue included two articles
published in immediate proximity to each other. One dealt with the still
ongoing Project for the Protection of Sarajevo's Human Environment
and the second with the Olympic candidacy. The former sought to explain
the changing attitudes in the city towards the protection of the environment. According to this article, a more humane city was emerging with
the Project, and the change was affecting residents' relationships to their
city and its environment. Shortly put, their social conduct in the urban
environment was changing.[43] According to the second article, there was
strong support in the city for its Olympic candidacy. According to the
daily's journalists, if they won the candidacy, Sarajevans would be ready to
roll their sleeves up and do their best to prepare their city for the Olympics.[44]
Yet, as we will see in the next section, Olympic preparations were not only
about building and improving the infrastructure; they were as much about
changing certain attitudes and modes of social conduct.

---

[40] 'Uspjela operacija na srcu grada', *Oslobođenje Žurnal* 10.8.1980, 2.

[41] For example in the 1975 edition of *Sarajevo* (Prohić and Balić 1975).

[42] Z. Elez, 'Raport na kraju mandata. Iza akcije ostao trag', *Oslobođenje* 19.3.1982, 10.

[43] E. Mesihović, 'Za ljepši, humaniji grad', *Oslobođenje* 3.5.1978, 6.

[44] M. Borojević & J. Krešakljaković, 'Podrška i očekivanja', *Oslobođenje* 3.5.1978, 6.

## 3.3    DISCIPLINING SARAJEVANS FOR THE OLYMPICS

One special trait of the modernity dimension of the Olympics is their quality of 'performance' or 'exhibition'. This aspect is not only evident in official ceremonies and sporting competitions, but it encompasses the whole Olympic event, from bidding for Games to the closing ceremony and even beyond. Implicated in the notion of performance and exhibition are the spectators, that is, the real and the imagined global audience. Consequently, hosting the Olympics serves as a key occasion for host cities and their populations to construct and present images of themselves 'in the eyes of the world' (Roche 2000, 6), and in this respect Sarajevo was no exception. From the very beginning Sarajevo's urban political leadership paid considerable attention to the image Sarajevans performed before the world. A meeting of the city's section of the SSRN in February 1981 exemplifies this focus. Held after the city had started to receive substantial global attention and an increasing number of tourists and news reporters, the meeting was closely monitored by the local press, including *Oslobođenje*. Compiling its reports on the meeting as a collage comprising a main text and several related text boxes, the newspaper surveyed the meeting's various discussion topics and the conclusions that were reached. Two of the text boxes were numbered and used as two halves of the header for the main text. One informed readers that the SSRN had drawn up a working strategy comprising the most important activities and tasks that had to be accomplished in relation to hosting what was called 'this large sporting event'. It was complemented by the second text box insisting, among other things, that '[t]he Olympics are our collective act that cannot be imagined without the participation of all Sarajevans, from kindergartens, schools, work units, local communities to the Academy of Science'. Together, these two text boxes were presented as if providing a to-do Olympic preparation list for all Sarajevans. Given this content, it is not surprising that *Oslobođenje* chose to call the article as a whole, 'We are all the Olympic [Organising] Committee', implying that even though the Olympics were considered a sporting mega-event, responsibility for Olympic success was placed on all Sarajevans collectively and not on any individual sporting or political body in the city.[45]

There was still much more in this article. For instance, another text box sought to explain how the Olympics were Sarajevo's 'exam in front of the

---

[45] H. Arifagić & R. Kolar, 'Svi smo olimpijski komitet', *Oslobođenje*, 23.2.1981, 7.

entire world', resembling in this phrasing the afore-presented argument that the Olympics are performed in front of a global audience (both real and imagined). For this reason, the text box had it, the SSRN would work on making the city cleaner and more orderly, creating an atmosphere that would make athletes, journalists and visitors feel welcome. Yet another text box dealt with the criticism of slow service at one of the city's hotels mentioned by a German journalist in an otherwise very positive *Frankfurter Allgemeine Zeitung* article. Based on this criticism, the text box, entitled, 'And a Few Criticisms', stressed how important it was for overall Olympic success to improve the quality of service in Sarajevo before the Games. Commenting on this episode, Ahmed Karabegović, Secretary-General of the Olympic Organising Committee, explained that international journalists simply 'write what they see'. It was therefore up to the people of Sarajevo to make the journalists see things in the best possible light. Yet another text box claimed that the Olympics were providing new opportunities within the spheres of sport and tourism. Very much in the manner described in the previous chapter, it pointed out how important this 'exam in front of the world' was for the city's future as a tourist centre. This framed the Olympics as an occasion when the city could project itself onto the world screen for the purpose of its future development. In more general terms, we see here how the staging of the Olympics in the spotlight of the global media provided a setting for a dramaturgical re-making and representation of the host city (Short 2012, 257).

Finally, in the introduction to the article's main text, *Oslobođenje*'s journalists told readers about public 'Olympic debates', mentioning that they were occurring more and more often and becoming more extensive. These debates, argued the authors, were important occasions in which the broader populace could participate and offer suggestions and evaluations. The reason being, the two authors insisted, that the Olympics concerned all Sarajevans. Worded this way, the introduction in fact served as an invitation to Sarajevans to participate in the city's preparations for the Olympics even more eagerly and in even larger numbers. The text then elaborated on several important topics discussed at the meeting, including the need to, and the importance of, cleaning up the city, learning foreign languages and becoming familiar with the details of the Olympic programme in order to be able to provide the necessary service and hospitality to Olympic guests. The article then presented selected statements by different members of the SSRN concurring with its content.[46]

---

[46] H. Arifagić & R. Kolar, 'Svi smo olimpijski komitet', *Oslobođenje*, 23.2.1981, 7.

Material like this illustrates that the SSRN, the largest and most influential mass political organisation in Yugoslav society and supported by the Olympic Organising Committee and the local media, saw preparations for the Olympics as not simply being about completion of the Olympic infrastructure. It was not enough to create a modern and greener city. Residents also had to be prepared for the Olympics. To this end, city elites and political leaders, as well as the local media, drew on Sarajevans' civic pride, underlining that ensuring the success of the Olympics was a collective responsibility and calling for the strong and unrestrained engagement of the populace. Needless to say, this was not something only expressed at the SSRN meeting in February 1981. It was a common theme during the whole Olympic preparation period. We find a very similar example in two different reports on 'The Pre-Olympic Days in Sarajevo' in April 1982, the cultural festival mentioned in the previous chapter. First, in a report on the opening event, based on interviews with people from the SSRN and the Olympic Organising Committee, *Oslobođenje* argued that every single Sarajevan should by that time be feeling a duty and a responsibility towards the Olympics. Very much in this spirit, the article was titled, 'Five rings everybody should wear', referring to the Olympic symbol, and insisted that the Olympics were the responsibility of all Sarajevans, one that was ever-present.[47] The second report, covering the conclusion of the festival, was even more specific. It insisted that it was clear from the moment that the city won its Olympic bid that some things had to be changed and improved, and this concerned every single inhabitant of the city. Summarising the different debates and talks held in relation to the festival, the daily stressed the trending topics discussed. They concerned, among other things, various traffic issues, the general cleanliness of the city and the allegedly bad habits of residents in public. There had been some improvements since the city won the Olympic bid, the daily's journalist claimed. However, much work still had to be done to prepare the city for the Olympics so that it could present itself at the Games as a serious winter tourism centre—or 'maybe not that much', added the journalist in parentheses, if everybody fully engaged in the process.[48]

By 1982, the general impression was that substantial improvements had been made. Hence, while the 'Pre-Olympic Days' festival was going on,

[47] E.I., 'Pet prstenova da ih svako nosi', *Oslobođenje* 7.4.1982, 6.
[48] R. Ćerimagić, 'Predolimpijski dani. Da dodamo. Novi duh grada', *Oslobođenje* 18.4.1982, 11.

*Oslobođenje* published a report claiming that the city was becoming cleaner and public transport more punctual and orderly.[49] However, despite these important advancements, judging by the attention that the newspaper continued to pay to problematic issues in its reporting, the latter appeared to be multiplying. I argue that this impression was misleading for at least two reasons. First, time was getting short and accordingly, as the Games approached, a sense of urgency was becoming even more apparent. This was rather clearly expressed in an *Oslobođenje* article in June 1982, not long after the festival, in which it was argued that there was not much time left for discussion. Everybody had to get down to their own tasks immediately if the city were to stand any real chance of fulfilling its Olympic ambitions. It went on to refer to the President of the Olympic Organising Committee, Branko Mikulić, who had already addressed the issue at a meeting for the City Assembly at which he insisted that employees in the service and tourism sectors should raise their standards to meet expectations at the coming Olympics.[50] Second, with most of the infrastructural work nearing completion, longstanding problems with poor service or standards of cleanliness appeared more salient and critical. This was clearly enunciated in *Oslobođenje*'s criticism of Sarajevo's Tourist Board in March 1983 which addressed the problems of missing city-limit signs and littering on highways. Pointing to one example of missing signage, journalist Josip Vričko accentuated how important such guidance was 'in modern times', adding that the fact that the city was now closely associated with 'the Olympic rings' was anything but irrelevant to the matter.[51]

Analysis of *Oslobođenje*'s coverage of the issue indicates that the daily took a proactive position in this situation, which was interesting because *Oslobođenje* was the largest and by far the most influential newspaper in the whole of Bosnia and Herzegovina.[52] Even before the February 1982 festival, one of the newspaper's journalists, N. Idrizović, had pointed out that Sarajevo offered the impression of a 'foul and unkempt city'; however, he did not stop there, also mentioning the lack of professionalism among the

[49] A.H., 'Grad čistiji, saobraćaj uredniji', *Oslobođenje* 17.4.1982, 13.

[50] D. Stanojlović, 'Olimpijska razmišljanja. Ugostiteljski san i java', *Oslobođenje* 14.6.1982, 6.

[51] J. Vričko, 'Gdje su nam kapije grada? Vrata širom—zatvorena', *Oslobođenje* 20.3.1983, 7.

[52] According to official statistics in the Olympic period, *Oslobođenje* was among the ten top selling newspapers in Yugoslavia and the biggest seller in Bosnia and Herzegovina (*VGAJ* 1987, 225).

city's taxi drivers. Although this was not an article specifically about the Olympics, but about visitors to the city in general, the Olympic reference was clear. Idrizović concluded the article by pointing out, in the first person, that the standards of cleanliness should concern all citizens of the Olympic city—'to which guests have already started arriving'.[53] The next day, yet another article stressed the importance of the upcoming Olympic context and the city's position as a tourist centre. Yet, while advocating the need to clean up the city for the Games, it explicitly argued that this should not just be for the visitors, but first and foremost for those 'who spent all their lives' in Sarajevo. It is also noteworthy that this article explicitly argued that the goal of cleanliness was not only about cleaning up the city itself, but also about the population's habits, a message reflecting the article's title, 'Washing Up the City. Water Won't Wash Habits'.[54]

As the Olympics approached, *Oslobođenje* started broadening its focus to cover these 'habits' and, by 1983, we see an increasing number of articles dealing with the quality of service and politeness to customers. It was particularly diligent about reporting on Sarajevans who would be directly engaged in interactions with Olympic guests, either as workers in the service and tourism sectors or in private business. Thus, reporting on the readiness of families choosing to rent private rooms to Olympic guests, the newspaper demanded, in March 1983, 'a major change in habits' among Sarajevans.[55] A couple of months later, in a report on preparations for the Olympics, 'habits' were stressed again, with the dictum, 'smiles are more important than commodities'.[56] This implicitly announced the newspaper's upcoming serial, which would last almost nine months: 'Our Project: The Olympic Smile' (*Naša akcija: Olimpijski osmijeh*). The premise for the serial was that a smile, including 'the Olympic' one, symbolised politeness, friendliness and hospitality; yet it did not stop there, further linking 'the smile' to a number of concerns about preparations for the Olympics (Image 3.3).

The serial was launched on 1 June 1983 and presents an interesting source for analysis of the process of 'fixing', or preparing, Sarajevo's inhabitants for their role as Olympic hosts. It was originally conceived as

---

[53] N. Idrizović, 'Po jutru se dan poznaje. Utisak zapuštenog grada', *Oslobođenje* 15.3.1982, 9.

[54] D. Stanojlović, 'Počelo je umivanje grada. Voda ne pere navike', *Oslobođenje* 16.3.1983, 9.

[55] Ž. Rodić, 'Sarajevski predolimpijski dani. Navike treba mijenjati', *Oslobođenje* 1.3.1983, 2.

[56] E. Isaković, 'Pripreme za olimpijadu. Osmijeh važniji od robe', *Oslobođenje* 13.5.1983, 9.

OD SUTRA NAŠA AKCIJA

# Olimpijski osmijeh

Sutra i mi krećemo u konkretne pripreme za Olimpijadu. Rukovođeni seznanjem da ćemo pozitivne poene kod nekoliko stotina hiljada takmičara i gostiju, uz borilišta i zvaničan doček, steći za-sigurno u turističko--ugostiteljskoj branši, is-pitivaćemo kako su se ljudi iz ove oblasti pripremili za ovaj svjetski događaj, istovremeno i svojevrstan poslovni izazov. Jer, Olimpijada će rezultate pokazati tek nakon igara.

Zaći ćemo u »Evropu«, »Bristol«, »Srbiju«... ali, i u privatne restorane, kafane, picerije. Gostovaćemo i razgovarati sa gosti-ma. Pomagaće nam i gradska inspekcija. Gledaćemo sve: od ispeglane bluze, dočeka, kvaliteta jela i pića, preko uslužnosti, cijena, zakidanja, do osmijeha...

Znači, od sutra smo u svim poznatijim restoranima i kafanama grada i šire.

**Image 3.3**  *Oslobođenje* announcing its serial 'The Olympic Smile' with an interesting opening sentence: 'From tomorrow we are also starting with the actual preparations for the Olympics'. ('Od sutra naša akcija. Olimpijski osmijeh', *Oslobođenje* 1.6.1983, 9)

reportage on the situation in the city's catering industry. More precisely, as the serial's initial series outlined, the newspaper was interested in testing 'how ready or prepared Sarajevo was for the international guests coming to the city' for the Olympics.[57] With this in mind, the quality of food and service, prices and the cleanliness and cordiality of staff in the city's eateries, including canteens, restaurants, cafés and hotels, were subject to inspection. It is noteworthy that, when investigating these places, the journalists were often accompanied by official inspectors from the city's Commission for Hygiene. Besides the listed criteria, particular attention was paid to cases of shortchanging, failure to give customers bills and knowledge of foreign languages. Unsatisfactory service did not only lead to bad reviews; it could also provoke fines levied by the accompanying inspectors. In the worst cases, the businesses responsible were temporarily closed.[58]

After the initial 43 reports from the catering industry, the newspaper extended the serial, this time visiting the city's shops and examining the

[57] 'Od sutra naša akcija. Olimpijski osmijeh', *Oslobođenje* 1.6.1983, 9; R. Kolar, 'Naša akcija: Olimpijski osmijeh. Usluga naša, zadovoljstvo vaše', *Oslobođenje* 2.6.1983, 8.

[58] M.G., 'Naša akcija: Olimpijski osmijeh (7). "Kristal" do daljnjeg—zatvoren', *Oslobođenje* 8.6.1983, 9.

quality of the service they provided, with a slight expansion of focus. In addition to general levels of service and cleanliness, the friendliness of the staff and their knowledge of foreign languages, the daily now also paid special attention to the proper display of prices. The general impression provided by this series of reports was somewhat worse than in the first, probably due to shop workers' generally being less concerned with customer satisfaction than those working in restaurants, hotels or cafés. Hence, not surprisingly *Oslobođenje* wrote about 'the sour smile of shop workers'.[59] Specifically in relation to the city's position as Olympic host city, a common criticism concerned the unavailability of Olympic souvenirs,[60] or, as one instalment stated in its title, Vučko, the mascot, was not even to be found in the window display.[61]

This series of reports was then followed by one focusing on the service provided at post offices, in public administration offices, various sales outlets and so on. Named 'Counters', it followed up on efficiency, language skills, general politeness and professionalism among employees. One of the major complaints in this series concerned long queues. Another interesting detail concerned the ability of personnel to provide customers with the correct information about the Olympics and the city, which used wording resembling that of the report from the February 1981 meeting of the SSRN mentioned above.[62] The next series focused on taxis and public transport, with punctuality, cleanliness, shortchanging and transparency of prices guiding reportage. Interestingly, with every new theme increasing numbers of features were examined and controlled. Moreover, in the series on taxis and public transportation the newspaper also began to com-

---

[59] S. Lučkin, 'Naša akcija Olimpijski osmijeh—Trgovina: Gorki trgovački osmijeh', *Oslobođenje* 17.8.1983, 9.

[60] It is nevertheless quite interesting in this context that during the Olympics (including the immediate pre- and post-Olympic period) Sarajevo's shops were well supplied, provoking comments in *Duga* and *Polet*, among other magazines, that the city was like a 'left-over oasis of Yugoslavia from the prosperous 1970s'. Milomir Marić, 'Sve o zimskoj olimpijadi: Pred početak olimpijade. Sneško belić u bosanskom loncu', *Duga*, 28.1.1984, 22–23; Zoran Simić, 'Poletov bob dvosjed u Sarajevu', *Polet* 251, 9.2.1984, 13.

[61] B. V. 'Naša akcija Olimpijski osmijeh—Trgovina (13). Vučka ni u izlogu', *Oslobođenje* 30.7.1983, 13.

[62] For instance, in one case, workers at the bus station were criticised for being unable to provide information on how, and how often, Jahorina could be reached from the city. Ja. B. 'Naša akcija Olimpijski osmijeh—Šalteri (8). Ne znam kako će te do Jahorine', *Oslobođenje* 25.8.1983, 8.

ment on how bus and taxi drivers were dressing.[63] The newspaper then launched another inspection of the service and politeness offered by the catering industry, revisiting the places that had proved unsatisfactory in the first round, as well as some previously unvisited establishments. When all the service sectors had been covered, in late November 1983 the newspaper launched a new project dealing with cleanliness of the city in general, which had journalists visiting various neighbourhoods, parks, bus and train stations and so on. Then, in December 1983, with less than two months until the Olympics commenced, the two final, somewhat more specific, series of reports were launched in quick succession. These examined the new payment forms, like credit cards and cheques, and general shop supplies, respectively.[64]

The serial as a whole comprises an interesting source because it discloses a process of inculcating desirable attitudes and habits seen as necessary to transform Sarajevans into modern, global citizens ready to host the Olympics. It worked on the general principles of disciplining modern subjects, in Norbert Elias' sense (1994, 447), in that 'requirements' were not only imposed directly or indirectly on each individual by an authority (the newspaper, the Commission for Hygiene, the Olympic Organising Committee and the Socialist Alliance of Working People), they also took the form of self-disciplining. Through self-disciplining the imposed 'requirements' were mediated by the individual's own reflections on the consequences of other patterns of behaviour. Playing an important role in this context was the risk of financial consequences and public shaming if identified as providing unsatisfactory services, given the rising civic pride and urban solidarity resulting from the city's position as Olympic host. Conversely, the reports also offered a 'carrot' in the form of good reviews for establishments and workers conforming to norms and expectations, of which arguably the most illustrative example is found in an article in the first round in which a restaurant's waiters were lauded as 'the Olympic waiters'.[65] Finally, it should be stated that the serial did not only address deficiencies among employees, that is, service providers, it also addressed impoliteness and

[63] 'Naša akcija. Olimpijski osmijeh—o GRAS-u (1). Ne može. Čekaj!', *Oslobođenje*, 21.9.1983, 9.

[64] There were, the whole serial included, over 200 reports.

[65] 'Naša akcija: Olimpijski osmijeh (5). Malo sam se preš'o', *Oslobođenje* 6.6.1983, 6.

undesirable behaviour among customers,[66] placing emphasis on the situation in which a social practice was conducted and not only on one side of the exchange: all Sarajevans were to act properly and according to expectations during the Olympics, not only employees.

From the first series of inspection reports, the serial became very popular and the project gained broad support, most notably from the Sarajevo Tourist Board which praised the project and offered financial help.[67] The Sarajevo Tourist Board was one of the driving forces behind the organisation of the Games and the promotion of the city so its interest in the serial was not surprising. Furthermore, after every series a roundtable was held which presented its results and sought to make the project even more effective. Referring idiomatically to the sense of dignity and prestige that the city attached to hosting the Olympics, the first roundtable insisted that Sarajevo would 'meet the world with an honest face'. Furthermore, it also commended the 'engaged journalism' of the project and encouraged broad public engagement in it.[68] As a result, with the second series of reports, Sarajevans started contacting the newspaper, either calling to report irregularities themselves or writing readers' letters on the topic,[69] thereby taking ownership of the event in order to defend their communal pride. This offers a clear illustration of how Olympics 'tap into large reservoirs of civic pride and deep feeling of urban community', as John R. Short (2012, 255) phrases it.

Uplifted by the success, the serial's journalists became increasingly self-confident. By the midway evaluation of the second round of reports (the one on shop workers), they insisted that 'a smile was worth more than gold'.[70] Here we see a symbolic inflation in the worth of 'the Olympic smile' from its being 'more important than commodities' in May 1983 to being 'worth more than gold' in August of the same year. It is in this con-

[66] This could for, instance, be a matter of ill-mannered guests or customers not respecting the queues. For instance in El. Ka., 'Naša akcija: Olimpijski osmijeh—Šalteri (4). I ljubazni i nekulturni', *Oslobođenje* 21.8.1983, 6; or S. L. 'Naša akcija: Olimpijski osmijeh—Šalteri (12). U red druže!', *Oslobođenje* 29.8.1983, 6.

[67] M.G., 'Naša akcija: Olimpijski osmijeh (43). Sarajevo na dlanu', *Oslobođenje*, 14.7.1983, 8.

[68] M.G., 'Okrugli sto o Našoj akciji "Olimpijski osmijeh". Može i kreč umjesto lamperije', *Oslobođenje*, 15.7.1983, 7.

[69] H.I., 'Naša akcija. Olimpijski osmijeh—Trgovina (5). Kafa (jedino) za prijatelje', *Oslobođenje*, 22.7.1983, 8.

[70] 'Naša akcija. Olimpijski osmijeh—Trgovina. Manjak i pored zakidanja', *Oslobođenje*, 4.8.1983, 8.

text of 'the Olympic smile' that the daily announced in October 1983—some four months before the Games, as the second round of inspecting the catering industry began—'Now, it is up to Sarajevans'.[71]

## BIBLIOGRAPHY

### BOOKS, ARTICLES, REPORTS, BLOGS AND WEBSITES

Anderson, Raymond H. 1972b. Yugoslav Enterprise Prospers. *The New York Times*, October 7, 1972, 43. https://www.nytimes.com/1972/10/07/archives/yugoslav-enterprise-prospers-stress-on-efficiency-builds-a.html.

Baum, Drago. 2002. *Emerik Blum. Monografija*. Sarajevo: Sahinpašić.

Berg, Adam P. 2016. *Denver '76: The Winter Olympics and the Politics of Growth in Colorado during the Late 1960s and Early 1970s* (Doctor of Philosophy, The Pennsylvania State University).

Čihák, Jan. 2016. *Tramvaji i trolejbusi / Tramvaje a trolejbusy*. Ústí na Labem: Jan Čihák.

Dabac, Tošo. 1953. Ing. Juraj Neodhardt: Ovako ćemo izgraditi Sarajevo u budućnosti. *Mozaik*, September 1953. http://www.yugopapir.com/2013/08/ing-juraj-neidhardt-ovako-cemo.html.

Edwards, Paul N. 2003. Infrastructure and Modernity: Force, Time, and Social Organization in the History of Sociotechnical Systems. In *Technology and Modernity*, ed. Thomas J. Misa, Philip Brey, and Andrew Feenberg, 185–226. Cambridge: MIT Press.

Elias, Norbert. 1994. *The Civilizing Process*. Oxford: Blackwell.

Harvey, David. 1996. The Cities or Urbanization? *City: Analysis of Urban Trends, Culture, Theory, Policy, Action* 1 (1–2): 38–61.

Jokić, Gojko. 1984. Gradovi-Metropole - Sarajevo. In *Čudesna Jugoslavija*. Svjetlost, 250–253.

Kulić, Vladimir. 2014. The Scope of Socialist Modernism: Architecture and State Representation in Postwar Yugoslavia. In *Sanctioning Modernism: Architecture and the Making of Postwar Identities*, ed. Vladimir Kulić, Timothy Parker, and Monica Penick. Austin, TX: University of Texas Press.

Levinston, Charles. 2013. East-West Trade and the Unions. In *International Trade Unionism*, 142–202. London: Routledge.

Ličina Ramić, Aida. 2017. Od ekološke katastrofe do olimpijskog grada—Sarajevo 1971–1984. In *Poplava, zemljotres, smog: prilozi ekohistoriji Bosne i Hercegovine u 20. stoljeću: zbornik radova*, ed. Amir Duranović, 115–147. Sarajevo:

---

[71] 'Sad je na sarajlijama', *Oslobođenje*, 3.10.1983, 2.

Udruženje za modernu historiju/Udruga za modernu povijest (Edicija Zbornici; knj. 3).

Morrison, Kenneth. 2016. *Sarajevo's Holiday Inn on the Frontline of Politics and War*. Palgrave Macmillan.

Prohić, Kasim, and Sulejman Balić. 1975. *Sarajevo*. Sarajevo: Turistički savez Sarajevo.

————. 1983. *Sarajevo*. Sarajevo: Turistički savez Sarajevo.

Roche, Maurice. 2000. *Mega-events and Modernity: Olympics, Expos and the Growth of Global Culture*. London: Routledge.

Sarantakes, Nicholas Evan. 2010. *Dropping the Torch. Jimmy Carter, the Olympic Boycott, and the Cold War*. Cambridge: Cambridge University Press.

Short, John R. 2012. Globalization, Cities, and the Summer Olympics. In *The Making of Olympic Cities: Critical Concepts in Urban Studies, Volume I: Contexts and Overviews*, ed. John R. Gold and Margaret M. Gold, 235–262. London and New York: Routledge.

SSRNBiH (Gradska konferencija SSRNBiH Sarajevo). 1984. *Sarajevo—Olimpijski grad: Ljudi i akcija*. Sarajevo: NIŠRO Oslobođenje.

TSOOC: The Sarajevo Organizing Committee of the XIV Olympic Winter Games Yugoslavia. 1984b. *Sarajevo '84. Yugoslavia 8-19.02*. Final Report Published by the Organizing Committee of the XIV Winter Olympic Games 1984 in Sarajevo. Sarajevo: Oslobođenje.

*U znaku Sarajeva. Kako su xiv zimske olimpijske igre opisane u jugoslovenskoj štampi i JRT*. 1984. Eds. Zlatan Husarić, Dušan Paravac, Dževad Tašić, Hidajet Delić, Ante Jelavić and Velimir Jojić. Sarajevo: Organizacioni komitet XIV zimskih olimpijskih igara.

*VGAJ (Veliki geografski atlas Jugoslavije)*. 1987. Ed. Ivan Bertić. Zagreb: Liber.

Vuic, Jason. 2015. *The Sarajevo Olympics: A History of the 1984 Winter Olympic Games*. Amherst and Boston: University of Massachusetts Press.

RECORDS (ISCOGRAPHY)

ZP (Zabranjeno pušenje). 1984a. Abid. *Das ist Walter*. Zagreb: Jugoton.

CHAPTER 4

# Catching Up With the West with the Sarajevo Olympics

In his discussion on different dimensions of the Olympic Games, Maurice Roche argues that their development parallels the growth and spread of 'modernity'. According to this argument, the Olympics are important because they offer national and international audiences something dramatic and extraordinary, beyond the rationality and routine of modern everyday life. Consequently, they tend to become readily identifiable and memorable public events that people use as temporal and cultural markers which orient their individual and collective 'identity work'. Thence, although short-term sporting events, the Olympics serve as important points of reference with long-term cultural perspectives, meaning they can be seen as cultural mega-events that contribute to modernity's pace and direction of change (Roche 2000, 6–7).

Roche further argues that, as 'modern' cultural events, Olympics are 'progressive' because they typically involve non-religious/secular values, ideologies and principles of organisation connected with 'Western civilization', including positive roles for science and technology (or 'techno-rationalism'), capitalism, universalistic humanism, urbanism and transnational levels of organisation, communications and transport. However, precisely because of their 'modernity' and 'progressiveness' and because of the reflexivity this implies, notions of the Olympics inherently contain implicit or explicit references to modernity's changing versions of the past and future. In other words, the Olympics can at times contribute

Z. Jovanovic, *A Cultural History of the 1984 Winter Olympics,
Modernity, Memory and Identity in South-East Europe*,
https://doi.org/10.1007/978-3-030-76598-9_4

to social change and thus to the process of modernisation in which preceding periods are seen as 'traditional' and pre-modern (Roche 2000, 8–9).

The extent to which an early post-Olympic serial in *Oslobođenje* corresponds with Roche's description of the modernity dimension of the Olympics is interesting in this context. Entitled 'Sarajevo: Postolimpijske refleksije' ('Sarajevo: Post-Olympic Reflections'), it was written by one of the leading members of the Organising Committee of the Sarajevo Olympics, Aziz Hadžihasanović.[1] Its premise is expressed in the first sentence of the opening article: The Sarajevo Olympics, according to Hadžihasanović, were 'a ground-breaking step' in the city's history. Against this opening, the author then moves on to claim that the Olympics changed Sarajevo forever, reckoning, '[t]he Olympics, obviously, like a gigantic wave splashed all the pores and margins of [previously] existing Sarajevan life, and offered something new, something different, and something bigger'.[2] This observation strongly resonates with the extraordinariness of the Olympics and the social change they engender described by Roche in his discussion of the modern/non-modern dimension of Olympic mega-events.

In the second article of the serial, Hadžihasanović pointed out several aspects of social change caused by the Sarajevo Olympics. Suggesting that as a result of the 'collective effort' and 'common will' of all Sarajevans to make their city a 'prettier, cleaner and more kind' place to be in, Hadžihasanović claimed that during the Olympic period Sarajevo transformed into a 'world city of order and cleanliness'.[3] 'In this way', he wrote, 'by organizing the 14th Winter Olympics, the city rediscovered itself',[4] deviating 'from previously existing norms, according to which the sights and attractions in the city were enough in themselves, and no further effort was needed to also make their immediate surroundings pretty, orderly and ennobled'. Rediscovered, the Olympic city now put much more effort into arranging its shop windows, whitewashing its facades, putting up info-visual boards and cleaning businesses, shops, restaurants

---

[1] Recently Hadžihasanović published a book using some of the same material and reflections. See (Hadžihasanović 2010).

[2] Aziz Hadžihasanović, 'Sarajevo: Postolimpijske refleksije (I). Novo u starom', *Oslobođenje* 28.3.1984, 3.

[3] Aziz Hadžihasanović, 'Sarajevo: Postolimpijske refleksije (II). Red za ugled', *Oslobođenje* 29.3.1984, 3.

[4] Aziz Hadžihasanović, 'Sarajevo: Postolimpijske refleksije (III). Ram za lijepo', *Oslobođenje* 30.3.1984, 3.

and streets. In Hadžihasanović's view, this development revealed that the Olympics had a 'strong pedagogical dimension', as modernising the city and *putting it in order* had spurred self-discipline among its residents, engendering, according to the author, 'the needed respect and endeavour to behave nicely in the pleasant, newly created physical ambience of the city'.[5] Hadžihasanović's interpretation of the development in Olympic Sarajevo strongly resembles Roche's argument that, as cultural mega-events, the Olympics offer modernity the pace and direction of change.

Moreover, the self-discipline which Hadžihasanović mentioned also greatly resembles the process of disciplining discussed in the previous chapter, once again illustrating the social change resulting from the city's position as an Olympic host city. It is also interesting how, in relation to this process, the author defined the preceding periods as 'traditional' and hence pre-modern, and how he saw the cutting edge of change as being qualitatively different from the present. As we see in more detail later in this chapter, several times in his articles Hadžihasanović, implicitly or explicitly, counterposed modernist universalism and techno-rationalist positivism with what he called '*čaršija* mentality',[6] 'bazar traditionalisms'[7] and 'Balkan manners and its historical [Ottoman] heritage and mentality'.[8] In doing so, he made use of the general and at that time dominant discourse on 'modernity' and the common *Balkanist* (self-)representation. According to this form of self-representation, the Balkans' principal

[5] Aziz Hadžihasanović, 'Sarajevo: Postolimpijske refleksije (III). Ram za lijepo', *Oslobođenje* 30.3.1984, 3.
[6] Aziz Hadžihasanović, 'Sarajevo: Postolimpijske refleksije (I). Novo u starom', *Oslobođenje* 28.3.1984, 3.
*Čaršija mentality (čaršijski mentalitet)* refers here to the trope of *čaršija*. In the Balkans, particularly in Bosnia and Herzegovina and Macedonia, the *čaršija* represents an urban structure typical of the Ottoman era when it was, most commonly, found in the centre of the city and concentrated much of its economic and commercial activities. According to Dušan Grabrijan (1984, 37–53) the architectural features of the *čaršija* gave the city its identity and reflected its spirit. It was usually organised around a mosque and contained various stalls and the city administration and official buildings. Today (if still preserved after the departure of the Ottomans) the Čaršija has changed its original function; back is the reference to the 'premodern' times of the Ottoman Empire and their corresponding *čaršijski mentalitet*.
[7] Aziz Hadžihasanović, 'Sarajevo: Postolimpijske refleksije. Novo u starom', *Oslobođenje* 28.3.1984, 3. & Aziz Hadžihasanović, 'Sarajevo: Postolimpijske refleksije (III). Ram za lijepo', *Oslobođenje* 30.3.1984, 3.
[8] Aziz Hadžihasanović, 'Sarajevo: Postolimpijske refleksije (II). Red za ugled', *Oslobođenje* 29.3.1984, 3.

characteristic was the region's alleged backwardness vis-à-vis Western Europe (Čolović 2013). Consequently, the Balkans' only way into modernity was via eradicating its non-Western cultural traits engendered in 'Balkan manners' and 'Ottoman *čaršija* mentality'. This, according to Hadžihasanović's argument, is a goal that Sarajevo and Sarajevans finally attained during, and thanks to, the Olympic Games.

Interestingly, according to Hadžihasanović, the cutting edge of change was to be found in the retail sphere, in consumer culture and, in particular, customer services. Most notably, in the ninth of the serial's twelve articles, he argued that the lowly shop counter developed an important social dimension as, particularly during the Olympic period, it became the 'point of the most immediate communication between the city and the *foreign visitor*' (emphasis added).[9] The importance of good customer service did not, in this context, only refer to Sarajevo's newly won position as a potentially global tourist centre. Hadžihasanović was also drawing attention to the current economic situation in Yugoslavia, arguing that the retail sector, commerce and trade had the potential to show the way out of the economic crisis that had hit the country while Sarajevo was preparing for the Olympics. It is also noteworthy that the author saw Olympic success as closely connected to Yugoslavia's socialist self-managing system,[10] a particularly interesting claim when compared with the link between the Olympics and capitalism suggested by Roche.

In this respect, it is pertinent that Hadžihasanović began his discussion with reference to a commentary published in the *Los Angeles Times* a couple of days after the opening of the Sarajevo Olympics. The commentary asked what Los Angeles, as the host city for the 1984 Summer Olympics, had to do in order to achieve the same prominence as Sarajevo.[11] In Hadžihasanović's article, the *Los Angeles Times* quote was placed in a continuation of the article's subheading reading 'The counter's new clothes.

[9] Aziz Hadžihasanović, 'Sarajevo: Postolimpijske refleksije (IX). Novo ruho tezge. Kako dostići Sarajevo,' *Oslobođenje* 5.4.1984, 3.
[10] Aziz Hadžihasanović, 'Sarajevo: Postolimpijske refleksije (V). Izazov nove ere', *Oslobođenje* 1.4.1984, 2; 'Sarajevo: Postolimpijske refleksije (VII). Grad na nogama', *Oslobođenje* 3.4.1984, 3; and—'Sarajevo: Postolimpijske refleksije (IX). Novo ruho tezge. Kako dostići Sarajevo', *Oslobođenje* 5.4.1984, 3.
[11] Aziz Hadžihasanović, 'Sarajevo: Postolimpijske refleksije (IX). Novo ruho tezge. Kako dostići Sarajevo,' *Oslobođenje* 5.4.1984, 3.

How to catch up with Sarajevo.'[12] Paired this way, the subheading and the quotation invoked some important cultural references concerning the idea of modernity in Yugoslavia. For instance, the notion of *catching up* used here is inherent to the general idea of 'modernity' in Yugoslavia and the Balkans, expressed in the omnipresent aspiration and ambition of 'catching up' to the West in terms of economic, cultural and political development.

Against this background and bearing in mind Maurice Roche's argument that the Olympics involve values, ideologies and principles of organisation connected with capitalism, in the following section, I discuss the notion of 'catching up' in relation to Yugoslavia's then status as a socialist country vis-à-vis the capitalist West. Yet I want to emphasise that the chapter should not be read as a discussion of whether Yugoslavia and Sarajevo in fact achieved this catch up. Instead, my primary interest is to examine and explain the impact of the Olympics on cultural practices and understandings. In pursuing this endeavour, I proceed by introducing the topic of socialist consumer culture and placing Yugoslav consumer culture in the context of global capitalist economy. While my focus in the first section is mostly on the whole of Yugoslavia, in the second section I zoom in on Sarajevo and—given I am interested in changes in cultural representations of the city—in that section I examine those representations reflecting the notion that, with the Olympics, Sarajevo, finally—even if only for a short while—managed to catch up with, or even surpass the West. It is also from this perspective that the section discusses the city's Olympic 'catching up' in relation to its Ottoman past.

## 4.1    'THE FIRST WINTER OLYMPICS EVER HELD IN A COMMUNIST COUNTRY': YUGOSLAVIA BETWEEN COMMUNISM AND CAPITALISM

'An essential part of being modern is thinking that you are modern' and 'up with the times', observes C.A. Bayly (2004, 10) in his seminal work, *The Birth of the Modern World*. Tracing cultural transformations that were shaped by and in turn also shaped the forces of globalising modernity, Bayly argues that 'modernity' is best understood as a process of emulation and borrowing across the world's regions in order to 'be up with the times'. While explicitly referring to time, and thus to the temporality of

---

[12] Ibid.

modernity, Bayly seems to be somewhat more concerned with the spatial dimension of modernity, judging by his focus on its relationship with globalisation. Relating this to the argument I presented above—that reflexivity is inherent to the notion of 'modernity' as the term implicitly and/or explicitly refers to the non-modern, in particular the 'pre' modern—it can be claimed that this reflexivity has an important spatial dimension, with some regions of the world being regarded as having certain 'pre' modern characteristics. In this respect, scholars dealing with the topic of modernity in Eastern and Southeastern Europe have argued that 'modernity' can be understood as a specific Western perception that can be traced back, at least, to the Enlightenment (von Puttkamer 2014, 19). At the core of this perception lies the notion of 'us' and 'them', of modernity and backwardness. Seen from this perspective, as part of the modern world of Western Europe's closest periphery, Eastern and Southeastern Europe emerged as Western Europe's most immediate backward 'other' in the course of the eighteenth century. Ever since, this 'otherness' shaped common perceptions—including also self-perceptions—of 'Eastern Europe' and 'the Balkans' and their alleged inferior position vis-à-vis Western Europe.

During the last few decades, discomfort with this has become one of the driving forces in historical debates on Eastern Europe and the Balkans. Starting with the mid-1990s' works of Larry Wolff (1997) and Maria Todorova (1997), the historiography of the region experienced what has recently been coined 'the spatial turn in historical debates on Eastern Europe' (Holubec et al. 2014, 9). As a derivative of the cultural turn in social and human sciences, the spatial turn arose from the idea that a given geographical space and its natural conditions do not predetermine the history of peoples and societies. Rather, peoples and societies shape space by creating infrastructure and symbolic orders, with the notion of 'catching up' being one of the symbolic orders that has dominated perceptions and self-perceptions of Eastern Europe vis-à-vis Western Europe. As early as the late sixteenth century a metaphorical understanding emerged of Eastern Europe as a younger sister learning from her older, more developed sibling, Western Europe, with the former trying to 'catch up' with the more mature and developed latter—economically, but also culturally and politically. This developed into the idea of a backward, non-modern Eastern Europe from the eighteenth century. In this situation, the leaders of the Eastern European states that emerged from the eighteenth century on reacted with a mixture of resignation and frenzied determination to catch up to the West by accelerating economic development through different statist policies (von Puttkamer 2014, 26).

In the twentieth century, and with the arrival of communism and the establishment of the Soviet Union, a new, ideological, component was added to this East-West perception. In the USSR in the 1920s and 1930s a discourse of 'Russian backwardness' appeared, which expressed the need 'to catch up and overtake' the most developed capitalist countries economically. After the Second World War, with most of Eastern and Southeastern Europe becoming communist, this ideologically laden discourse of competition between communism and capitalism became even more widespread in the USSR. During the Cold War, and in particular under Khrushchev and Brezhnev, 'catch up and overtake' became a common metaphor in the USSR that depicted the country's relationship to its archenemy, the USA. This was voiced in Khrushchev's use of a metaphor 'catch up and overtake America in the per-capita production of meat, milk and butter' in 1957 (Scherrer 2014, 10–11). Throughout this period, it became common practice among politicians and also ordinary citizens, not only in the USSR but in the whole Eastern bloc, to measure what was happening in their countries against the standards of the capitalist West. This practice became particularly widespread among the youth and in the sphere of popular consumer culture which, from the 1960s, increasingly defined the everyday life of the citizens in Eastern Europe and their related idea of modernity (Luthar and Pušnik 2010, 11).

As a socialist country situated in the south-east sector of the continent, Yugoslavia exhibited many of the same traits as Eastern European countries. As Igor Duda (2017, 391–408) argues in his history of everyday life in Yugoslavia, the central metaphor in its consumer cultural development was also 'catching up with Europe', meaning the western part of it. However, because Yugoslavia was not part of the Eastern Bloc and was relatively open to the West and its influence, another important dimension of 'catching up' surfaced in Yugoslavia. As Breda Luthar and Maruša Pušnik (2010, 11) have argued in their work on everyday life in Socialist Yugoslavia, there was a constant sense of 'secondariness' in Yugoslav identity vis-à-vis the capitalist West. According to this argument Yugoslavia was symbolically the result of a Western gaze imposing its hegemony on its non-Western periphery. This defined the otherness of Yugoslavia in terms of its peripheral geographical position, relative economic backwardness and the particularities of its socialist ideology and values. Consequently, Yugoslavia's citizens depended on Western evaluations of the state-of-things in Yugoslavia to shape the image of their country abroad and their own cultural identities.

In Sarajevo, this sense of secondariness reached new heights during the Olympic period. Due to their nature as a cultural festival, combining the two major subgenres of 'exhibition' and 'performance', the Sarajevo Olympics—like any other Olympics—were performed/exhibited to the real and the imagined global audience (Roche 2000, 8–9). Consequently, right from the start of the Olympic preparation period, *Oslobođenje* began reposting news on Sarajevo that appeared in the international press. Gradually, international coverage of preparations for the Games became everyday news in the Sarajevan media, increasing in frequency with the approach of the Games.[13] As we saw in the previous chapters, a sense of the world's gazing on Sarajevo was constant and increasingly omnipresent, strongly affecting Sarajevans' self-image and cultural representations. Hadžihasanović caught this very vividly in the last, twelfth, article of his serial in *Oslobođenje*, when he pointed out that during the Olympics it became the norm for Sarajevans to 'see themselves reflected in the eyes of the world'.[14] This implied that international reportage on the city's Olympic performance worked as a mirror in which the city populace evaluated itself, its deeds and accomplishments and, on the basis of such self-evaluation, constructed its cultural identity.

Hadžihasanović himself was not immune to this sense of secondariness, which materialised most clearly in his choice to include, in each of the serial's articles, short messages selected either from one of many letters sent in the immediate post-Olympic period to the Mayor of Sarajevo by people from the West, or quoted from the Western press or news agencies—like the comment from the *Los Angeles Times* that he used as an epigraph for his aforementioned article focusing on the customer services in Olympic Sarajevo (Image 4.1). As already argued, Hadžihasanović's use of it created the impression that during the 1984 Winter Olympics Yugoslavia appeared to have finally managed, at least for a short while, to catch up to and even overtake the West. It is interesting that Hadžihasanović included this comment in an article dealing with consumer culture and consumption practices in Olympic Sarajevo titled, 'The counter's new clothes', in which he addressed the issue of capitalist consumption practices:

[13] As we saw in the first chapter, in 1982 longer and more interesting coverage from all over the world began to appear. By the turn of the year 1983–1984 they were published on a daily basis.

[14] Aziz Hadžihasanović, 'Sarajevo: Postolimpijske refleksije (XII). Osmijeh sa obavezom', *Oslobođenje* 8.4.1984, 2.

**Image 4.1**   The title and the heading for an article in an *Oslobođenje* post-Olympic serial: 'How to catch up with Sarajevo. "… What, for God's sake, do we need to do in Los Angeles before the beginning of the Summer Olympic Games, in order to secure that we achieve the same prominence as Sarajevo?"' (*Los Angeles Times* 10.2.1984). (Aziz Hadžihasanović, 'Sarajevo: Postolimpijske refleksije (IX). Novo ruho tezge. Kako dostići Sarajevo', *Oslobođenje* 5.4.1984, 3)

It has already been said that Sarajevo's retail sector will increasingly face customers—guests looking for a better and more varied selection than the one available now in terms of supply and services. A more and more demanding customer, pampered by the uncompromising competitive psychology of capitalist service, will be ever more present. As our Olympic experience has particularly shown us, such a customer will expect and require a greater selection of products, more attractive design and, above all, impeccable service.

Customer service—in all its aspects, from a kindly welcome to the farewell smile—is increasingly becoming a very refined expression of the general business and cultural situation in the city. Hence, the need to provide good and fair customer service, in its widest sense, becomes an imperative of [our] time.[15]

---

[15] Aziz Hadžihasanović, 'Sarajevo: Postolimpijske refleksije (IX). Novo ruho tezge. Kako dostići Sarajevo,' *Oslobođenje* 5.4.1984, 3.

Seen through the lens of the described otherness of Socialist Yugoslavia and its widespread sense of *secondariness* to the West, and in light of Roche's argument on the links between the Olympics, modernity and capitalism, the article seems to be implying that becoming a global tourist centre, which Sarajevo was hoping to do, meant that customer service in the socialist country had to be synchronised with capitalist consumption practices and expectations. Seen from this perspective, the title of the article indicates that the Olympics had contributed to social change in Sarajevo, very much in line with Roche's argument. In addition, Hadžihasanović implicitly argued that it was desirable to follow established capitalist norms and consumer practices because customer service 'was increasingly becoming an expression of the general business culture in a city', just as 'good and fair customer service' was becoming 'the imperative of the time'. This idea of specific praxis being 'the imperative of the time' leads us back to Bayly's definition of modernity as incorporating the idea of being 'up with the times'.

This was, however, far from the only place in the *Oslobođenje* serial where Hadžihasanović's interpretation of the impact of the Olympics on Sarajevo resonated with Bayly's framing of modernity. In fact, analysis of the serial indicates that 'the imperative of the time' seems to be at its core, as Hadžihasanović put considerable effort into explaining Olympic impact in the fields of tourism, culture, art and consumption in terms of their being 'in the spirit of time',[16] meeting 'the challenges of the new era'[17] and 'work in accordance with new [rules]'.[18] One expression of this appears to have been the longer opening hours of the city's stores, in particular supermarkets, which, as several sources mentioned, stayed open late during the Olympics.[19] Hadžihasanović himself addressed this new phenomenon in the article dealing with consumer culture and practices in Olympic Sarajevo, where he argued that the longer hours of operation strongly

[16] Aziz Hadžihasanović, 'Sarajevo: Postolimpijske refleksije (IV). Riznica na dlanu', *Oslobođenje* 31.3.1984, 3.
[17] Aziz Hadžihasanović, 'Sarajevo: Postolimpijske refleksije (V). Izazov nove ere,' *Oslobođenje* 1.4.1984, 2.
[18] Aziz Hadžihasanović, 'Sarajevo: Postolimpijske refleksije (IX). Novo ruho tezge. Kako dostići Sarajevo,' *Oslobođenje* 5.4.1984, 3.
[19] F. N., 'Olimpijsko radno vrijeme', *Borba* 24.1.1984, 10; Aziz Hadžihasanović, 'Sarajevo: Postolimpijske refleksije. Novo u starom', *Oslobođenje* 28.3.1984, 3; Aziz Hadžihasanović, 'Sarajevo: Postolimpijske refleksije (IX). Novo ruho tezge. Kako dostići Sarajevo,' *Oslobođenje* 5.4.1984, 3.

affected urban and social life in the city. In fact, Hadžihasanović was very eager to explain how the city's position as an Olympic host city affected local consumption culture in general and to depict social changes relating to new consumer practices that emerged with the Olympics.

Most notably, he argued that longer opening hours for the city's stores, 'despite often being a mechanical and not thoroughly studied' phenomenon, quickly gave the city a new 'dimension of life, activities and practicability'. Thanks to the stores being open late at night, wrote Hadžihasanović, Sarajevo attained the different character of a 'more lively and more immediate city' and generated a sense of previously unseen relaxation in locals' everyday life as it gave them the opportunity to go out after work and shop in a more relaxed manner. Against this background, Hadžihasanović reckoned that the end result of this new situation was not only that customers would probably buy more, but also that late night shopping would become a habit and, with time, an unavoidable necessity.[20]

Hadžihasanović's observation indicates that Sarajevans happily embraced new practices that were based on the ideas, values and principles that we commonly associate with capitalism. Moreover, from the perspective of Roche's argument about the close relation between modernity, the Olympics and capitalism, it makes sense to pose the hypothetical question of whether Sarajevo and Yugoslavia were becoming capitalist with the Olympics. In order to avoid drawing an overhasty conclusion, however, by uncritically conflating modernity and consumption with capitalism, we need to place the social changes occurring in Olympic Sarajevo in the socio-politico-historical context of socialist consumption and an alternative socialist road into modernity.

In this respect, it is important to point out that over the past couple of decades there has been a wave of path-breaking scholarship dealing with different aspects of popular consumer culture in socialist Eastern Europe. Many of the recent works have directed their analytical focus to the everydayness of socialism and socialist modernity during the so-called late socialist period, lasting from the early 1960s until the late 1980s. At the centre of the chronological demarcation of late socialism lies a recognition that by the 1960s, the Eastern European countries had not only recovered from the damage suffered during the Second World War but had also developed into modern industrialised and increasingly urbanised states

---

[20] Aziz Hadžihasanović, 'Sarajevo: Postolimpijske refleksije (IX). Novo ruho tezge. Kako dostići Sarajevo,' *Oslobođenje* 5.4.1984, 3.

(Krylova 2014). With this acknowledgment, a new research trend developed among scholars of the history of socialism, a cultural history that explored the materiality of everyday life in the era of late socialism. They sought to provide an alternative to persistent post-socialist interpretations of 'real' life under socialism that rely exclusively on macro-studies of social structures, as well as political and institutional histories which lack accounts of the texture of life in the margins of society, including narratives of the feelings, experiences and practices of ordinary people. Explicitly or implicitly criticising the institutional histories of socialism by analysing the *Lebenswelt* of ordinary Eastern Europeans, their popular experience, and the 'lived culture' of socialism, this new cultural and material history focuses on the margins of society—on everyday life on the fringes of, or away from, official institutions and political organisations. As Paul Betts and Katherine Pence (2008, 10) have argued in their work on the GDR, it is by examining everyday cultures in arenas such as work, consumption, domesticity and youth subcultures that a more complex picture of the relationship between a modernising socialist state and its citizenry emerges. The study of what has been described as 'real existing socialism' cannot be limited to top-down transformative efforts by state and Party but should also examine the experience of the 'socialist modern' in everyday life and popular culture—and such 'socialist modern' is less about avant-garde modernity than popular music, fashion, consumption and film (Luthar and Pušnik 2010, 9–10).

Embedded in this new history of socialism is also a criticism of the still persistent and simplified 'totalitarian paradigm' in the history of socialist Eastern Europe which rests on a dichotomous picture of a totalitarian region in which state and society, official ideology and everyday practices are sharply distinguished as oppositional pairs (Luthar and Pušnik 2010, 3). By defining late socialist Eastern Europe as authoritarian, or even 'post-totalitarian'—rather than merely totalitarian (Bren and Neuburger 2012, 12)—the new cultural history of socialism emphasises the complexity of the relationship between the socialist state and its subjects. In regard to the relationship between the official and the unofficial discourses in everyday life in socialist Eastern Europe, historians have called for a distinction to be made between the strict official proclamations of the party-elites' programmes and the substantially more relaxed pragmatism exhibited in praxis (Betts and Pence 2008, Introduction).

Despite the achievements of the new history of socialism, the presence of the West, in particular in the form of different consumer and popular-cultural products in Eastern European space, is still very commonly (mis)interpreted as a sign of socialist citizens' opposition to socialism. Even more problematic is that an admiration for the Western lifestyle is commonly equated with a longing for Western liberal democracy. As Vladislav Zubok, among others, argues in his study of late socialist USSR, the generations growing up in the 1960s, particularly the students of the late 1960s—who would later become the final cohort of Soviet intelligentsia—saw the West through the lens of its consumer culture, rather than through the opposition between liberal democracy and socialism. These students were, according to Zubok (2009, 318), more interested in the West's presumed consumerist paradise than in its liberal democracy. In fact, as Patrick Hyder Patterson's (2011) work on socialist consumer culture shows, we must resist the tendency to interpret the history of the socialist East as a perpetual conflict between state elites and society, between the party-state and its citizens. In the end, very few Eastern Europeans actually engaged in politics. For the vast majority of the population in the socialist countries, access to participation in popular consumer culture took priority over any political needs. Popular demand in the socialist countries, as Krisztina Fehérváry (2013, 89) notes in her study of Hungary, was most closely related to an 'appraisal and appropriation of the ever-changing modern world commodities as an essential part of one's material order and well-being'. Consequently, as Paulina Bren and Mary Neuburger (2012, 13) suggest in their work on consumption in Cold War Eastern Europe, many Eastern Bloc citizens came to see abundant consumption—often of Western and Western-inspired cultural and material products—as the primary signifier of progress and modernity in their own societies.

As mentioned, the 'consumer turn' of the 1960s was built primarily on the foundation of Eastern Europe's post-war recovery. Yet Eastern Block citizens did not call for capitalism on that basis, something particularly important to acknowledge in this context. On the contrary, consumption became a 'normality to everyday life under communism' (Bren and Neuburger 2012, 12). In fact, as Neringa Klumbytè and Gulnaz Sharafutdinova (2012, 7) write when dealing with late socialist USSR, 'the popularity of Lee jeans among Soviet citizens did not mean the westernisation of the USSR and the subversion of socialist ideals'. Rather, as Alexei Yurchak (2005, 158–206) argues in his work on the topic, Soviet citizenry—in particular the youth—constructed an 'imaginary West' and localised and domesticated various Western cultural forms, creatively adapting them to the socialist context in which they lived. In re-contextualising them, Sergei Zhuk (2011, 89) notes in his work on Ukrainian rock music, Soviet/Ukrainian citizens simultaneously deployed Western cultural forms as constituent elements of their own socialist selves. In addition, although the 'consumer turn' had much to do with post-war recovery, it was also closely related to the ideological relaxation of the post-Stalin era. Fehérváry has made a particularly strong case for under-standing socialist modernity as a shift away from the miseries of the Stalinist era, while at the same time trying to keep a distance from, and avoid the callous injustice of, capitalism. Thus, modernity and consumption in the Eastern Europe of the 1960s should not be viewed through the lens of the ideological construction of the 'New Socialist Man' of the Stalinist 1950s. Instead, the analytical focus of our studies should be placed on the 'Person of Today' and related processes of transforming a largely rural population into a modern and increasingly demanding citizenry (Fehérváry 2013, 84).

What these observations on material and popular culture(s) across the Eastern bloc make plain is that the sphere of economics in the 'Sovieticized world' was never limited to the production of quotas and the politics of provisions, but rather gave form to a host of 'cultural' questions about identity, allegiance and even nationhood. In this regard, as Fehérváry (2013, 78, 85–87) notes, socialist modernity was very much about pro-ducing and cultivating demanding citizens who would be able to distin-guish between kitsch and a 'modern', superior way of living which was increasingly being equated with urban 'good life'. As a result of this devel-opment, societal shift from production and citizens as worker-producers to consumption and citizens as worker-consumers occurred, as Kacper Poblocki (2012, 68–69) argues in his work on Socialist Poland. This to a certain level disrupted class hierarchies—understood in the Marxian sense—and led to the construction of a socialist consumer identity instead. This was so because identities are less about belonging to some theoretical a priori category, and more about problem-specific phenomena that stress personal senses of values of what is really important about life, as Patterson (2011, 298) puts it in his study of Socialist Yugoslavia's consumer culture.

And indeed, as a communist country, Yugoslavia shared most of these trends with Eastern Europe. Most notably, just like in other socialist coun-tries, a fully developed consumer society emerged in the course of the 1960s, resulting in the societal shift from citizens as worker-producers to citizens as worker-consumers. Even the titles of some recent works on Socialist Yugoslavia reflect this: for example, Maša Kolanović's (2011)

*Worker! Rebel? Consumer* … (*Udarnik! Buntovnik? Potrošač* …) focusing on popular literature in Socialist Croatia; and Zoran Janjetović's (2011) *Od 'Internacionale' do komercijale: Popularna kultura u Jugoslaviji 1945–1991*, which examines Socialist Yugoslavia's popular culture from the perspective of a shift from the Communist 'Internationale' to what he calls in slang, *komercijala*, implying that Yugoslav popular culture became increasingly commercialised and commodified.

This said, there were, nevertheless, a number of substantial differences between Yugoslavia and the Eastern Bloc countries due to the former's geopolitical uniqueness as more open to the West.[21] Openness to Western visitors, and the freedom to travel and work in the West, made an inflow of Western material and cultural products into the country virtually untrammelled—something unimaginable in the socialist countries of the Eastern Bloc. According to William Zimmerman (1987, 140), Yugoslavia's open borders policy tied the popular consumer culture in Yugoslavia inextricably to the West European consumer culture. Developing from the mid-1960s to the mid-1980s, it played a significant role in the *Lebenswelt* of Yugoslav citizens, particularly their popular culture and everyday life practices (Kolanović 2011, 1). It is therefore not surprising that Yugoslavs, especially young people, saw their cultural universe as part of the Western popular-cultural hemisphere (Pogačar 2010, 199–224). This sense of belonging to and with the West conveniently matched official identity policy in Socialist Yugoslavia in which the significant 'other' playing a central role in identity construction was not Western capitalism but Soviet-style socialism.[22] The analyses of socialist self-representation in Yugoslavia's youth cultures of the early 1980s clearly indicate that the USSR was seen as the ultimate 'other' among the Yugoslav youth of the time (Jovanovic 2014, 54–83).

Yugoslav consumer culture emerged in this socio-politico-historical context which meant that the country's consumer culture was marked by many outward similarities to the classic consumer societies of the capitalist West. As Patterson (2011, 12) puts it in his work on Socialist Yugoslavia's popular consumer culture, it was remarkable just how 'un-communist' it

---

[21] It is as well important to keep in mind that there existed big differences both between the individual Eastern Bloc countries and between different regions and administrative units within each country; thence we must resist the tendency of the post-socialist discourse to paint all the countries and their subnational units with the same brush.

[22] On the construction of the USSR as a 'significant other' in Yugoslavia see (Jović 2003).

felt to many, both Yugoslavs and foreign visitors. Patterson argues, however, that Yugoslavia ultimately did not generate a genuinely, distinctively, or purely 'socialist' version of consumer culture. With the country's economic system remaining socialist, the culture of consumption that developed in Yugoslavia was a hybrid form. Thus, with regard to consumption, Yugoslav socialism proved to be open, experimental and extraordinarily amenable to practices and values that the political leaders and economic managers of other communist states were much more likely to squelch in short order as undesirable ideological deviations (Patterson 2011, 4–7).

This was not least the case with the country's advertising practices. According to Patterson (2011, 2), the industry literature makes it clear that many Yugoslav enterprises recognised relatively early that advertising, marketing, and public relations could be an important part of their efforts to penetrate international markets. They felt that something had to be done and it had to be done quickly in order to improve the competitiveness of the comparatively backward state. Thus, although Yugoslavs had much 'catching up' to do, in order to meet Western standards, during the 1950s and early 1960s, by the late 1960s it had become rather difficult to distinguish between the styles and techniques employed in Western Europe and the USA and those in Yugoslavia. Receiving substantial institutional support from the Yugoslav socialist state, this development further accelerated in 1973, when a pan-Yugoslav professional association, the Advertising Federation of Yugoslavia (*Savez ekonomskih propagandista Jugoslavije*) was established (Patterson 2011, 93). This coincided with the period in which the idea of Sarajevo's Olympic nomination was starting to gain serious ground. Thus, by the time Sarajevo won its Olympic bid, advertising and Western-style consumer culture in general were no longer novelties, but rather normality in Socialist Yugoslavia, which made it even easier for the Yugoslav political elites and ordinary Yugoslavs to embrace the principles and practices associated with the capitalist West.

That said, the Olympics nonetheless pushed this development to yet another level, with Western advertisements beginning to appear even in newspapers like *Oslobodenje* and no longer, as had been customary, exclusively in specialist literature or the so-called lifestyle magazines. Moreover, in the same period, advertisements for Western products like Coca-Cola and Mitsubishi appeared next to advertisements for Yugoslav products. It is as well important to note that Coca-Cola, Mitsubishi and a number of other Western companies also served as official sponsors for the Sarajevo Olympics, along with Yugoslav enterprises. Yet another development during the Olympics concerned TV advertising, with some sources going so far as claiming that there was too much of it during the Olympics.[23] Others were pleased that the Olympics were attracting so many sponsors, proudly citing 'the impressive number of 103 [domestic and international] sponsors' compared with the 'barely twenty-something' sponsors attracted by the forthcoming Los Angeles Summer Olympic Games.[24]

Celebrated as yet another success for the Sarajevo Olympics, the sponsorship issue discloses an interesting story about the strategy behind the financing of the Olympics. According to the General Questionnaire (*Sarajevo. General Questionnaire* n.d., Ch. IV), which the Preparation Committee for the Sarajevo Olympics had to answer and submit along with the nomination, the Organising Committee of the Sarajevo Olympic Games did not distinguish between public and private contributions. The event was supposed to be financed through a specific system involving a number of different participants, including budgetary contributions from the three-level government (City of Sarajevo, the Socialist Republic of Bosnia and Herzegovina and the Yugoslav Federation), voluntary citizens' donations, a lottery, sales of TV rights and various sponsorship agreements with Yugoslav and foreign companies.

As it comes to expression in the *Final Report of the Sarajevo Olympics* the financing of the Games was originally planned in accordance with general practices in financing international sport events in Yugoslavia, particularly following practice at the 1979 Split Mediterranean Games (TSOOC 1984, 182):

> Important international sport events in Yugoslavia are financed through a specific system which includes a number of different participants, because we are of the belief that they are of general importance to the entire country, regardless of the location of the event.
>
> This was the case with … a great number of world sports events … held in Yugoslavia.
>
> Extending the system and the source of financial participation, the Mediterranean Games were organized in Split, 1979, for which the whole of Yugoslavia participated in financing. This system was also used for financing the XIV [Olympic Winter Games].

---

[23] Smail Festić, 'Dobra Ulaznica', *Nedeljna Borba* 25–26.2. 1984, 3.
[24] Enver Demirović, 'Svijet je vidio šta možemo', *Nedeljna Borba* 25–26.2. 1984, 3.

Following this practice, the public funding package for the construction of the new facilities for the Sarajevo Olympic Games was conceived of as follows (*Sarajevo. General Questionnaire* n.d., ch. IV):

- One third of the necessary funds will be provided by the Municipality of Sarajevo;
- One third by the Government of the Socialist Republic of Bosnia and Herzegovina;
- One third will be made available from the funds of the Ports Lotto and other Lottery run on the federal level.
  Revenue (from gate receipts, photography licensing, share of the receipts from television rights, support from the Federal Government) will be used to cover the operational expenses of organising the Games.

However, due to certain disagreements between stakeholders, as well as the economic crisis that hit the country shortly after the city won its Olympic bid, a disproportionately large part of the funding ultimately came from the sales of TV rights (approximately 35%) and sponsorship agreements with Yugoslav and foreign companies (9%) (TSOOC 1984, 170 et seq.). This meant, in short, that much of the financing of the Sarajevo Olympics was secured by selling TV broadcasting rights to the American ABC and by accepting Western brands as sponsors for the Games. This development supports Patterson's argument about Yugoslavia proving itself to be extraordinarily open to Western cultural, ideological and commercial influences.

It should nevertheless be noted that securing a substantial part of Olympic financing by selling TV rights was not something exceptional for Sarajevo. As several scholars working on the topic have observed, since 1980 the sale of TV rights has secured a disproportionately large percentage of funding at all the Olympic Games, with the single exception of the 1984 Los Angeles Summer Olympics (Roche 2000, 138–140; Barney et al. 2002, 181–202). With no notable variation between Yugoslavia and other Olympic host countries, apart from the USA, differences between those in the capitalist West and Socialist Yugoslavia appear, in fact, to be smaller than those between the USA and other capitalist economies. In other words, it was rather the USA than Yugoslavia that was the exception in this regard.

This brings me back to Patterson's observation that Yugoslavia felt 'un-communist' to many foreigners, something supported by a number of sources from the immediate post-Olympic period. For example, *Olympic Games 1984*, a book published by the US Olympic Committee shortly after the 1984 Los Angeles Summer Olympics, covering both the Sarajevo and the Los Angeles Olympics. In its coverage of the opening ceremony in Los Angeles, the book offered an interesting commentary on Yugoslavia. According to the author of the piece, three countries at the Los Angeles opening ceremony drew the particular attention of the audience: China, Romania and Yugoslavia. It was the ideology of the first two that attracted attention, with the author explicitly naming them as 'the two communist countries' participating at the Los Angeles Games, while, in contrast, Yugoslavia was noteworthy, according to the author, because it was the host nation of the recently finished Winter Olympics (Schaap 1984). The case exemplifies how common it was, among international observers, not to count Yugoslavia amongst the communist countries.

In contrast to *Olympic Games 1984* the Yugoslav press and a number of officials often emphasised, and indeed did so with pride, that the Sarajevo Games were the first winter Olympics ever held in a socialist country. Both *Politika* and *Borba* stressed how the Olympics made some international visitors completely change their idea of what life in a communist country was like.[25] The President of the Olympic Organising Committee, also the highest positioned member of the Bosnian branch of the League of Communists, Branko Mikulić, notably argued in an interview for *The Times* that Sarajevo's Olympic advertising success proved that high levels of business-mindedness were not solely the province of capitalism.[26] Hadžihasanović did not put his argument as unequivocally in his *Oslobođenje* serial, but nevertheless linked Sarajevo's Olympic success directly to Yugoslavia's socialist self-managing policies. In several of the articles, he spoke of socialist self-management as a prime structural force behind not only the Olympic success but also behind the societal change occurring during the Olympic period.[27] According to his arguments, the structural force of 'the self-managing life' encouraged creativity and pro-

---

[25] 'Narod divne, plemenite duše. (Drugi o nama: Olimpijska "Knjiga utisaka")', *Politika* 17.2.1984, 13; Z. Mandžuka, 'Olimpijada svih nas', *Borba* 18–19.2.1984, 1.

[26] Here from Knežević-Čečez et al. (1984, 104).

[27] Aziz Hadžihasanović, 'Sarajevo: Postolimpijske refleksije (IX). Novo ruho tezge. Kako dostići Sarajevo,' *Oslobođenje* 5.4.1984, 3.

moted new and authentic ideas. Therefore, claimed Hadžihasanović, the Olympic success could be seen as proof that the socialist self-managing system was working.[28]

While certainly being significantly ideologically laden, this argument is interesting when seen from the perspective of recent scholarship on socialist economies in the 1980s. In his provocative and well researched *Europe Since 1989*, Philipp Ther (2016) argues that there existed many commonalities between capitalist and socialist economies of the 1980s. In contrast to the still prevalent common-sense Cold War paradigm that tends to see capitalism and socialism as having been discrete economic systems during the period, Ther argues that capitalism and socialism in fact shared a great many features; attributing this to the rise of *neoliberalism*, he speaks of 'the neoliberal turn in east and west' (Ther 2016, 39). Johanna Bockman goes even further in her *Markets in the Name of Socialism* (2011) and explicitly argues for the socialist origin of the phenomenon of neoliberalism. It is noteworthy that, in relation to this development, Bockman (2011, 168) points out Yugoslavia's socialist self-managing system, whose ultimate goal was the realisation of true *worker(s') self-managing market socialism*, that is, a market socialism self-managed by the workers. According to the principal ideologue of the system, Edvard Kardelj, socialist self-management differed from the state socialism of the Eastern Bloc countries in that, while the latter aimed to establish social property, socialist self-management experimented with different forms of non-private, non-state ownership. Kardelj criticised state socialism and social property for leading to managerial, rather than worker, control. Kardelj's theoretical underpinnings are clearly visible in Hadžihasanović's serial, with the latter claiming that socialist self-management proved capable of mobilising workers and spurring modern dynamic urban life in Olympic Sarajevo.[29]

This does not mean that Hadžihasanović had adopted his economic views necessarily directly from Kardelj. As Bockman explains (2011, 168–169), most Yugoslav economists of the 1970s and 1980s were advocates of competitive markets. One of the country's leading economists of

---

[28] Aziz Hadžihasanović, 'Sarajevo: Postolimpijske refleksije. Novo u starom', *Oslobođenje* 28.3.1984, 3; Aziz Hadžihasanović, 'Sarajevo: Postolimpijske refleksije (VII). Grad na nogama', *Oslobođenje* 3.4.1984, 3; Aziz Hadžihasanović, 'Sarajevo: Postolimpijske refleksije (IX). Novo ruho tezge. Kako dostići Sarajevo,' *Oslobođenje*, 5.4.1984, 3.

[29] Aziz Hadžihasanović, 'Sarajevo: Postolimpijske refleksije (VII). Grad na nogama,' *Oslobođenje* 3.4.1984, 3.

the time, Aleksandar Bajt, argued that 'the only acceptable model of socialist economy [was] the model of free competition'. Yet, according to the Yugoslav economists, securing the free competitive market required certain socialist institutions, one of which was entrepreneurship. This being said, continues Brockman, Slovenian economist Tea Petrin argued that it was not only in socialist, self-managing Yugoslavia that entrepreneurship emerged as one of the fundamental institutions in the 1980s. Rather, as Petrin put it, '[t]he eighties will be remembered as an era of entrepreneurship', with an entrepreneurial movement emerging globally, in the West as well as the East.

It is therefore interesting that Hadžihasanović talked at length of entrepreneurship, returning to the topic several times throughout the serial and always speaking of it in positive terms.[30] Furthermore, he did not stop there, but also tried to identify the agents most eagerly engaged in this new trend. These were, according to Hadžihasanović, 'the young professionals'—a category in which he also included students. According to Hadžihasanović, the emerging imaginativeness of young Yugoslav men and women had initiated and eventually resulted in a previously unseen creativity in the sphere of culture, service, arts, design and entertainment.[31] In relation to this development, Hadžihasanović spoke of the professionalism, activism and innovativeness of young specialists, arguing that they offered new ideas and new solutions and that their entrepreneurship should be taken into account in general city policies.[32] Finally, in his reading of the motivation for this development, Hadžihasanović stressed neither socialism (that is socialist self-management) nor capitalism, but a drive among these young professionals to be up with times.[33]

In light of Hadžihasanović's focus on the younger generation, including students, it makes sense to examine the content of Sarajevo's youth

[30] Most notably in Aziz Hadžihasanović, 'Sarajevo: Postolimpijske refleksije. Novo u starom,' *Oslobođenje*, 28.3.1984, 3 and Aziz Hadžihasanović, 'Sarajevo: Postolimpijske refleksije (V). Izazov nove ere', *Oslobođenje* 1.4.1984, 2.

[31] Aziz Hadžihasanović, 'Sarajevo: Postolimpijske refleksije. Novo u starom,' *Oslobođenje*, 28.3.1984, 3; & Aziz Hadžihasanović, 'Sarajevo: Postolimpijske refleksije (III). Ram za lijepo,' *Oslobođenje* 30.3.1984, 3.

[32] Aziz Hadžihasanović, 'Sarajevo: Postolimpijske refleksije. Novo u starom,' *Oslobođenje*, 28.3.1984, 3; & Aziz Hadžihasanović, 'Sarajevo: Postolimpijske refleksije (III). Ram za lijepo,' *Oslobođenje* 30.3.1984, 3.

[33] Aziz Hadžihasanović, 'Sarajevo: Postolimpijske refleksije (III). Ram za lijepo', *Oslobođenje*, 30.3.1984, 3.

periodical, *Naši dani* and find out how its journalists covered the topic. Here, one of the most interesting articles in relation to this discussion, written by Miroslav Arapović, was published in the periodical's first post-Olympic issue. In it, the author explained with amusement how an American visitor to the city was surprised to discover that Yugoslavia was a socialist country.[34] The very fact that the author made fun out of this episode indicates that for young Sarajevans (and Yugoslavs) Yugoslavia was unquestionably socialist. It is, however, at least equally interesting to see that Arapović's vision of socialism could hardly be more removed from the ideas of socialism that still dominate the common Cold War paradigm. In the article, Arapović told his readers, '[t]here were no fights during the Sarajevo Olympics other than the sporting ones (and of course commercial ones)'.[35] Although his main argument concerned Yugoslavia's widely recognised success in overcoming the rising tensions between the two Cold War blocs in the early 1980s, Arapović's comment was even more interesting in light of what he placed in the parentheses. While pointing out Yugoslavia's success in allegedly 'depoliticising' the Games, that is, divorcing sport and Cold War politics, Arapović treated the relationship between sport and business ('commercial fights') as unproblematic. Hence, they did not need to be separated in the same way as sport and politics. Implicated in this statement is a reference to sponsorship and advertising, which some sources considered excessive during the Olympics, as we saw in the above discussion concerning the Olympic sponsorship. In conclusion to this point, it can be noted that Arapović's acceptance of the logic of a free competitive market advocated by Yugoslav economists of the time, coupled with his amusement that a visitor had not been aware that Yugoslavia was a socialist country, both support and reflect Patterson's discussion of Yugoslavia's hybridity.

Arapović's article echoed the dominant economic discourse of the period in other ways as well. Like the Yugoslav political elites, he argued that the real (Olympic) race was only about to start. This race was not about sports medals but, rather, was a competition within the global winter sport tourism business. In line with the general discourse on the Olympics as an extraordinary business opportunity, he named the article 'Zov biznisa'—The Call of Business. In respect to the modernity aspect of the Olympics, we should also remember that using English words, like

---

[34] M. Arapović, 'Postolimpijske misli i ... Zov biznisa', *Naši dani* 805, 24.2.1984, 10.
[35] Ibid.

'business', had since the 1950 been a marker of modernity among Yugoslavs—particularly among the younger generations. Another English term that surfaced during the Olympic period was 'publicity management', which appeared in the same issue of *Naši dani* in the two-page coverage of advertising during the Olympics. Named 'The Best Know What's Best' and consisting of a short lead article and several text boxes, it covered a number of recognised brands and their advertisement technologies and strategies. The lead article was written by two of the periodical's journalists, with help from a colleague from Youth Radio in the Croatian capital of Zagreb. In a similar manner to Arapović, they argued that 'the Olympics were not only a competition for sport medals, but also a competition for consumers'. Explaining the logic of the title of the piece, they pointed out that the goal of every brand was to get the leading athletes to use their products. If the globally known stars used a certain brand, then the masses would follow. This was the logic behind the philosophy of 'publicity management', argued the journalists, adding, in explanation of the term, that it can also be referred to as commercials or 'epp'—the latter being an acronym for The Economic Propaganda Programme, the Yugoslav term for advertising in the broad sense. Leaving an impression of serious journalism, the piece used an interesting subtitle: 'Epp at the Olympics (A Contribution to Advertisementocracy)'. Put this way, 'advertisementocracy', or *reklamokratija*, appeared as a system of government by the advertisement industry. Finally, the journalists explained that, although the focus in the text boxes accompanying the lead article was on individual international brands, they wanted to draw attention to the situation in the city of Sarajevo, which was, they claimed, filled with advertisement billboards, advertising domestic and international Olympic sponsors.[36]

From this point of departure, in the following section I zoom in on Sarajevo. Before that one last interesting issue relating to Hadžihasanović's serial should be mentioned. Arguably the most interesting article in terms of Hadžihasanović's commentary also appeared in the same issue of the youth periodical. Entitled, 'Oh Daddy Find Me a Stranger', and using once again an English word—'stranger' in the Serbo-Croatian transcription 'strendžer'—the article dealt with the change in habits among young Sarajevans caused by the Olympics, based on a number of interviews

---

[36] Haris Prolić & Hrvoje Batinić, 'Epp na Olimpijadi. Najbolji znaju šta je najbolje (Prilog izučavanju reklamokratije)', *Naši dani* 805, 24.2.1984, 8–9.

carried out among the demographic. According to the periodical, one of their hottest conversation topics during the Olympic event was their employment by US companies like TV broadcaster and major Olympic sponsor, ABC, or the Coca-Cola Company, which were offering young Sarajevans previously unimaginable high salaries. Naturally, not all Sarajevan youth were equally interested in working for the US companies, but those who did take the jobs quickly experienced changes in lifestyle and habits. Students got a chance to meet foreigners through their jobs and to practice and improve their English, which was at the time becoming an important asset in terms of securing Sarajevo a position in global tourism. Some worked longer hours, trying to make the most possible out of the event. Having well-paid jobs could also mean that youngsters developed new interests, changed their leisure activities and even altered their ideas of the good life. 'We really needed these Olympics', claimed a young woman who worked as a tourist guide during the Olympics. 'You learn to aim more and are not satisfied with what you had before', she explained. Another young Sarajevan, a male student of English language at the University of Sarajevo and an amateur car-rally driver, told the periodical: 'I did not have a particularly clear idea about the Olympics until the very last pre-Olympic days. I thought that everything was a bit exaggerated, and hence was not prepared for it.' But then, just a few days before the opening of the event the student filled in an application for a job as a driver for ABC. He got the job, which thoroughly changed his view about the Olympics and also made him proud of his country. According to the periodical, he was now planning to travel to Los Angeles for the Summer Olympics a few months later.[37]

## 4.2   GLOBAL CULTURE AND SARAJEVO AS AN OLYMPIC SHOWCASE

'Since the revival by Count de Coubertin at the end of the nineteenth century', writes Christian Tagshold (2012, 26), 'the Olympic Games have served as a symbol of modernity'. In explaining the close relationship between Olympics, modernity and the nation, he points out that the Olympics offer new-born nations a clear path to international recognition as modern states: first by joining the International Olympic Committee, then sending a delegation to the Olympics, eventually winning medals and

[37] Veso Đorem, 'Nađi mi babo strendžera!', *Naši dani* 805, 24.2.1984, 11.

finally hosting the Olympics themselves (Tagshold 2012, 26–27). Prior to the Sarajevo Winter Olympics, Yugoslavia won all its Olympic medals in summer sports disciplines. Then, at the Sarajevo Olympics, on the home field, Slovenian Jure Franko won the silver medal in the giant slalom—the first medal ever won by Yugoslavia at a Winter Olympics—potentially further strengthening the association between Yugoslavia's modernity and the Sarajevo Games.

For Sarajevans, modernity came in many versions. Firstly, as we saw in the previous chapter, the 1984 Winter Olympic Games became an opportunity to modernise Sarajevo by securing major urban infrastructural change in the city, which transformed it radically, turning it into a new modern urban metropolis. As a part of the infrastructural change, public transport in the city was substantially improved by renovations of the tram system and the introduction of trolleybuses and scheduled night buses.[38] In *Oslobođenje*'s wording, Sarajevo was getting 'modern public transportation for the Olympics'.[39] This type of wording shows how modernity and the Olympics were becoming more and more discursively inseparable from each other.

Meanwhile, other sources indicate that the modernisation of the city's public transportation was very successful. Probably the most telling assessment of Olympic Sarajevo's public transport came from taxi drivers who had travelled to Sarajevo from other parts of the country in hopes that the Olympics would provide them with the opportunity to earn some extra money. As witnessed by an article in the Zagreb youth periodical, *Polet*, published during the Olympics, the taxi drivers interviewed by the journal were disappointed, complaining that public transport in Olympic Sarajevo functioned so well that it prevented them earning what they had expected to earn during the Olympics.[40] According to the Belgrade daily, *Sport*, the international press voiced the same impression, insisting that the public buses run to such precision that the watches could be set according to their timetable.[41]

In addition to public transport, both Sarajevo's airport and its central train station were restored and modernised for the Olympics. Indeed, the airport was modernised to such an extent that the Final Report of the

[38] S. Lučkin, 'Ponoćna vožnja Sarajevom. Bez gužve i sa osmijehom', *Oslobođenje* 29.1.1984, 11.

[39] D. Stanojlović, 'Moderan prevoz u olimpijskom gradu', *Oslobođenje* 18.1.1983, 12.

[40] Zoran Simić, 'Poletov bob dvosjed u Sarajevu', *Polet* 251, 9.2.1984, 13.

[41] 'Sarajevo donosi ozdravljenje olimpjskog pokreta', *Sport* 6.2.1984, 8.

Sarajevo Olympics claimed that 'a modern airport' had been built for the Olympics (TSOOC 1984, 191). The thoroughly renovated airport was reopened a few weeks before the Olympics, or as Belgrade's *Borba* put it, 'for the Olympics'.[42] The daily went on explaining that the renovated airport now possessed the most modern equipment to help navigate aircrafts landing and taking off during serious weather conditions.[43] Meanwhile, *Oslobođenje* labelled the renovated airport the city's 'bridge to the world'.[44] A few days before the Games started, *Borba* told its readers that the thoroughly renovated airport could now accommodate even the biggest types of planes and repeated once again that the most modern airport equipment had been acquired.[45] To the joy of the local political and economic elites and tourism promoters, record numbers of passengers passed through the restored airport during the Olympic period, as early Olympic counts had shown.[46] Almost needless to point out is that, along with trains, automobiles and skyscrapers, airports were icons of modernity; thus a 'new' airport also had symbolic value in relation to the modernity brought by the Olympics.

The renovated Sarajevo train station played a somewhat different role in the Olympic modernisation narrative, as it was already one of the modernist symbols of the city. However, during the Olympic period, it became a part of the story of a functioning and reliable railway system. As we saw in the discussion on the relationship between infrastructure and modernity, the latter is often defined by its reliance on the former. It is, therefore, worth mentioning that some sources claimed that during the Olympic period trains started running punctually for the first time,[47] providing some basis for the claim that the sense of modernity in Olympic Sarajevo was strengthened by a newly functional and reliable railway system. Furthermore, in line with modernity's implying a mastery of space, in addition to public transport, the PTT—the postal, telegraph and telephone service—was also thoroughly modernised in order to meet the needs of the Olympics, giving the title, 'Olympic Sarajevo Calling', to an

---

[42] 'Aerodrom za ZOI', *Borba* 17.1.1984, 12.

[43] Ibid.

[44] H. Ibišević, 'Otvoren aerodrom "Sarajevo". Vazdušni most sa svijetom', *Oslobođenje*, 18.1.1984.

[45] D.S. 'Za ZOI 400 aviona', *Borba* 2.2.1984, 1.

[46] 'Pao i aero-rekord', *Politika* 8.2.1984, 9.

[47] Sead Lučkin, 'Jedan dan na … Željezničkoj stanici Sarajevo: Na vrijeme krenuti, na vrijeme stići', *Oslobođenje—Nedeljni prilog* 26.2.1984, 5.

*Oslobođenje* article covering this issue.[48] Finally, relating to the idea that modernity is most of all about 'being up with the times', as well as the thereto related widespread sense of *secondariness* to the West, it is quite noteworthy that in its early February 1984 report on western coverage of the approaching Sarajevo Olympics, Belgrade's *Politika* stressed how a journalist from West German TV insisted that the new Olympic TV studio in Sarajevo was so modern and well-equipped that it could easily have been somewhere in the USA or Western Europe.[49]

For some, modernity came at a cost. Most notable among these were the inhabitants of the suburb of Dobrinja, whose homes had to be destroyed in order to make room for the modern Olympic village that would accommodate domestic and international journalists during the Olympics.[50] Quite differently from the sports installations and arenas raised for the Olympics—particularly the Olympic Hall, Zetra, which was built with the intention of leaving a lasting symbolic Olympic legacy in Sarajevo—Dobrinja was integrated into the city in a very different way. Along with the Mojmilo Olympic Village, which hosted athletes during the Games, after the Olympics Dobrinja was utilised as a new suburb to house Sarajevo's growing population. As an exception to the rule in international terms, both Mojmilo and Dobrinja became regular residential areas of the city after the event. As Jaen-Loup Chappelet (2012, 84) shows in his comparative analysis of the seven Winter Olympic Games held in the period from 1980 to 2002, this practice was quite unusual. Besides Sarajevo, only the Japanese city of Nagano—the host city of the 1994 Winter Olympics—did the same, by turning its Imai Olympic Village into residential apartments.[51] In Sarajevo, during the post-Olympic period, Dobrinja would in fact bear the main brunt of the demographic explosion that the newly formed urban municipality of Sarajevo-Novi Grad (Sarajevo New Town) experienced in the 1980s.[52] Even beyond the limits of the

[48] E. Isaković, 'Danas pišemo ... o modernizaciji telefonskog i telegrafskog saobraćaja: Ovdje olimpijsko Sarajevo', *Oslobođenje* 7.2.1983, 7.

[49] B. Dikić, 'Majnc pozdravlja Sarajevo', *Politika* 6.2.1984, 13.

[50] D. Stanojlović, 'Od Dobrinje do Olimpijade', *Oslobođenje* 13.1.1981, 9.

[51] Chappelet further explains that other Olympic Villages built in the period were either dismantled (Lillehammer) or turned into student residences (Calgary and SLC), hotel and tourist apartment complexes (Albertville) or into a low security prison (!) in the case of the 1980 host, Lake Placid.

[52] The population of this municipality more than doubled, from 60,000 to over 136,000, in the period from the constitution of the municipality in 1974 to the last Yugoslav census in 1991.

municipality, Dobrinja became the main construction area in the city after the Olympics. Moreover, shortly after the Olympics, both Mojmilo and Dobrinja achieved the status of desirable modern residential neighbourhoods among Sarajevans.[53] Undoubtedly, one of the reasons for this development was that Mojmilo and Dobrinja were built on the route of the new modern trolleybus system that was introduced in the city shortly after the Olympics. A new and cleaner means of transportation now traversing the whole city and connecting Dobrinja in the west to the northern suburb of Vogošća via the city centre and the Koševo Valley, certainly left an impression of a very different city to the pre-Olympic one.

The modernity of Olympic Sarajevo also transpired in symbolic ways, which included the insistence that the Mojmilo Olympic Village was the first in history that would not separate women from men.[54] This symbolic universalism could be seen as representing the process of female emancipation, which is one of the central subprocesses of socio-cultural modernisation. Thus, unisex accommodation in Mojmilo served as an important signifier of Sarajevo's modernity. Another such signifier was a modern and very popular discotheque that opened in the Olympic Village, which soon became highly praised among its temporary residents.[55] Outside the West, discotheques had emerged as symbols of modernity, a role emphasised by Sergei I. Zhuk (2011, 87–117) of the late 1970s and early 1980s in terms of new leisure pursuits among Soviet youth. This should be seen from a perspective of the expansion of 'leisure time societies' as the ultimate expression of the modern era and the development of the modern welfare state—in the East and the West alike (Holubec et al. 2014, 8). In the same manner, in an article titled 'Vučko Learning Bon-ton', *Naši dani* stressed the importance of the city's '300 cafés' in defining the experience of city life in Olympic Sarajevo.[56] Zagreb's youth periodical, *Polet*, wrote about Sarajevo during the Olympic period—and in reference to emerging New

---

[53] It is quite noteworthy that the aforementioned official 1984 publication on the Olympics in Sarajevo and Los Angeles, *1984 Olympics*, by the US Olympic Committee pointed out that the Mojmilo Olympic Village marked a big improvement over the 'cramped Lake Placid quarters', while Don Miller, the executive director of the US Olympic Committee, argued that 'the Sarajevo Olympic Village was the best Olympic village built to date' (Schaap 1984, 14).

[54] 'U "selu" kao u velegradu', *Sport* 6.2.1984, 8–9.

[55] 'Šetnja kroz olimpijsko selo u Mojmilu: Sve utihne tek u ponoć', *Sport* 7.2.1984, 8.

[56] Risto Motika, 'Predolimpijska kulturna razmišljanja. Vučko uči bon-ton', *Naši dani* 763, 26.11.1982, 19.

Primitivism subculture—as offering 'the best party in the whole country'.[57] Nor did the Federal Government's organ *Borba* fail to mention the city's discotheques. In fact, with reference to writings in the international press, the sports daily explained that during the Olympics, 'the city changed its clothes', 'woke up from the lethargy of quiet and boring petit bourgeois life' and 'offered its visitors a brand new face with boutiques, disco-clubs, and imported products of the highest quality'.[58] Leisure and in particular consumption appeared once again as the defining characteristics of the new Olympic city. Seen through this optic, it does not come as a surprise that the Belgrade sports daily used the same vocabulary as Hadžihasanović in speaking of the 'new clothes' of the city and the shop counter.

In continuation of Roche's argument that the Olympics at times contribute to social change and the process of modernisation, this linkage between consumption and the notion of modernity is very interesting in terms of how Olympic Sarajevo's modernity became manifest in changes in consumer practices in the city. Here, we need to remember, as Frank Trentmann (2006, 1–27) points out, that modern history is to a significant extent defined by the evolution of the consumer into a master category of our collective and individual identities. In this respect, Trentmann has sought to redirect our analytical attention to the processes whereby *consumers as such* emerged as vital subjects of modernity. Yet, as he stresses, before there could be a popular notion of consumer sovereignty, the consumer had to be cultivated. As we saw in the previous section, the Olympics brought longer opening hours to Sarajevo's stores, altering the previously dominant patterns of shopping behaviour. In addition, a whole set of innovations relating to retail activities appeared during the Olympic period. For instance, cheques and credit cards, previously a rarity, were introduced everywhere. Even smaller shops in *Baščaršija* accommodated these new payment methods.[59] Meanwhile, the wholesale enterprise Magros was one of the larger companies that chose to introduce cheques and credit cards during the Olympic preparation period. In May 1983, in an *Oslobođenje* report on the preparations for the Olympics, a Magros manager responsible for the 'Olympic supply' announced that later the same month it would be possible to pay with traveller's cheques, 'euro-

---

[57] Miro Purivatra, 'Primitivci na Polet platzu!', *Polet* 25.5.1983, 236–237.

[58] 'Novo gradsko ruho', *Nedeljna Borba* 28–29.1.1984, 9.

[59] Sl. Dakić 'Naša akcija "Olimpijski osmijeh": Umjesto novca—kartica', *Oslobođenje* 9.12.1983, 9.

cheque', American Express credit cards, and any other payment methods used globally. The practice was to be introduced in all the company's shops in Sarajevo. The manager explained that this was an important novelty, as previously it had only been possible to pay by cheque or credit cards in a very few shops in the city.[60] Once again, we see how the Olympics had become an opportunity to modernise Sarajevo not only by securing major urban infrastructural change, but also by affecting common everyday practices in Sarajevo. This said, and as we saw with regard to the introduction of practices and values associated with capitalism, changes occurring in the city during the Olympics represented the continuation of processes that had started some time before. This being said, the Olympics, in line with Roche's argument, could nevertheless now emerge as providing important momentum that contributed substantially to the overall process of modernisation.

Thus, in the same manner, international credit cards like Diners Club had already been introduced in Yugoslavia in the early 1960s, making Yugoslavia an exception among socialist countries (Underwood 1960). By the early 1970s, there were already several thousand Diners Club holders in the country (Anderson 1972a), although still only a tiny minority of Yugoslavs had a credit card when Sarajevo hosted the Olympics, with cheques being somewhat more common. However, despite the tiny minority and although the introduction of credit cards as an acceptable payment method was primarily meant to satisfy the needs of Western visitors to the city, news of innovations like these had the strong potential to strengthen the general sense of modernity, a sense of the city following and being up-to-date with global consumer trends. A review of *Oslobođenje* indicates that the daily was eager to tell its readers about the introduction of credit cards and cheques in Sarajevo's stores, as well as about the new 'computer receipts' that were going to be printed out to guests and customers in the Holiday Inn—'Sarajevo's Olympic hotel'. In its articles the daily placed these new developments within the frame of preparations for the Olympics and related modernisation processes.[61] This eagerness should be seen from the perspective of the wider coverage of preparations for the Olympics, whereby these news and reports became bricks in the general story of modernisation relating to Sarajevo's position as an Olympic host city (Essex and Chalkley 2004, 222).

---

[60] E. Isaković, 'Pripreme za olimpijadu. Osmijeh važniji od robe', *Oslobođenje* 13.5.1983, 9.
[61] J. Vričko, 'Na licu mjesta. Hotel u oktobru', *Oslobođenje* 28.7.1984, 14.

Even if the local population did not itself benefit most from the introduction of new payment methods and could only learn about them, and the new 'computer bills', from news media, their experience as customers was certainly strongly affected by the enlarged range of goods available in the stores during the Olympics. This was observed by a number of sources. Some even argued that the supply was much greater than the actual need.[62] Most interesting in this respect were the comments from journalists and visitors from other parts of Yugoslavia. Zagreb's youth periodical, *Polet*,[63] and Belgrade's magazine, *Duga*,[64] both remarked that Olympic Sarajevo's shops looked more like Yugoslavia in the prosperous 1970s than in the crisis-stricken 1980s, years in which sporadic shortages in certain products occurred across the country.[65] In Sarajevo's shops 'there is nothing missing', claimed another *Duga* journalist;[66] 'there are twenty different types of soap and sixteen types of toothpaste', wrote another.[67] As the country's showcase for the Winter Olympics, supply exceeded demand, making Sarajevo an exception in Yugoslavia at the time and framing the city as a Yugoslav success story.

Sarajevo also changed visually with the Olympics. As already suggested, during the preparation period the city attained elements of a modern *velegrad* or metropolis,[68] including the addition of large commercial billboards, some of which were illuminated, substantially changing the city's aesthetic appearance. An *Oslobođenje* article in autumn 1981 provides an interesting opinion on the topic, not least because it linked the phenomenon to the Olympics:

> Day by day, with the realisation of the *Project for the Protection of the Human Environment* and the approach of the XIV Olympic Winter Games, Sarajevo attains new aspects of a metropolis. And one of the inevitable 'flavours' of

---

[62] A. Ahmetašević, 'Olimpisjki osmijeh—kako se pripremamo: Više i od potreba', *Oslobođenje* 5.1.1984, 7.

[63] Zoran Simić, 'Poletov bob dvosjed u Sarajevu', *Polet* 251, 9.2.1984, 13.

[64] Milomir Marić, 'Sve o zimskoj olimpijadi: Pred početak olimpijade. Sneško belić u bosanskom loncu', *Duga 259*, 28.1.1984, 22–23.

[65] B.V., 'Naša akcija "Olimpijski osmijeh (12)": Maslac skriven među sapunima', *Oslobođenje* 29.7.1983, 10.

[66] P.I., 'Nema šta—nema!', *Duga* 28.1.1984, 26.

[67] Milomir Marić, 'Sve o zimskoj olimpijadi: Pred početak olimpijade. Sneško belić u bosanskom loncu', *Duga 259*, 28.1.1984, 22–23.

[68] Boro Radosavljević, 'Sarajevo u tonovima velegrada', *Oslobođenje—Žurnal* 13.9.1981, 8–9.

big cities are billboards that add the final touch to plazas, busy streets [and] the most prominent buildings in the city. Sarajevo had already been 'decorated' in this way, but with the XIV Olympic Winter Games [in sight], interest among the major world companies in advertising in the capital city of Bosnia and Herzegovina has multiplied.

...

In light of this, every advertising space in Sarajevo has become precious.[69]

From here the journalist went on to note that, once put in place, the advertising billboards quickly grew into a permanent feature of the city.[70] According to reactions and remarks in the Yugoslav press, this was particularly the case with illuminated billboards, especially that of the Slovenian electrical and electronic equipment manufacturer Iskra (Spark), one of the leading Yugoslav electronic brands of the time. As *Sport* put it, the continuously lit Iskra billboard became one of the trademarks of Olympic Sarajevo that every visitor to the city immediately noticed.[71]

Advertisements for international consumer and retail brands likewise contributed to the general sense of modernity in the Bosnian capital city. A very interesting example thereof was provided by the Coca-Cola Company which, as one of the official Olympic sponsors, dedicated a new can design to the 1984 Sarajevo Winter Olympics. For Yugoslavs, this had special significance as it also marked the first introduction of soft drink cans to Yugoslavia; and for Sarajevo this meant that the city was now associated with one of those Western cultural and material products that functioned as primary signifiers of modernity in Socialist Yugoslavia and Eastern Europe. Sarajevo was hence turning into a symbol of the whole country's modernity.

The story of the Japanese car manufacturer Mitsubishi, one of the major international sponsors of the Sarajevo Olympics, is equally interesting. Serving as Olympic sponsor and the official car supplier for the Olympics, Mitsubishi's advertisements appeared regularly in *Oslobođenje* during the period, not least for the company's innovative 1984 four-wheel drive, 4WD, yet another symbol of the modernity of Olympic Sarajevo. In one such advertisement we see the Olympic mascot, Vučko, driving one of the new vehicles. The image of an apparently excited Vučko was accompanied by a longer statement from the Mitsubishi Motors Corporation that,

[69] Ibid.
[70] Ibid.
[71] 'Džet-set u Šeheru. Bujrum, pa birajte!', Sport 5.2.1984, 9–10.

among other things, promised to 'help everything go smoothly and successfully' at the Sarajevo Olympics (Image 4.2).

Vučko, the mascot, is himself interesting in terms of the articulation of modernity during the Olympic period. A common animal across the country and a prominent figure in Yugoslavian fables, the wolf embodies a frightening wild animal, full of strength. However, with his smiling facial expressions, Vučko turned the wolf into a rather friendly character. As the early post-Olympic book on the coverage of Sarajevo in the Yugoslav press explained, in the period from early 1981 to mid-1983 the Olympic mascot appeared no less than 316 times in the titles of the Yugoslav press, which succeeded in cultivating or even emancipating the wolf, transforming it into a harmless, darling Vučko (*U znaku Sarajeva* 1984, 91). This said, Vučko's 'transformation' did not stop there. During the Olympic period, Vučko was commonly represented and depicted as 'the modern cosmopolitan character',[72] who even became a master of *bon ton* for the Olympics.[73] Hence, he in fact became 'more of a Disney character, than a scary wild animal', as one source suggested.[74] Turned into a popular-cultural figure, Vučko now frequently appeared in cartoons and commercials, as in the one in which he drove a Mitsubishi 4WD. Finally, he became an imagined consumer: modern history's master category of collective and individual identity and the vital cultivated subject of modernity, in Frank Trentmann's sense of the term. In line with this, and in its typical joking manner, approximately a month before the Games event started *Naši dani* carried a fictional pre-Olympic interview with Vučko. Asked about different topics relating to the Sarajevo Olympics and the city's and his own global popularity, (fictive character) Vučko did not waste the opportunity to explain to the periodical's journalist, that he naturally knew the purpose of owning a Diners Club credit card—to spend money on credit.[75]

Given the capacity of the Olympics to serve as an opportunity for a nation to gain international recognition of its modernity, Sarajevo's updated public transport, supplies of retail commodities and visual

[72] Milomir Marić, 'Sve o zimskoj olimpijadi: Pred početak olimpijade. Sneško belić u bosanskom loncu', *Duga* 259, 28.1.1984, 22–23.

[73] Risto Motika, 'Predolimpijska kulturna razmišljanja. Vučko uči bon-ton', *Naši dani* 763–764, 26.11.–3-12.1982, 19.

[74] Melita Karalić, 'Drugi o Olimpijadi. Duga između svijetova i vjekova—Vučko', *Oslobođenje* 14.1.1984, 5.

[75] Miroslav Arapovich, 'Olimpijada jeeeeeeeeee!!!—Interview: Vučko (glavom I bez brade) "Auuuu!"', *Naši dani* 803, 10.1.1984, 11.

**Image 4.2**  Vučko, the Olympic mascot, driving Mitsubishi's new 4WD, exemplifying the close relationship between modernity and the Olympics. (*Oslobođenje* 16.2.1984, 21)

appearance were at least partly intended to provide a showcase for late Socialist Yugoslavia in front of a global audience. In the end, as one Yugoslav periodical insisted, people would come to Sarajevo to see and experience Yugoslavia.[76] When the Games ultimately proved to be an enormous success, as the Olympic Games and modernity are intricately interconnected, Sarajevo became a symbol of Yugoslavia's modernity. This did, however, not occur in a cultural vacuum, but in a specific socio-cultural context. In its character as a cultural event, the Olympics carried

---

[76] 'Utisci direktora svetskih novinskih agencija. Sve—odlično!', *Duga 259*, 28.1.1984, 25.

salient cultural connotations enabling it to affect culture and cultural understandings in the city and beyond. Most notably, the Sarajevo Olympics—like other Olympic Games events—occurred in the cultural-historical context of the growth of global culture that Roche speaks about. As the development of the modern Olympics has paralleled the growth and spread of modernity, this culture was closely related to the dominant discourse on 'modernity'.

This leads me back to another of Roche's arguments concerning the modernity dimension of the Olympics. According to this argument, ideologies and principles behind the organisation of the Olympic Games event are closely connected with 'Western civilization', including the ideas of universalism and 'techno-rationalism', that is, of positive roles for science and technology. As we have seen time and again in this chapter, the early post-Olympic serial of articles by Aziz Hadžihasanović strongly resonated with Roche's description of the modernity dimension of the Olympics. For this reason, in the remainder of this chapter, I return to this serial and show how it also supports Roche's discussion of universalism and 'techno-rationalism'. My goal is to give some general conclusions on global(-ising) Olympic culture and its impact on cultural representations of Olympic Sarajevo.

In his serial, Hadžihasanović observed that shops' longer opening hours heralded changes in everyday life practices in the city and in its residents' experience of urban life.[77] He also praised the quality and precision of the city's substantially improved public transportation during the Olympics, pointing out that Sarajevo had exceeded most expectations. In fact, he claimed, there had been some 'gloomy forecasts' concerning the city's public transportation before the Olympics although, ultimately, everything went more than well. Sarajevo presented itself to the world, as Hadžihasanović put it, as the modern, dynamic 'city on wheels'.[78]

Hadžihasanović furthermore dedicated one of his articles to the new aesthetic dimension of the city that, according to his interpretation, emerged with the Olympics. He linked this development to the young professionals and students of the Academy of Fine Arts of Sarajevo, who were, he wrote, most responsible for the new aesthetic look of the city.

[77] Aziz Hadžihasanović, 'Sarajevo: Postolimpijske refleksije (IX). Novo ruho tezge. Kako dostići Sarajevo,' *Oslobođenje* 5.4.1984, 3.
[78] Aziz Hadžihasanović, 'Sarajevo: Postolimpijske refleksije (II). Red za ugled,' *Oslobođenje* 29.3.1984, 3.

The enthusiasm of these young specialists was, according to this argument, the driving force behind the emergence of a completely new perception of this aspect of the city. During the Olympic period the young specialists developed new ideas and offered important new solutions which, he suggested, materialised in modern solutions for shop windows arranged by the academy students. On this basis Hadžihasanović related these new aesthetic ideas to retail and consumption.[79]

He did not explicitly speak of Sarajevo's relationship to other Yugoslav cities in the serial, as his focus was exclusively on Sarajevo. However, his interpretation of developments in Olympic Sarajevo clearly falls within the dominant discourse on 'modernity' and common *Balkanist* (self-)representations. According to these, the region's Ottoman past was the major cause for its backwardness vis-à-vis Western Europe. As explained in the first section of this chapter, according to this discourse, in order to catch up with Western Europe, the region had to eradicate its Ottoman cultural habits. This had translated into an idea of the internal hierarchy according to which the southern and south-eastern parts of Yugoslavia were trying, more or less successfully, to catch up with the north and north-west because the former had been longer under the Ottomans and were allegedly reciprocally less capable of becoming modern and Western. In this context, due to its strong Ottoman cultural heritage, Sarajevo was considered a southern city, always lagging behind the northern cultural metropoles, despite being one of the leading economic and cultural centres in the country throughout the post-Second World War period.

It is noteworthy in this respect that Hadžihasanović began the article in which he discussed public transport in Sarajevo by explaining that, before the Olympics, there were 'some malicious reporters' who, 'in the most pejorative manner accentuated our Balkan manners and historical heritage and the corresponding mentality'. It is particularly interesting that, although Hadžihasanović was critical of these reporters, he nevertheless accepted the premise of this argument, adding that 'some earlier episodes and habits' of Sarajevans provided legitimacy for the assertions.[80] In fact, supporting the theoretical view that the modernity dimension of the Olympics always unavoidably contain some references to the preceding

---

[79] Aziz Hadžihasanović, 'Sarajevo: Postolimpijske refleksije (III). Ram za lijepo', *Oslobođenje* 30.3.1984, 3.

[80] Aziz Hadžihasanović, 'Sarajevo: Postolimpijske refleksije (II). Red za ugled,' *Oslobođenje* 29.3.1984, 3.

periods, which are seen as 'traditional' and pre-modern, Hadžihasanović's articles frequently refer to the Balkans and 'Balkan traditionalisms' and 'Balkan manners', to '*čaršija* mentality', Ottoman cultural-historical character[81] and even 'the uncontrolled Orientalism' of pre-Olympic Sarajevo.[82] Ultimately, his claim that—not least in terms of aesthetic values—the Olympics prevailed over 'the provincial spirit' defined by the 'kitsch and mess of an Ottoman bazaar' served to draw a line and qualitatively distinguish between the Olympic present and the preceding pre-Olympic, 'pre-modern' period.[83]

Withal, very much in line with Roche's argument that the Olympics offer modernity a model for pace and direction of change, from the first article in the serial Hadžihasanović praised the achievements of the times and 'the fundamental transformation' of the city. He urged the need to continue development in accordance with 'the Olympic experience',[84] warning against 'any possible *recourse to mentality of čaršija*' (emphasis added), which he suggested was based on 'narrowness, self-sufficiency and autarky of partial interests, without any broader understanding, perspective or reasoning'.[85] In a similar manner, in the article on the aesthetic dimension of the Olympics, Hadžihasanović argued that the Olympics helped unleash an enormous professional potential as young Sarajevan professionals liberated themselves from all 'particularistic interests' and offered solutions based on a broader reasoning.[86] He concluded that, drawing from the Olympic experience, it was 'time for a codex' that would standardise aesthetic dimensions and provide foundations for Sarajevo's future urban policies.[87] Accordingly, Hadžihasanović criticised 'particularistic interests' throughout the serial.[88] This reflects his advocacy of

---

[81] Basically, this goes through the whole serial.

[82] Aziz Hadžihasanović, 'Sarajevo: Postolimpijske refleksije (VI). Predah sa porukom,' *Oslobođenje* 2.4.1984, 3.

[83] Aziz Hadžihasanović, 'Sarajevo: Postolimpijske refleksije (III). Ram za lijepo', *Oslobođenje* 30.3.1984, 3.

[84] Aziz Hadžihasanović, 'Sarajevo: Postolimpijske refleksije (VII). Grad na nogama', *Oslobođenje* 3.4.1984, 3.

[85] Aziz Hadžihasanović, 'Sarajevo: Postolimpijske refleksije. Novo u starom', *Oslobođenje* 28.3.1984, 3.

[86] Aziz Hadžihasanović, 'Sarajevo: Postolimpijske refleksije (III). Ram za lijepo', *Oslobođenje* 30.3.1984, 3.

[87] Ibid.

[88] Insisting that the Olympics were 'the time for the courageous' and those ready for change, Hadžihasanović stressed this explicitly already in the opening article of the serial:

universalistic    solutions    grounded    in    'well-informed    scientific'
formulations,[89] evoking once again Roche's argument that the modernity
dimension of the Olympics is connected with 'Western civilization',
including positive roles for science and technology ('techno-rationalism')
and universalistic humanism. Indeed, Hadžihasanović counterposed this
'techno-rationalism' and its belief in the positive role of science and technology with 'Balkan manners, traditionalisms, [Ottoman] heritage and
*čaršija* mentality'.[90]

It is equally interesting that in his article dealing with public transport,
Hadžihasanović offered a view of infrastructural improvement in Olympic
Sarajevo that closely corresponds with the theoretical position presented
in the previous chapter. There I argued that infrastructure, besides being
about technology, organisation and reliability, is also important for the
way that infrastructural projects create commitments, foster responsibilities and expectations, and, not least, enable certain imaginaries. Very much
in this manner, Hadžihasanović argued that having the necessary infrastructure was not enough in itself. In fact, in his view, the mode in which
that infrastructure was operated was much more important, thereby cred-
iting the change in manners, behaviour and social conduct that occurred
during the Olympic period, in particular the rise in self-discipline, consciousness and collective responsibility.[91]

Lastly, it is important to underline that Hadžihasanović's interpretation
was not unique in this regard; on the contrary, sources indicate that his
interpretation was representative. For instance, in an interview with the
*US News & World Report* on 13 February 1984, Sarajevo's mayor Uglješa
Uzelac spoke about the 'renaissance of consciousness' taking place in
Sarajevo as a result of the Olympics. Thence, he explained to the *Report's*
Stewart Powell (1984, 35) that '[t]here have been changes not only in the
faces of buildings, but also in the heads of the people'.

---

Aziz Hadžihasanović, 'Sarajevo: Postolimpijske refleksije. Novo u starom', *Oslobođenje*
28.3.1984, 3.
[89] Aziz Hadžihasanović, 'Sarajevo: Postolimpijske refleksije (IV). Riznica na dlanu',
*Oslobođenje* 31.3.1984, 3.
[90] Ibid. & Aziz Hadžihasanović, 'Sarajevo: Postolimpijske refleksije (VI). Predah sa porukom,' *Oslobođenje* 2.4.1984, 3.
[91] Aziz Hadžihasanović, 'Sarajevo: Postolimpijske refleksije (III). Ram za lijepo',
*Oslobođenje* 30.3.1984, 3; Aziz Hadžihasanović, 'Sarajevo: Postolimpijske refleksije (VI).
Predah sa porukom,' *Oslobođenje* 2.4.1984, 3; & Aziz Hadžihasanović, 'Sarajevo:
Postolimpijske refleksije (VII). Grad na nogama', *Oslobođenje* 3.4.1984, 3.

# BIBLIOGRAPHY

BOOKS, ARTICLES, REPORTS, BLOGS AND WEBSITES

Anderson, Raymond H. 1972a. Diners Club or Just Dinars, Yugoslav Consumer Is King. The New York Times, August 16, 1972. https://www.nytimes.com/1972/08/16/archives/diners-club-or-just-dinars-yugoslav-consumer-isking.html.

Barney, Robert Knight, Stephen R. Wenn, and Scott G. Martyn. 2002. Monique Berlioux Zenith: Sarajevo and Los Angeles Television Negotiations. In *Selling the Five Rings. The International Olympic Committee and the Rise of Olympic Commercialism*, ed. Robert Knight Barney, Stephen R. Wenn, and Scott G. Martyn, 181–202. Salt Lake City: University of Utah Press.

Bayly, C.A. 2004. *The Birth of the Modern World 1780–1914. Global Connections and Comparisons*. Malden, MA: Blackwell.

Betts, Paul, and Katherine Pence. 2008. Introduction. In *Socialist Modern. East German Everyday Culture and Politics*, ed. Paul Betts and Katherina Pence, 1–34. Ann Arbor: University of Michigan.

Bockman, Johanna. 2011. *Markets in the Name of Socialism: The Left-Wing Origins of Neoliberalism*. Stanford, CA: Stanford University Press.

Bren, Paulina, and Mary Neuburger. 2012. Introduction. In *Communism Unwrapped: Consumption in Cold War Eastern Europe*, ed. Paulina Bren and Mary Neuburger, 3–19. Oxford: Oxford University Press.

Chappelet, Jean-Loup. 2012. From Lake Placid to Salt Lake City: The Challenging Growth of the Winter Games Since 1980. In *The Making of Olympic Cities. Critical Concepts in Urban Studies, Volume I: Contexts and Overviews*, ed. John R. Gold and Margaret M. Gold, 74–93. London and New York: Routledge.

Čolović, Ivan. 2013. Balkanist Discourse and Its Critics. *Hungarian Review* 4 (2): 70–79. http://www.hungarianreview.com/article/balkanist_discourse_and_its_critics.

Duda, Igor. 2017. Everyday Life in Both Yugoslavias. Catching up with Europe. In *Yugoslavia From a Historical Perspective*. Eds. Latinka Perović et al., 391–408. Belgrade: Helsinki Committee for Human Rights in Serbia.

Essex, Stephen, and Brian Chalkley. 2004. Mega-Sporting Events in Urban and Regional Policy: A History of the Winter Olympics. *Planning Perspectives* 19 (2): 201–232.

Fehérváry, Krisztina. 2013. *Politics in Color and Concrete: Socialist Materialities and the Middle Class in Hungary*. Bloomington and Indianapolis, IN: Indiana University Press.

Grabrijan, Dušan. 1984. *The Bosnian Oriental Architecture in Sarajevo: With Special Reference to the Contemporary One*. Ljubljana: Tiskarna Tone Tomšič.

Hadžihasanović, Aziz. 2010. *1984. Olimpijada trijumfa i šansi.* Sarajevo: Rabic.

Holubec, Stanislav, Włodzimierz Borodziej, and Joachim von Puttkamer. 2014. Introduction. In *Mastery and Lost Illusions: Space and Time in the Modernization of Eastern and Central Europe,* ed. Włodzimierz Borodziej, Stanislav Holubec, and Joachim von Puttkamer, 1–14. Munich: Walter de Gruyter GmbH.

Janjetović, Zoran. 2011. *Od 'Internacionale' do komercijale: Popularna kultura u Jugoslaviji 1945–1991.* Beograd: Institut za noviju istoriju Srbije.

Jovanovic, Zlatko. 2014. *'All Yugoslavia Is Dancing Rock and Roll'. Yugoslavness and the Sense of Community in the 1980s Yu-Rock.* PhD Thesis, Faculty of Humanities, University of Copenhagen.

Jović, Dejan. 2003. Communist Yugoslavia and Its Others. In *Ideologies and National Identities,* ed. John Lampe and Mark Mazower, 277–302. New York, NY: Central European University Press (CEU Press).

Klumbytè, Neringa, and Gulnaz Sharafutdinova. 2012. Introduction: What Was Late Socialism? In *Soviet Society in the Era of Late Socialism, 1964–1985,* ed. Neringa Klumbytè and Gulnaz Sharafutdinova, 1–14. Lanham, MD: Lexington Books.

Knežević-Čečez, Gordana, Ljiljana Smajlović, and Mirsad Zorabdić. 1984. *Svijet o Sarajevu. Svjetska štampa, televizija i radio o XIV Zimskim Olimpijskim igrama.* Sarajevo: Organizacioni komitet XIV Zimskih Olimpijskih igara Jugoslavija.

Kolanović, Maša. 2011. *Udarnik! Buntovnik? Potrošač…: Popularna kultura i hrvatski roman od socijalizma do tranzicije.* Zagreb: Naklada Lievak.

Krylova, Anna. 2014. Soviet Modernity: Stephen Kotkin and the Bolshevik Predicament. *Contemporary European History* 23 (2): 167–192.

Luthar, Breda, and Maruša Pušnik. 2010. Introduction: The Lure of Utopia: Socialist Everyday Spaces. In *Remembering Utopia: The Culture of Everyday Life in Socialist Yugoslavia,* ed. Breda Luthar and Maruša Pušnik, 1–33. Washington, DC: New Academia Publishing.

Patterson, Patrick Hyder. 2011. *Bought and Sold: Living and Losing the Good Life in Socialist Yugoslavia.* Ithaca and London: Cornell University Press.

Poblocki, Kacper. 2012. 'Knife in the Water' Competitive Consumption in Urbanizing Poland. In *Communism Unwrapped: Consumption in Cold War Eastern Europe,* ed. Paulina Bren and Mary Neuburger, 68–86. Oxford: Oxford University Press.

Pogačar, Martin. 2010. Yugoslav Past in Film and Music: Yugoslav Interfilmic Referentiality. In *Remembering Utopia: The Culture of Everyday Life in Socialist Yugoslavia,* ed. Breda Luthar and Maruša Pušnik, 199–224. Washington, DC: New Academia Publishing.

Powell, Stewart. 1984. Winter Olympics' Real Winner Is Sarajevo. *US News & World Report,* February 13, 1984, 35.

Roche, Maurice. 2000. *Mega-events and Modernity: Olympics, Expos and the Growth of Global Culture*. London: Routledge.

*Sarajevo, Bosnia and Herzegovina, Yugoslavia. General Questionnaire*. n.d.

Schaap, Dick. 1984. *The 1984 Olympic Games: Sarajevo/Los Angeles* (The Official Book of the US Olympic Committee).

Scherrer, Jutta. 2014. 'To Catch Up and Overtake' the West: Soviet Discourse on Socialist Competition. In *Competition in Socialist Society*, ed. Melanie Ilic and Katalin Miklóssy, 10–22. Abingdon and New York: Routledge.

Tagshold, Christian. 2012. Modernity, Space and National Representation at the Tokyo Olympics 1964. In *The Making of Olympic Cities. Critical Concepts in Urban Studies, Volume III: Critical Concepts in Urban Studies*, ed. John R. Gold and Margaret M. Gold, 26–37. London and New York: Routledge.

Ther, Philipp. 2016 [2014]. *Europe since 1989: A History* (Orig.: *Die neue Ordnung auf dem alten Kontinent: eine Geschichte des neoliberalen Europa*. Translated by Charlotte Hughes-Kreutzmüller). Princeton, NJ: Princeton University Press.

Todorova, Maria. 1997. *Imagining the Balkans*. Oxford and New York: Oxford University Press.

Trentmann, Frank. 2006. Knowing Consumers—Histories, Identities, Practices: An Introduction. In *The Making of the Consumer: Knowledge, Power and Identity in the Modern World*, ed. Frank Trentmann, 1–27. Oxford: Berg.

TSOOC: The Sarajevo Organizing Committee of the XIV Olympic Winter Games Yugoslavia. 1984. *Sarajevo '84. Yugoslavia 8-19.02*. Final Report Published by the Organizing Committee of the XIV Winter Olympic Games 1984 in Sarajevo. Sarajevo: Oslobođenje.

Underwood, Paul. 1960. Credit Cards' Gain: Yugoslavia Acting to Ease Exchange Troubles for the American Tourist. *The New York Times*, February 28, 1960. https://www.nytimes.com/1960/02/28/archives/credit-cards-gain-yugoslavia-acting-to-ease-exchange-troubles-for.html.

*U znaku Sarajeva. Kako su xiv zimske olimpijske igre opisane u jugoslovenskoj štampi i JRT*. 1984. Eds. Zlatan Husarić, Dušan Paravac, Dževad Tašić, Hidajet Delić, Ante Jelavić and Velimir Jojić. Sarajevo: Organizacioni komitet XIV zimskih olimpijskih igara.

von Puttkamer, Joachim. 2014. Mastery of Space and the Crises of Modernity in Central and Eastern Europe. In *Mastery and Lost Illusions. Space and Time in the Modernization of Eastern and Central Europe*, ed. Włodzimierz Borodziej, Stanislav Holubec, and Joachim von Puttkamer, 17–29. Munich: Walter de Gruyter GmbH.

Wolff, Larry. 1997. *Inventing Eastern Europe: The Map of Civilization on the Mind of the Enlightenment*. Stanford: Stanford University Press.

Yurchak, Alexei. 2005. *Everything Was Forever, Until It Was No More*. Princeton, NJ: Princeton University Press.

Zhuk, Sergei I. 2011. The 'Closed' Soviet Society and the West - The Consumption of Western Cultural Products, Youth and Identity in Soviet Ukraine During the 1970s'. In *The Crisis of Socialist Modernity. The Soviet Union and Yugoslavia in the 1970s*, eds. Marie-Janine Calic, Dietmar Neutatz and Julia Obertreis, 87–117. Göttingen/Oakville, CT: Vandenhoeck & Ruprecht.

Zimmerman, William. 1987. *Open Borders, Nonalignment, and the Political Evolution of Yugoslavia*. Princeton, NJ: Princeton University Press.

Zubok, V.M. 2009. *Zhivago's Children: The Last Russian Intelligentsia*. Cambridge, MA: Belknap Press of Harvard University Press.

# PART III

# Sarajevo, 'An Oasis' (National/Non-national Dimension of the Sarajevo Olympics)

# CHAPTER 5

# Inventing Sarajevo as the Ultimate Olympic City

Scholars of urban studies suggest that in the context of a global media spotlight that is characteristic for the Olympics the spectacular staging of the Olympics becomes a setting for a dramaturgical representation of the city (Short 2012, 235–262). However, due to the event's global context, this representation becomes also important in the 'story of a country', a people, a nation. For that matter, Olympics have always represented and continue to represent key occasions on which nations can construct and present images of themselves for comparison with other nations and 'in the eyes of the world' (Roche 2000, 6).

Given that Olympic representations do not emerge in a vacuum but are always constructed in specific socio-politico-historical contexts, they are never free of ideological connotations, most commonly echoing the dominant political mythology of the host nation. In this regard, the relationship between ideology and political mythology becomes highly important. As Chiara Bottici argues in her work on the relationship between mythmaking and identity building, ideology uses political mythology in order to make the ideological message more easily accessible to the populace by utilising narratives through which the populace orients itself, feels about its own socio-political world and acts in it. On this basis, Bottici (2007, 13–14) defines myth as 'the work on a common narrative by which the members of a social group provide significance to their (socio-political) experience and deeds'. This entails, Pål Kolstø (2003, 20) writes in his

Z. Jovanovic, *A Cultural History of the 1984 Winter Olympics, Modernity, Memory and Identity in South-East Europe*, https://doi.org/10.1007/978-3-030-76598-9_5

work on the topic, that myth is about perceptions and not about histori-cally validated truths. For this reason, as George Schöpflin (1997, 19) argues, it is the content of the political myths that matters and not their accuracy.

This in turn implies that it is possible—and most commonly quite probable—that members of a community are well aware that the myth they accept is not strictly accurate. Still, they accept it because it is not history and historical accuracy that is its most crucial function. It is more important that the myth's content provides the members of a community with significance. Consequently, political mythology should be seen not only as an ideological product, but also as the producer of collective identities. Put differently, political mythology has an impor-tant identity-building function. In that sense, we can say that myth con-stitutes a community's common identity and is therefore best approached as 'a set of beliefs, held by a community about itself, regarding certain propositions as normal and others as perverse and alien' (Schöpflin 1997, 19–20). Put more directly, myth seeks to establish the sole way of ordering the world and defining world-views and is therefore, according to Schöpflin, one of the crucial instruments in cultural reproduction. The identity-building function of political mythology rests to a substan-tial extent in such cultural reproduction and, in that regard, as Pierre Nora (1996, 13) has argued, in building our cultural identities 'we seek not our origins but a way of figuring out what we are from what we are no longer'.

Against this theoretical backdrop and looking more closely into the international dimension of the Sarajevo Olympics, this chapter places non-aligned Yugoslavia's political mythology at the centre of discussion. Following the argument proposed by Christopher G. Flood (2002, 44) that we should approach political mythology by exploring and highlight-ing the political ideology behind it, I want to draw attention to the afore-mentioned article on this topic by Kate Meehan Pedrotty, 'Yugoslav unity and Olympic ideology at the 1984 Sarajevo Winter Olympic Games'. In this article, Pedrotty (2010, 337) discusses how the image of non-aligned Yugoslavia as a particularly peace-loving country was used by different Yugoslav Olympic and tourist organisations in order to promote the coun-try and increase tourist revenues in a time of growing economic crisis. In this respect, Pedrotty appropriately depicts how these organisations stressed the presumed natural harmony of the country's non-alignment stance and international Olympic brotherhood. Arguing that this was an ideological construct, Pedrotty conducts an excellent analytical deconstruction of its content.

However, while Pedrotty's interpretation provides a number of important insights and valuable arguments, in this chapter I offer quite a different reading of this image of Yugoslavia as a particularly peace-loving country in the Cold War world. My primary interest is to examine the impact of this image in Yugoslavia and in particular in Sarajevo. Departing from theoretical reflections concerning the identity-building function of political mythology, instead of investigating the historical accuracy of the country's political myths, I seek to contextualise the content of this mythology and provide some comments regarding the populace's readiness to accept it. In doing so, I focus the analysis on, while not reducing it to, several high-circulation, influential Sarajevan and Yugoslav newspapers. These newspapers present an interesting source of historical information concerning the broader socio-political relations in the country. Besides, and given that, until the late 1980s, Yugoslav media were to a substantial extent controlled by the state and projected the authorities' political and ideological priorities, they also constitute an interesting entry to the analysis of the country's political mythology.

Applying this frame, in the first section of the chapter, I examine how the internationally promoted image of Yugoslavia as a particularly peace-loving country was reflected by the political leaderships of both Bosnia and Herzegovina and Yugoslavia, by the Olympic Organising Committee, which mainly consisted of persons from Bosnia and Herzegovina, and by the local Sarajevan and broader Yugoslav media. In exploring this dimension of the Sarajevo Olympics and in the spirit of this book, I pay special attention to the historical context of the 1970s and 1980s—the so-called *Détente* and post-*Détente* years—and explain how the geopolitical situation provided non-aligned and neutralist Yugoslavia with an opportunity to imagine and project itself as the leader of world peace and also as the saviour of the crisis-ridden Olympic movement. Following this discussion, in the chapter's second section, I zoom in on Sarajevo and discuss how hosting the Olympics affected the city's image, nationally and internationally. From previously being most commonly associated with the assassination of the Austrian Archduke Franz Ferdinand and the beginning of the

First World War, with the Olympics, an image of Sarajevo as a global centre of peace and friendship emerged. Yet, as we will see, this development was not only important in terms of the new image of the city that surfaced as a result of its position as an Olympic host city. The presumed and widely emphasised breach between the old and the emerging image of the city was at least equally important. The latter related closely to the identity-building function of Yugoslavia's (geo)political mythology. Or, in Nora's terminology, the new global identity of Sarajevo was not about defining the city's 'natural' character and properties but rather figuring out and stressing what Sarajevo was no longer.

## 5.1    'The Most Sportsmanlike and the Least Politicised Games Ever'

In discussing the relationship between sport and international politics, Barrie Houlihan (1994, 12–16) identifies three aspects of the relationship between sport and ideology, one of which concerns sport as a tool for ideological manipulation which is at the disposal of a government. A second aspect is the way sport reflects the underlying political and economic structures of a society. Finally, the third aspect sees sport as a potential source of counter-ideology. Expatiating on his argument concerning the first of these three aspects, Houlihan further discusses three different types of uses, or purposes, to which sport may be put by a government: the process of socialisation, shaping the image of the state and the establishment of international leadership. In terms of socialisation, Houlihan explains that governments often focus on the utility of sport as a means of inculcating certain attitudes and values in the population. For this reason, sport has frequently been fostered by governments precisely because of its capacity to inculcate desirable values, whether national, middle class, capitalist or socialist—just to mention a few of the arguably most common. Hence, as several scholars have stressed, Houlihan argues sport has been used as a vehicle for inculcating values appropriate to the capitalist economy, while others have pointed out that post-Second World War communist states recognised the utility of sport as a tool for revolutionary inculcation and the development of socialist and communist values.

Probably the most common use to which sport is put by governments, according to Houlihan, is that of providing a vehicle for shaping and projecting an image of the state and its political and ideological priorities.

Interestingly, in relation to this book's topic, Houlihan mentions that the Mexican government, while hosting the 1968 Summer Olympics, sought to use the event to project an image of the state as modern, North American and stable. In order to achieve this image, Mexico City was cleared of the homeless, and the government effectively used military force to destroy the vigorous left-wing student movement. We saw in the previous two chapters that the modernity dimension was equally important for the Yugoslav state in relation to its position as the Olympic host nation. While nothing like the harsh measures seen in Mexico were utilised in Yugoslavia, the Sarajevo Olympics also meant cleaning up the city and disciplining the populace by somewhat different means. It is also noteworthy that despite the creeping economic crisis, Yugoslavia, as we saw in the previous chapter, succeeded in showing itself as a functioning modern state with high-quality services.

Finally, Houlihan notes that a number of states have found sport a valuable tool in attempting to establish international leadership, specifically mentioning Indonesia and Cuba. After being banned from participating in the 1964 Olympics for preventing Israel from participating in the 1962 Asian Games—in solidarity with other Muslim states—Indonesia organised an alternative 'anti-imperialist Asian Olympics', thereby establishing itself, at least symbolically, as the leader in Asia. Cuba, on the other hand, used its international sporting success to enhance its claims to leadership in the non-aligned world. These are rather interesting points, as Yugoslav political elites always saw Yugoslavia as one of the leading members of the non-alignment movement and, as we will see shortly, they used the country's position as Olympic host to claim a role for it as both the leader of world peace and the saviour of the Olympic movement that due to Olympic boycotts found itself in a deep existential crisis. These claims strongly affected (self-)representations in Sarajevo and Yugoslavia, eventually even altering understandings of why the country was awarded the Olympics in the first place.

As the analysis in the first part of this book illustrated, arguably the main reason for choosing Sarajevo as the host city for the 14th Winter Olympics at the IOC meeting in Athens on 18 May 1978 was that Sarajevo could schedule all Olympic activities within a radius of 25 kilometres. Emphasising this feature was also the main tactic that Artur Takač, 'the Yugoslav man' in Lausanne, employed in eliminating Sarajevo's main competitor, Swedish Gothenburg (Vuic 2015, 34–36). While the early official Yugoslav response to winning the Olympic bid recognised this and explicitly stated that the IOC chose Sarajevo due to the close proximity of all the activities, the official Yugoslav interpretation added another, political layer, according to which the IOC also credited Yugoslavia for its socialist non-aligned policy by awarding the Olympics to a Yugoslav city.

The first reaction of the Yugoslav ambassador in Athens, Radko Močivnik, on hearing Sarajevo had won the bid, clearly illustrates how this transpired in official Yugoslav discourse. As Močivnik explained to Belgrade sports daily, *Sport*, on the day the news became public:

> By choosing Sarajevo as the Olympic host city, the members of the IOC—it should be emphasized—both chose the economically sustainable solution (as all future sites are concentrated in a rather small area) and at the same time paid recognition to Socialist Yugoslavia and her non-aligned policies.[1]

Yugoslav source materials, including official documents and various Yugoslav newspapers from the immediate months after the city was awarded the Olympics, indicate that, although Yugoslav officials were proud of the win on behalf of both Yugoslavia and Sarajevo, they were also somewhat anxious about it, as winning the bid also meant commitment to years of hard work building all the necessary facilities. This was a quite big endeavour for a country such as Yugoslavia, which despite a significant increase after the Second World War still in 1978 had much lower GDP per capita than any other Winter Olympic host country. Pointing—in a similar manner—to the fact that Yugoslavia's GDP per capita was way below those of rival countries, Sweden and Japan, *Sport*'s journalist covering the host selection at the IOC's meeting in Athens, claimed that winning the bid was only the beginning—and there was no time to waste.[2] This anxiety was persistent in the Sarajevan and Yugoslav media for about a year or even a bit longer, as if Bakarač's joke from 1973 that Sarajevo should submit its Olympic bid, but nevertheless pray to God not to win it, had gained some currency. It was often stressed, during the first year-to-year-and-a-half of the Olympic preparation period, that, besides being a great honour, being awarded the Olympics also carried huge responsibility. Or as put in the title of an *Oslobođenje* article published a couple of days after winning the bid: 'Congratulations that oblige'.[3]

---

[1] Milan Nikolić, 'Sarajevo domaćin Zimske Olimpijade 1984', *Sport* 19.5.1978, 18.

[2] Milan Nikolić, 'Posla odluke MOK. Nema vremena za predah', *Sport* 20.5.1978, 2.

[3] One example which catches this excellently is Alija Resulović, 'Čestitke koje nose obavezu', *Oslobođenje* 20.5.1978, 16.

Then, during the fall of 1979, it all started changing rapidly. In September 1979, Yugoslavia hosted the Mediterranean Games in the Croatian coastal city of Split. As the largest sporting event Yugoslavia had organised to date, the 1979 Split Mediterranean Games (September 15–29, 1979) were naturally perceived as being closely associated with the Sarajevo Olympics. In fact, the Yugoslav media and officials widely interpreted the Mediterranean Games in Split, as 'the general test' and 'the main rehearsal' for the Sarajevo Olympics, and 'a step towards' them.[4] It was also a logical step for the Organising Committee of the Sarajevo Olympics to borrow the formula for financing the Olympic Games from the 1979 Split Mediterranean Games (TSOOC 1984b, 182). Moreover, the two manifestations were connected even on a very personal level: Artur Takač served as Vice President of the Organising Committee of the Split Games as well as being one of the central personalities in the whole process of Sarajevo's nomination and being awarded the 1984 Winter Olympics. In addition, with Takač serving as a member of the IOC, the Organising Committee of the Split Games was thereby also closely connected to the IOC, which also recognised the link between the two events. This was clearly demonstrated by the visits of the IOC's President, Lord Michael Killanin, and Vice President Juan Antonio Samaranch to both Split and Sarajevo during the 1979 Mediterranean Games. Their visits and subsequent comments in the Yugoslav media had the apparent potential to increase the sense of connectedness between the two sporting events.[5]

The 1979 Split Mediterranean Games were quickly and widely recognised as successful and praised for their organisation and also the modernist architecture of the newly built sports arenas. Indeed, the Yugoslav newspapers claimed that in some respects 'the Split Games were better organised than any Olympics held up to that date'.[6] The success in Split boosted Yugoslav self-confidence, not least among the officials engaged in preparations for the Sarajevo Olympics and the media covering them. This was, however, not the only event in late 1979 that helped boost Yugoslavs' pre-Olympic morale. In the final days of the year, Yugoslavia's unique geopolitical position in the bipolar Cold War world suddenly gained cur-

---

[4] D. Vasović, 'Stepenik prema Olimpijadi', *Borba* 15.9.1979, 13.

[5] 'Vaše iskustvo garancija uspeha', *Sport* 15.9.1979, 12; 'Olimpijske igre goleme i skupe', *Sport* 20.9.1979, 2; D. Vasović, 'Stepenik ka Olimpijadi', *Borba* 15.9.1979, 13; 'Impresioniran sam onim što sam video', *Borba* 20.9.1979, 12.

[6] Miša Vasiljević, 'Blistava baklja mladosti čarobne splitske noći', *Sport* 30.9.1979, 10–11.

rency in relation to Sarajevo's hosting the Olympics. On Christmas Eve 1979, less than three months after the Split Mediterranean Games, the Soviet military invaded its Central Asian neighbour, Afghanistan. One of the results of the Soviet invasion of Afghanistan was that its archenemy, the USA, along with another sixty-four countries (not all close allies of the USA), ultimately boycotted the 1980 Summer Olympics in Moscow. Many of the boycotting countries chose instead to participate in the Liberty Bell Classic, an athletic event organised in Philadelphia in the USA. Four years later, the Soviets and most of the East Bloc countries retaliated to the American boycott by not participating in the 1984 Los Angeles Summer Olympics.

In the context of the Olympic boycotts, Roger I. Abrams (2013, 150–151) has observed that during the Cold War, the competition between the two global superpowers was always couched in ideological terms, with both sides seeking to define the terms of the dialogue. Claiming to be the democratic defenders of the true faith, the USA labelled the Soviet Union a godless dictatorship. The Soviets, on the other hand, decried the USA as the epitome of imperialist capitalism, run by bourgeois entrepreneurs for their own private gain at the expense of the proletariat. In contrast to the USA, the Soviet Union was the land ruled by the masses where everyone received what was needed in order to flourish.

As Abrams (2013, 150–151) puts it, both these depictions were caricatures of the real situation. Furthermore, behind the ideologically framed discussion, both superpowers were most motivated by non-ideological concerns about national security and the capture of economic markets. In realpolitik terms, both the USA and the Soviet Union needed (and sought) to provide safety for their populations, purchase raw materials and sell their industrial products.

In the larger picture, the Soviet invasion of Afghanistan marked the end of the period of the Cold War known as *Détente* and the beginning of the so-called Second Cold War. In contrast to the open antagonism, constant threat of armed conflict and armament race that defined the 1960s, *Détente* was a period from 1970–1979 during which the two sides became more cooperative, participating in joint summits and accords and signing several armaments control acts; meanwhile, however, they continued to fight each other in proxy wars and support their allies around the world. This makes it reasonable to argue, as historian Nicholas Evan Sarantakes (2010, 54) has done in his work on the politics behind the Olympic boycotts, that *Détente* was a period of 'managed competition' and a 'time when the Cold War was "less dangerous" but, nevertheless, still ongoing'.

For example, during this time the CIA backed a right-wing coup in Chile that eventually led to a military dictatorship, and the USA supported anti-leftist state terror campaigns in several Latin American countries.[7] For their part, the Soviets backed left-wing guerrillas in Asia, supporting them both ideologically and with material. In addition, despite increased cooperation during the era, both sides continued to be highly sceptical of each other's foreign policies. There was a strong anti-*Détente* agenda among some Soviet officials who believed that the Soviet Union was making too many concessions to the USA and its Western allies (Sarantakes 2010, 54), while a number of American officials argued that *Détente* was working for the Soviets. One of the latter was National Security Advisor, Zbigniew Brzezinski, who believed that the Soviets were trying to use *Détente* to spread their communist ideology (Sarantakes 2010, 55). It was also in this situation that both Moscow and Los Angeles—as well as Sarajevo—won their Olympic bids.

In the meantime, on the European front, Yugoslav politicians together with their colleagues from neutral Finland and Austria, did an important job in mediating between the two power blocs, seeking to establish a dialogue on peace, disarmament and civil rights. This culminated in the Conference on Security and Cooperation in Europe (CSCE), arguably the most important achievement of which was the signing of the 1975 Helsinki Accord at the summit meeting in the Finnish capital, a declaration that was intended to improve relations between communist East and capitalist West. Two years later, in 1977, a second summit was held in the Yugoslav capital of Belgrade. As a recent study shows, the Yugoslav drafts on national minority protection were in fact incorporated into the CSCE framework and are still valid for its successor organisation, the Organization for Security and Cooperation in Europe (OSCE). Minority rights were also an important field of action in the United Nations, but without the same strong impact that some Yugoslav proposals and concepts had on a European scale. Although its record in the field of civil rights, as well as the country's openness and affirmation of human rights internationally, stood in contrast to the country's record at home, the country's international activism helped establish and strengthen its neutralist position in the bipolar order of the Cold War period (Trültzsch 2017).

---

[7] Among others in Argentina, Uruguay, Paraguay, Bolivia and Brazil.

When the Soviet military invaded Afghanistan to shore up its ally in the country, massive Western criticism erupted, ultimately resulting in the US-led boycott of the 1980 Moscow Summer Olympics, although the invasion was far from the only reason why the Americans were unhappy with Moscow as an Olympic host city. Nicolas Evan Sarantakes' (2010, 32–45) work on the boycott shows rather well how American officials and analysts—not least the aforementioned Zbigniew Brzezinski—never really accepted the IOC's decision to hold the Olympics in Moscow. Indeed, from the very first day of its candidacy, various American officials began to express their hostility to the idea and advocate a boycott, arguing that the Games should only be held in 'the free world'. Others warned that the Soviets had failed to honour the Helsinki Accords, and that they might not admit Israel to the Games.[8] The *National Review*, a conservative political commentary journal, went so far as to declare that the Moscow Olympics were going to be 'a sinister and deadly-serious political operation disguised as sport'.[9] Lastly, besides specific US resentment about the Soviets as Olympic hosts, threats of Olympic boycott and the practice by organisers of banning individual nations from participation in sporting competitions had become more common throughout the 1970s, as Sarantakes' work shows, making such threats a more common weapon in political quarrels.

All these factors combined to contribute to the final US decision to boycott the Moscow Games, one result of which was retaliation by Moscow and its Warsaw Pact satellite regimes four years later. Boycotting the Los Angeles Summer Olympics, the Soviets and 13 other nations organised an alternative sporting event, symbolically calling it the Friendship Games. This sort of symbolic warfare became one of the defining characteristics of the period known as the Second Cold War. As Barrie Houlihan (1994, 117) notes in his discussion of the Olympics, with the boycotts of 1980 and 1984, the issue of the Soviet invasion of Afghanistan became rapidly confused with the controversy over the relationship between sport and government/politics.

---

[8] Different US sportsmen expressed strong opposition to the idea. One of them basketball player, Bill Bradley, winner of the 1964 Olympic gold medal, who, as early as 1976, argued that USA should discontinue its participation in the Moscow Games.

[9] Arguably Ronald Reagan's presidential campaign, based on an anti-*Détente* political platform, also contributed.

Drawing on its unique geopolitical position of not belonging to either of the two Cold War blocs, Yugoslavia joined this symbolic warfare in its own way. Equating the country's neutralist and non-aligned policies with the ideals of Olympism, Yugoslav officials sought to promote the country as particularly peace-loving, in fact, the most peace-loving country in the world (Pedrotty 2010, 333–363). Stressing the Olympic ideals of peaceful coexistence and cooperation among the world nations in times troubled by the American boycott of the Moscow Games and the looming Soviet retaliation, and with the Olympic movement and the IOC both in deep existential crisis, neutral Yugoslavia emerged as pretender to the position of champion of world peace and Olympism. Seen from this perspective, the participation of both superpowers (and their allies) at the Sarajevo Games appeared not only as a victory for the country's neutralist and non-alignment policies, but also as proof of its claimed position as the leader of world peace, of Olympic ideals and of the depoliticisation of international sport.

Yugoslav media picked up this thread and constructed an image of Yugoslavia as the ideal Olympic nation. In their writings, Yugoslav newspapers regularly supported this claim by referring to the international press and news agencies which, they stressed, were very positive in their evaluation of the Sarajevo Olympics and of Yugoslavia as Olympic host. Hence, in the Olympic preparation period, Yugoslavs could read that news agencies all over the world—from Angola to the USA to Czechoslovakia—claimed, among other things, that 'peace was the essence'[10] of the Sarajevo Olympics, that Sarajevo and Yugoslavia organised 'the most sportsmanlike and the least politicised games ever'[11] and finally that the capital city of Bosnia and Herzegovina had 'become 'the confluence of peace and international understanding'.[12] Yugoslav newspapers were not the only ones diligently passing on these reports from the international press. Shortly after the Olympics, the Sarajevo Olympics Organising Committee published the book, *World about Sarajevo. The International Press, TV and Radio Coverage of the XIV Olympic Winter Games*, in which many of the selected excerpts mentioned non-aligned, neutralist Yugoslavia's contribution to world peace (Knežević-Čečez et al. 1984). The quadrilingual Olympic guide, *Sarajevo '84: All on the Games*, left the same impression, in

[10] 'Sarajevo drugi put na mapi sveta', *Sport* 11.2.1984, 12.
[11] 'Veličanstven događaj', *Sport* 22.2.1984, 2.
[12] 'Sarajevska razglednica. Oaza prijateljstva', *Borba* 17.2.1984, 9.

particular in its sections 'In the Eyes of the World' and 'Sarajevo as the Others See It' (TSOOC 1984a, 13–20). Finally, *The Final Report*, also published by the Sarajevo Olympics Organising Committee, likewise insisted on Yugoslavia's contribution to the Olympic idea and linked the values of Olympism to Yugoslavia's non-alignment (TSOOC 1984b, 190):

> The XIV Olympic Winter Games, conceived as an event which will contribute to the promotion of humane values of Olympism, have undoubtedly succeeded as such.
>
> The atmosphere in Sarajevo during the Games proved the possibility of direct application of the universal Olympic idea. This was experienced not only by the athletes in a record number of participating countries, but also by members of the Olympic family, representatives of the mass media, guests and tourists. People all over the world were able to follow the Games via TV, radio and mass media.
>
> Held in such an atmosphere, the XIV OWG proved the desire, possibility and capability of Yugoslavia to contribute substantially to the expansion of the Olympic idea.
>
> The affirmation of Yugoslavia and Sarajevo through the XIV Olympic Winter Games, represents, above all, the affirmation of the Olympic movement, whose humane ideals are identical with the peace policy of Tito's non-aligned Yugoslavia.

While the Yugoslav media were naturally selective in their choice and presentation of international reportage, sources clearly indicate that the general impression from around the world was very positive. Indeed, a range of sources indicate that Yugoslavia in fact did appear as an extraordinarily peace-loving country in the troubled first half of the 1980s. The international news agencies and press that saw the Sarajevo Olympics as a great success in this and many other aspects were far from the only sources framing events this way. In the eyes of 'ordinary people' from around the world—those who saw the Olympics on their TV sets—Sarajevo, and Yugoslavia more broadly, seemed like important international agents working for world peace. The letters sent to the Mayor of Sarajevo in the immediate post-Olympic weeks by the people from across the world testify to this. Singling out a few of them serves to illustrate the point. One Canadian witness wrote that he saw Socialist Yugoslavia as being on 'the same side of the Cold War divide' as his native Canada. This was 'the peace side' he argued, praising Yugoslavia for its neutralist position in the bipolar

Cold War world.[13] 'You have made a strong contribution toward world understanding and peace', claimed an American that was watching the 1984 Winter Olympics from 'thousands of miles away in the Northwest Corner of the United States',[14] while an another American praised Yugoslavia and Sarajevo in his letter for 'showing the Olympic spirit at its best'.[15] Finally, it should be noted that *Oslobođenje* journalist, Aziz Hadžihasanović, in his serial, 'Sarajevo: Post-Olympic Reflections', used several of these letters to further his claim of Yugoslavia's allegiance to creating a more peaceful world.[16]

It is also important to mention that the members of the IOC were very pleased with the 14th Winter Olympics in Sarajevo, likewise emphasising Yugoslavia's declared commitment to peace, sport and the ideals of Olympism. In an open letter to the city of Sarajevo written immediately after the Games, the acting President of the IOC, Juan Antonio Samaranch, portrayed the Sarajevo Olympics as 'the triumph of sport, peace and Olympic ideals'.[17] In his capacity as President of the IOC, Samaranch argued that the Sarajevo Olympics had taught the world a lesson in how 'fraternity, friendship and cooperation can be achieved among all countries of the world'.[18] The existing historical record also clearly shows that Samaranch had always been very supportive of the Sarajevo Olympic Games and their Organising Committee, from the time he was Lord

[13] Letter from Scott Sanders to the Mayor of Sarajevo, 22.2.1984, Letter 228. Historijski Arhiv Sarajevo [Sarajevo Historical Archives], Sarajevo, Bosnia and Herzegovina.

[14] Letter from David James to the Mayor of Sarajevo, Letter 112. Historijski Arhiv Sarajevo [Sarajevo Historical Archives], Sarajevo, Bosnia and Herzegovina.

[15] Letter from Billy Edd Wheeler to the Mayor of Sarajevo, 21.2.1984, Letter 72. Historijski Arhiv Sarajevo [Sarajevo Historical Archives], Sarajevo, Bosnia and Herzegovina.

[16] Aziz Hadžihasanović, 'Ram za lijepo (Nije bilo uzalud)', *Oslobođenje* 30.3.1984, 3; 'Riznica na dlanu (letter Veliko hvala)', *Oslobođenje* 31.3.1984, 3; 'Izazov nove ere (Nezaboravno Sarajevo)', *Oslobođenje* 1.4.1984, 2; 'Predah sa porukom ("Ugrijali ste mnoga srca…")', *Oslobođenje* 2.4.1984, 3; 'Grad na nogama (Nada u bolji svijet)', *Oslobođenje* 3.4.1984, 3; 'Više od spomena ("Cijena nije važna…")', *Oslobođenje* 6.4.1984, 3; 'Ništa bez glasa (Grad magnet)', *Oslobođenje* 7.4.1984, 3; 'Osmijeh s obavezom (Gostoljubivost)', *Oslobođenje* 8.4.1984, 2.

[17] 'Otvoreno pismo gradu Sarajevu predsednika MOK Huana Antonia Samaranča: Trijumf sporta, mira i olimpijskih ideala (Veličanstven događaj)', *Sport* 22.2.1984, 2; 'Predsednik MOK uputio otvoreno pismo Sarajevu: Trijumf olimpijskom ideala i mira', *Borba* 21.2.1984, 10; 'Samaranovo pismo Sarajevu: Trijumf olimpijskog ideala i mira', *Politika* 21.2.1984, 13.

[18] 'Otvoreno pismo gradu Sarajevu predsednika MOK Huana Antonia Samaranča. Trijumf sporta, mira i olimpijskih ideala (Veličanstven događaj)', *Sport* 22.2.1984, 2.

Michael Killanin's deputy until long after the Sarajevo Olympics finished.[19] This said, Samaranch's position on the Olympic Games in general was fully in accordance with the official IOC position of promoting the ideals of Olympism. In fact, as Barrie Houlihan (1994, 109–131) argues in his discussion of the historical development of the Olympic Movement, many people involved in international sport have held the deep belief that sport works and should work for world peace, something manifestly woven into the very idea of the Olympic Movement. Given that the situation in international sport and related diplomacy in the early 1980s—one marked by the American boycott of the Moscow Games and the evident possibility of Soviet retaliation—could not have been further removed from this ideal, the IOC found itself in a deep existential crisis.[20] In this situation Yugoslavia's neutralist and non-aligned position and the prospect of both the USA and the USSR participating at the Sarajevo Games offered a sign of positive change and a remedy for the International Olympic Movement. Samaranch's satisfaction and enthusiasm for the Sarajevo Games should thus be seen from this perspective.

It is as well noteworthy that in its aforementioned first report from Athens after Sarajevo won its Olympic bid, *Sport*—the country's largest sports daily—claimed that by awarding Sarajevo the Olympics the IOC was showing its loyalty to the ideas held by the then organisation's President, Lord Michael Killanin. According to *Sport*, Lord Killanin held that 'it was necessary to broaden the circle of countries hosting Olympic Games, in order to also effectively spread the Olympic spirit to the new countries and regions of the world'.[21] Indeed, as Roger I. Abrams (2013, 150) shows in his work on the Olympics, when Lord Michael Killanin, a

[19] Already during his visit to Yugoslavia for the 1979 Split Mediterranean Games, Samaranch expressed strong belief that Sarajevo and Yugoslavia would be able to organise Olympic Games of the highest possible standard (D. Vasović, 'Stepenik prema Olimpijadi', *Borba* 15.9.1979, 13.). Later, shortly before the 1984 Sarajevo Olympics, he expressed his belief that these would in fact be the best Olympic Games organised to date (M. Blagojević, 'Huan Antonio Samaran o ZOI: Najbolje u istoriji!', *Oslobođenje* 13.1.1984, 9 and E. Demirović & R. Mučibabić 'Najbolja Olimpijada do sada', Borba 1.2.1984, 10.). Finally, in 1994, calling for a truce during the war in Bosnia, he left the Lillehammer Winter Games to pay a brief visit to Sarajevo.

[20] In fact, the Lord Killanin withdrew from the position after the US boycott of the Moscow Games, and when overtaking his position Juan Antonio Samaranch stressed that he saw the depoliticisation of sport as his main mission (in 'Depolitizacija sporta—osnovni zadatak', *Oslobođenje* 5.8.1980, 11).

[21] Milan Nikolić, 'Sarajevo domaćin zimske olimpijade 1984', *Sport* 19.5.1978, 18.

journalist, film producer and sports official, became the new President of the IOC in the 1970s, he pursued a policy of awarding the Olympics to countries with a range of political, religious and social views. According to Abrams, Killanin saw awarding the 1980 Summer Olympics to the capital of the Soviet Union as part of the Olympic Movement's effort to foster world peace. He believed, argues Abrams, that thanks to the Olympic Movement, countries that were very different ideologically would be able to come together in peace and compete in sports. His hopes would later prove impossible to fulfil. Nevertheless, even in that very first report from Athens, *Sport* implicitly supported the claim put forward by Radko Močivnik, the Yugoslav ambassador in Greece, that the award of the 14th Winter Olympics to Yugoslavia should be seen as a recognition of the country's non-alignment policies. This resonated with Lord Killanin's declared goal of disseminating the spirit of Olympism to countries with political views and ideological priorities that differed from Western liberal democracies. From the moment Sarajevo was awarded the Olympics, there emerged a common practice among the Yugoslav officials to interpret Killanin's goal as if he were favouring Yugoslavia as the Olympic host. This is the impression left by an interview with the Mayor of Sarajevo, Ante Sučić, published in *Oslobođenje* on 22 May 1978. As the title had it, awarding the Olympics to Yugoslavia meant 'a victory for Olympic principles'. In the interview, Sučić claimed that Sarajevo won the Olympic candidacy because 'Lord Killanin and some other members of the International Olympic Committee advocated, above all, Olympic principles'. For this reason, according to Sučić, they helped Sarajevo win, although he added that the fact that the Olympic venues were concentrated close to the city also played an important role.[22]

In a similar vein to Močivnik's and Sučić's references to international politics, the federal government associated *Borba's* correspondent Enver Demirović argued, in his first report from Sarajevo covering reactions to the news that the city had won the Olympic bid, that the award of the Olympics to Sarajevo signalled a 'recognition of Yugoslavia's non-alignment policies' and 'the reputation that the country enjoyed in the world'.[23] Even without specifying which reputation he was referring to, there was very little doubt that he was alluding to the country's position

[22] Borislav Radisavljević, 'Razgovor sa Antom Sučićem: Pobjeda principa olimpizma', *Oslobođenje* 22.5.1978, 3.
[23] E. Demirović, 'Priznanje našoj zemlji', *Borba* 19.5.1978, 6.

in the CSCE and its neutralist stance in regard to the bipolar Cold War world. Naturally, in the period immediately after Sarajevo was awarded the Olympics and until the Soviet invasion of Afghanistan, Olympism and the (de)politicisation of sport were not mentioned in relation to the Sarajevo Olympics in the Yugoslav newspapers or in any of the official statements from the Yugoslav Olympic Committee and the Organising Committee of the Sarajevo Olympics. One rare occasion, before the Soviet invasion of Afghanistan, on which sport and Yugoslavia's proclaimed peace agenda were linked to each other in the writings of the Yugoslav press, was during the Split Mediterranean Games, when the President of the League of Physical Culture of Yugoslavia, Trpe Jakovlevski, claimed in the federal government daily *Borba* that the Split Mediterranean Games were 'the Games with a peace mission'[24] and 'sport in service of the noble mission';[25] the latter with no doubt referring to world peace.

These two claims about the Split Mediterranean Games—'the best games ever' and 'the games for peace'—would later also become common phrases in the Yugoslav press when covering the Sarajevo Olympics some four-and-a-half years later. This came as the culmination of a process, lasting several years, of identifying Yugoslavia as a particularly peace-loving country and, for that reason, the ideal Olympic host nation, allegedly capable of organising the best games ever. This identification provided a strong contrast to the emergent situation of growing tensions and renewed armaments competition between the two Cold War blocs. Reflecting the controversial relationship between sport and politics, and occurring gradually and in consonance with global political developments in the immediate post-*Détente* period, the idea of the Sarajevo Olympics as 'the triumph of sport, peace and Olympic ideals' became one of the central elements of the Yugoslav Olympic narrative.

Bearing strong political connotations to the prevailing situation in international politics and sport in the early 1980s, the choice of the Olympic symbol for the Sarajevo Games, the Pahulja or Snowflake, is a product of this narrative. Once again *Oslobođenje* provides a good illustration of the point. Halfway through the period between the US boycott of the Moscow Olympics and the beginning of the Sarajevo Games, in May

[24] 'Intervju Predsednika SFKJ Trpeta Jakovlevskog Tanjugu (1): Igre u misiji mira', *Borba* 13.9.1979, 13.
[25] 'Intervju Predsednika SFKJ Trpeta Jakovlevskog Tanjugu (2): Sport u službi plemenitog', *Borba* 14.9.1979, 11.

1982, the daily's cultural section, 'KUN', carried an article titled 'Open to All Sides of the World'. Discussing the designs and the political messages of the symbols used by organisers of past Olympic Games, the author offered an interesting perspective on the Snowflake. According to his interpretation, despite appearing purely geometrical and apolitical, the shape of 'the crystal snowflake' bore, in fact, a deeper story and had clear and important political connotations. With its simple quadratic shape, opening outwards, it was meant to create the impression that Sarajevo and Yugoslavia were open to all sides of the world, argued the author. He did not stop there but went even further and claimed somewhat cryptically that the Sarajevo Snowflake 'defied the *Third World Peace*' (emphasis added). Implicit in this claim was an idea that the world was neither at war nor at peace in the post-*Détente* period of the early 1980s. Defined by the rising tensions between the two Cold War blocs, the post-*Détente* period was linked to the two World Wars and was hence 'the Third World Peace'. On the basis of his analysis, the author concluded that, with this Olympic symbol, the organisers of the Sarajevo Olympics aimed to 'remind the world' of 'the traditional principles of the Olympic Games in Ancient Greece', during which period, the author claimed, the world was at peace, quite unlike the world of the early 1980s.[26] Framed this way, the Sarajevo Games were placed in the service of much needed world peace, while Yugoslavia, as host nation, appeared not only as the leader in the struggle for global peace but also as the true carrier of the spirit of ancient Olympism at a time when sport had become a weapon in international politics, marked by the struggles between the two superpowers (Image 5.1).

As the official symbol of the Sarajevo Olympics, the Snowflake makes it apparent that we have to deal with the official narrative—and hence also the dominant discourse on the Olympics—which emerged from the country's neutralist position in the 1970s, but was further strengthened when the Soviet invasion of Afghanistan and the US-led boycott of the Moscow Games 'killed the Détente', as Sarantakes (2010, 13) has phrased it. In this situation, Yugoslav officials picked an opportunity to frame their country as the saviour of the Olympic movement. Accordingly, less than six months after the Moscow Olympics, when Lord Killanin stepped down and Juan Antonio Samaranch took over the presidency of the IOC, Branko Mikulić, a member of the Central Committee of the League of Communists of

---

[26] Radomir Vuković, 'Simbol i znak. Otvoren za sve strane svijeta', *Oslobođenje—kulturni dodatak 'Kultura Umjetnost Nauka'* (50) 29.5.1982, 1.

**Image 5.1** 'After you …', a cartoon featured in *Politika* showing the US and the USSR presidents, Ronald Reagan and Yuri Andropov, getting ready for a super-G race. An explicit criticism of the post-*Détente* nuclear arm race between the two superpowers, with even the name 'super'-G implicitly implying the race between the two Cold War 'super'-powers and contrasted to the sport-spirited Vučko, symbolising Yugoslavia. (Kušanić, 'Veleslalom', *Politika* 29.1.1984, 1)

Yugoslavia and the President of the Sarajevo Olympics Organising Committee, claimed that Yugoslavia's hosting the Sarajevo Olympics marked 'the affirmation of the Olympic movement'. In supporting his claim, Mikulić referred to Lord Killanin's statement that its slot between the competitions in Moscow and Los Angeles made the Games in Sarajevo particularly important, adding, 'we are not sufficiently aware how strong the influence of Yugoslavia is on the destiny of the Olympic movement'.[27]

---

[27] 'Afirmacija olimpijskog pokreta', *Oslobođenje* 3.1.1981, 3.

Following the same official narrative, Yugoslav reportage throughout the Olympic preparation period stressed that non-aligned Yugoslavia's hosting the Olympics meant 'the recovery of the Olympic movement'.[28] This explicit correlation of the country's policies of neutralism and non-alignment with the Olympic ideals of the role of sport in peaceful coexistence and cooperation among nations did not, however, emerge in a vacuum, but intertextually: that is, in relation to other narratives circulating at the time. Notable amongst the latter was that of the people engaged in international sport—including the IOC—who, as we saw, according to Barrie Houlihan (1994, 109–131) often had a deep belief that sport worked for world peace. For this reason, Samaranch argued in one of his first statements as President of the IOC, shortly after the closing of the Moscow Olympics, that the IOC's most important task was the depoliticisation of sport.[29] Naturally, Yugoslav officials and the press picked up this idea of depoliticisation and made it part of the Yugoslav Olympic narrative. The sources indicate that the closer we get to the Games, the more blurred became the distinction between Yugoslav neutralism and non-alignment and the ideals of Olympism in the Yugoslav press and the statements of Yugoslav officials. Hence, by the time the Olympics were about to begin, in February 1984, Yugoslavia appeared as the very embodiment of Olympism in the writings of the Yugoslav press: as the ultimate Olympic host nation and as a symbol of the world peace. In this situation, the (de) politicisation of the Olympics and world peace became two of the main themes in Yugoslav press coverage of the Games. Finally, during the Olympics, as for instance in *Sport*'s reporting, the Sarajevo Olympics and peace became virtually inseparable. Hence, according to the daily's main reportage published on their opening day, the Sarajevo Games were held 'in honour of peace'.[30] But even before the opening of the event, the daily—one of Yugoslavia's two exclusively sporting newspapers—depicted the Sarajevo Games as 'the Olympics of peace that were contributing positively in the current unfavourable situation in world'.[31] During the Olympic event, according to the daily, sport itself emerged as 'the real

[28] 'Sarajevo donosi ozdravljenje Olimpijskog pokreta', *Sport* (drugo izdanje) 6.2.1984, 8–9.

[29] 'Depolitizacija sporta—osnovni zadatak', *Oslobođenje* 5.8.1980, 11.

[30] 'Sarajevo u slavu mira', *Sport* 8.2.1984, 1.

[31] 'Igre mira i prijateljstva', *Sport* (Specijalni dodatak "Sporta" posvećen Zimskim Olimpijskim Igrama u Sarajevu) 5.2.1984, 7.

winner' of the Sarajevo Olympics, as those otherwise omnipresent political tensions of the time 'could not be felt in Sarajevo'.[32]

*Sport* was, of course, far from the only Yugoslav newspaper equating the Sarajevo Olympics with peace. By 1983 Sarajevo's major daily, *Oslobodenje*, frequently and explicitly stressed the link between Yugoslavia's non-alignment and Olympism. For instance, on 4 February the front page held an article that told readers that the Olympics were a chance to boost the reputation of non-aligned Yugoslavia.[33] By the summer *Oslobodenje* had become bolder, explicitly drawing a parallel between the ideology of Olympism and the Sarajevo Olympics, which were now 'the guiding light for Olympism'.[34] At the turn of the year, referring to the country's non-alignment policy, *Oslobodenje* described Yugoslavia as 'the ideal host for the Olympics',[35] while a few days later, in its first issue of the Olympic year, 1984, the daily raised a 'toast to peace and Olympism' on its front page.[36] Several other January issues had articles explicitly elaborating on non-aligned Yugoslavia's role as a particularly peace-loving nation and on Sarajevo's position as the symbol of peace in an otherwise troubled world. Delivering a message from the Yugoslav government and the Sarajevo Olympic Committee, the 13 January issue stressed how the fact that in contrast to several previous Olympic Games events, the fact that no country was boycotting the Games in Sarajevo should be seen as a recognition of Yugoslavia's commitment to international peace.[37] By February, the Sarajevo Olympics had turned into 'the Olympics of Peace'.[38] Then, in a self-congratulatory front cover article on the opening day of the Olympics, *Oslobodenje* insisted on the Sarajevo Games being held in 'the name of humanity', contributing to peace and understanding in the world.[39]

Clearly visible in these examples is that, by securing the participation of countries from both Cold War blocs, the Sarajevo Olympics appeared an unmitigated success—one that provided Sarajevo and Yugoslavia with the symbolic power to present themselves as the ideal Olympic hosts and the

---

[32] 'Sarajevo drugi put na mapi sveta', *Sport* 11.2.1984, 12.

[33] M. Pr., 'Olimpijada—izuzetan doprinos ugledu nesvrstane Jugoslavije', *Oslobodenje* 4.2.1983, 1.

[34] M. Borojević, 'Sedam dana programa (Pravi putokaz olimpizmu)', *Oslobodenje* 16.6.1983, 10.

[35] 'Olimpijska hronika: Jugoslavija idealan olimpijski domaćin', *Oslobodenje* 28.12.1983, 12.

[36] 'Zdravica miru i Olimpijadi', *Oslobodenje* 3.1.1984, 1.

[37] J.F., 'Olimpijske poruke mira', *Oslobodenje* 13.1.1984, 4.

[38] For instance in Faruk Midžić, 'Olimpijsko ruho zajedništva', *Oslobodenje* 4.2.1984, 8.

[39] Izudin Filipović 'U ime čovjeka', *Oslobodenje* 8.2.1984, 1.

champions of Olympism. Indeed, Yugoslavia, Sarajevo and their Olympics were presented as if they were synonymous with peace in the world. The same practice continued throughout the Games, with the newspaper taking the opportunity to explain to its readers how extraordinarily important Yugoslavia was to World Peace; for instance, on 10 February, when with reference to the international press, it claimed that by preventing any occurrence of boycott experienced at several previous Olympics, Yugoslavia managed to secure 'the spirit and charm of Olympism' and turn sport into 'the real winner' at the Sarajevo Olympics, making the Sarajevo Games into 'the Games of Peace'.[40] Finally, in the immediate days after the Olympics, the daily published articles written by journalists from other Yugoslav newspapers. On 22 February Čedomir Keco from the Novi Sad daily *Dnevnik* claimed that the Sarajevo Olympics added the sixth ring to the existing symbol of five Olympic rings representing the union of the five continents and the meeting of athletes from throughout the world at the Olympic Games. This was a ring inviting the whole of humanity to peace, understanding and cooperation.[41]

*Borba*, the Belgrade daily associated with the Federal Government, was equally explicit in drawing a parallel between the Sarajevo Olympics and Yugoslavia's international policies on the one side, and peace and Olympism on the other, claiming on 4 January 1984, like *Sport*, that the Sarajevo Olympics were 'the Olympics for peace'.[42] A couple of weeks later, a weekend edition of 21–22 January claimed that the Sarajevo Olympics were 'the Olympics for the whole world', which resonated with 'KUN's' comments on the Snowflake.[43] Another January issue had it that the Sarajevo Olympics would show by its own example that there was still the 'possibility for peaceful coexistence in the world', adding that the Sarajevo Olympics made an important contribution to world peace.[44] Several early February issues offered similar arguments. For instance, on 1 February the Sarajevo Olympics were described as 'the endowment for world peace',[45] while the following day's front-page article declared that the ideologies behind Olympism and non-alignment were in fact one and

[40] 'Sačuvan duh i šarm olimpizma', *Oslobođenje* 10.2.1984, 20.
[41] 'Za "Oslobođenje" pišu—Čedomir Keco ("Dnevnik", Novi Sad): Šest krug', *Oslobođenje* 22.2.1984, 11.
[42] 'Olimpijada za mir', *Borba* 4.1.1984, 10.
[43] 'ZOI za ceo svet', *Borba* 21–22.1.1984, 16.
[44] M. Blagojević, 'Olimpijada za primer', *Borba* 13.1.1984, 10.
[45] 'Odbrojavanje je počelo', *Borba* 1.2.1984, 1.

the same.[46] Thus, in its final pre-Olympic issues, *Borba* came full circle in relation to its writings six years earlier when, in its first report from Athens, it linked the ideology of Olympism, as expressed by Lord Killanin, to Yugoslavia's non-alignment policies. In the meantime, as we saw, the daily became rather bold in its writings on the topic, which carried through to its front-page article on the last day before the opening of the Olympics, titled, '*Neka bude mir!*', that is, 'Let There Be Peace!' In this, the daily's journalist proclaimed, 'Sarajevo is open', evoking once more the message of the Olympic symbol, the Snowflake, that the Bosnian capital city was open to all the people and nations of the world,[47] and also the claim by *Oslobođenje*'s cultural section that during the ancient Olympic Games the world was at peace.

Yet another Belgrade daily, with Yugoslavia's third highest readership at the time (*VGAJ* 1987, 225), *Politika*, also published a number of articles claiming the close relationship between the Sarajevo Olympics, Yugoslav foreign policies, peace and Olympism. Like the other mentioned newspapers, *Politika* repeated statements by members of the Yugoslav political elite. A couple of interesting examples can be found in its edition on the day of the Olympic opening ceremony and the one published the day after the closing ceremony. The former carried a page-long interview with the then Chairman of the Collective Presidency of Yugoslavia, high-ranking Croatian politician, Mika Špiljak, who told *Politika*'s journalist that the Sarajevo Winter Olympics were '"a festival of peace and friendship" among the world's nations'.[48] The latter brought a report from the press conference held by Branko Mikulić to mark the closing of the Olympics, in which he, as the President of both the Socialist Republic of Bosnia and Herzegovina and the Olympic Organising Committee, expressed his satisfaction with the Games' great success, emphasising that this success was 'not only in terms of sport'. Once again, as in early 1981, he referred to Lord Killanin, arguing that the Games were also a success because, by 'organising the Games between Moscow and Los Angeles, [we] contribute[d] to overcoming differences and relaxing tensions in the world'.[49] It is, however, interesting that, although Mikulić referred to Killanin, his statement closely resembled a remark by Killanin's successor,

[46] D.S., 'Butros Gali: Ideje nesvrstavanja', *Borba* 2.2.1984, 1.
[47] 'Sarajevo širom otvoreno' & 'Neka bude mir!', *Borba* 7.2.1984, 1.
[48] 'Igre počinju—srećno!', *Politika* 8.2.1984, 9.
[49] Vladimir Dedić, 'Na kraju—zadovoljstvo', *Politika* 20.2.1984, 12.

Juan Antonio Samaranch who, when visiting Bosnia and Herzegovina during the early autumn of 1983, claimed that Olympic Sarajevo was sending an 'important message' to the world: that 'the world can live in peace, understanding and friendship'.[50] Some four and a half months later Mikulić stressed that 'the messages sent from Sarajevo to the world during the Olympic event were messages of sport, peace and of friendship between the peoples of the world'.[51]

While Samaranch and Mikulić used the phrase 'sending messages' metaphorically, during the Olympic event *Oslobođenje* conducted a project in which they invited different statesmen and public personalities to send real Olympic messages of peace. The project was called '*Oslobođenje*'s Project: The Olympics of Peace' (Akcija Oslobođenja: Olimpijada mira), evoking in its name the project, 'The Olympic Smile' discussed in Chap. 3. Among those who sent such messages were Mika Špiljak, US President Ronald Reagan, and the Hungarian State Secretary and sports diplomat István Buda, who at the time also served as the President of the Hungarian National Physical Education and Sport Office. Stressing that Sarajevo could serve as an inspiration for the coming Summer Olympics in Los Angeles, Reagan argued that the Olympics 'show[ed] humanity at its best'.[52] Buda claimed that 'sport and peace are inseparable',[53] while Špiljak sent a message stating, among other things, that the Olympics served as a 'demonstration of peace and friendship' in the world.[54] While they all spoke of the Olympics in general, there is no doubt that the project itself was closely associated with the idea that the Sarajevo Olympics were somewhat special in this respect; and as discussed in the next section, the idea of 'the Olympics of peace' soon left an enormous impact on Sarajevo's image.

## 5.2   On the World Map for the Second Time

The idea of hosting the Olympic Games and developing tourism are, as already mentioned, inextricably interconnected. Among the main impacts the Olympics are assumed to have on their host cities are the short- and long-term economic effects of the flow of tourists into the city (Roche

---

[50] 'Velika poruka Sarajeva', *Oslobođenje*, 8.10.1983, 1.

[51] Vladimir Dedić, 'Na kraju—zadovoljstvo', *Politika* 20.2.1984, 12.

[52] 'Akcija "Oslobođenja": Olimpijada mira. Ronald Regan: Sarajevo kao inspiracija', *Oslobođenje* 19.2.1984, 14.

[53] 'Akcija "Oslobođenja": Olimpijada mira. Ištvan Buda: Sport i mir su nedjeljivi', *Oslobođenje* 19.2.1984, 14.

[54] 'Akcija "Oslobođenja": Olimpijade mira. Mika Špiljak: Praznik prijateljstva', *Oslobođenje* 8.2.1984, 1.

2000, 140). Sarajevo was exemplary in this respect. As we saw in Part One of this book, the idea of hosting the Winter Olympics in Sarajevo was linked to development of tourism and the inflow of, especially foreign, tourists into the city. Although it is difficult to estimate the direct *net* effect of the Olympics in the short-term, sources suggest that Sarajevo profited substantially from hosting them. In the ten-year period from 1977, when the city decided to place its Olympic bid, to 1986, the number of visitors and overnight stays rose much more in Sarajevo than in the country's two principal metropoles, Belgrade and Zagreb.[55] However, the difference, while present, was not as pronounced in comparison to Ljubljana and Skopje, Yugoslav republic capitals of a similar size and importance as Sarajevo. This perspective signals that it is difficult to estimate the short-term impact of the Olympics on Sarajevo in terms of the inflow of tourists. Further, as Kate Meehan Pedrotty (2010, 358) argues, the Olympics might have also boosted tourism to Yugoslavia in a general way. Other towns and cities—particularly in the already well-visited coastal areas—enjoyed increasing numbers of tourist arrivals, at least partly due to tourist promotion of Yugoslavia during the Sarajevo Olympics. Finally, the economic crisis and the rise of nationalist exclusivism that ultimately led to the dissolution of the country and the wars of Yugoslav succession, just a few years after the Sarajevo Olympics, further complicate measurement of the economic impact of tourism on the city.

In contrast to the uncertainty of estimates relating to the effects of the Olympics on tourism, the impact they had on the image of the city nationally and internationally already became clear during the Olympic period itself. This was probably most apparent in the image of the city that emerged in response to its position vis-à-vis the rising tensions between the two Cold War superpowers in the early 1980s. *Borba*, the mouthpiece of the Federal Government, provides an interesting example of how this crystallised in the country's newspapers. In its final, pre-Olympic Sunday edition, the daily's Sunday edition, *Nedeljna Borba*, published a special Olympic supplement. The first article in the supplement, 'We Welcome You, Olympics' presented the history of the Sarajevo Olympics from the conception of the idea by the OECD in 1967. Emphasis was placed on the shift from initial scepticism and doubt—including Boris Bakarač's famous remark, 'Ok, place your candidacy, if you insist on it so much, but pray to

---

[55] The number of overnight stays in Sarajevo more than doubled in the ten years from 1975 to 1984, rising 124%—almost three times as much as Zagreb, which rose 47%, while the number even declined by 12% in Belgrade (*VGAJ* 1987, 86).

God not to get it'—to overwhelming approval and self-congratulation. The newspaper also stressed that, due to its lack of winter sports traditions, even after the city won its candidacy the global sporting community was doubtful whether this 'Yugoslav adventure' was such a good idea. In the end, however, everything went more than well and the situation improved on a daily basis, with 'every visit to Sarajevo resulting in further affirmation of both the city and the whole country', as *Nedeljna Borba* put it, before concluding:

> We must not forget that Yugoslavia is the first socialist and non-aligned country in the world organising the Winter Olympic Games and, as such, making a special appearance in the history of the Olympic Games.
>
> Yugoslavia is gladdened that its Olympics have not been marked by the darkness of political disagreement that has characterised some of the latest Olympic gatherings and are threatening other Olympic events in the near or far future.
>
> We are pleased that all the world is coming to Sarajevo, that all are talking about feeling cordially welcomed and about nice venues [and] the good organisation [of the Games].
>
> We are proud to be hosts of a gathering that will, at least for these 12 days and at least to some extent, reconcile 'the irreconcilables'; that Sarajevo will be an assemblage of youthfulness, joyfulness, celebration, [and] in fact an important treasury of peace in this, otherwise, troubled world.
>
> We welcome you, Olympics![56]

Implicitly referring to the Olympic boycotts at the Moscow and Los Angeles Games, and contrasting them with the Sarajevo Games ('that the whole world is coming to'), *Borba* emphasised Sarajevo as an exception and thus nothing less but 'a treasury of peace in the troubled world'. In the same vein, during the Olympic event the daily claimed repeatedly that Sarajevo was a city of peace and friendship, often using the trope of 'oasis', which implied that Sarajevo was a rare haven of peace in the troubled times of the 'Second' Cold War. An example of this can be found in the daily column, 'Postcard from Sarajevo', which covered the international press and news agencies' reportage from Sarajevo. On 17 February, the daily claimed that almost all international reporting from the Olympics contained the sentence 'Sarajevo—an oasis of peace, friendship and

---

[56] 'Dobro nam došla Olimpijado', *Nedeljna Borba* (Specijalni dodatak povodom 14. Zimskih Olimpijskih Igara), 4–5.2.1984, 1.

understanding'. Moreover, it also observed that journalists from all over the world did not only cover sporting results and competitions, but frequently wrote about Yugoslavia's domestic and international policies. It was through the latter reports, *Borba* claimed, that Sarajevo emerged as an 'oasis of [international] friendship' in the troubled times of the early 1980s.[57] Similarly, just a few days later, two days after the closing of the Olympics, the daily published an editorial, 'The Oasis of Peace', in which the author insisted that in this period of increased international tensions, Sarajevo showed itself as an oasis of peace (Image 5.2).[58]

This trope of 'oasis', implying that Sarajevo was an exception in the intensified ideological exclusiveness of the early 1980s' Cold War world, was not something only used by journalists. It was also on the lips of 'ordinary people', who did not hesitate to use the term when talking about the Olympics and Sarajevo. For example, shortly before the opening of the Olympics, one visitor to Sarajevo from neighbouring Montenegro drew a parallel between the Sarajevo Olympics and the Olympic Games in Ancient Greece and stressed that Sarajevo was an 'oasis of sport and friendship' in the early 1980s' world,[59] once again implying that there was always peace or at least a truce during the ancient Olympic Games. This reference to Ancient Greece was commonplace in Yugoslav media during the Olympic period, as exemplified by *Oslobođenje*'s discussed analysis of the Olympic Snowflake. Woven into this reference was the implication that there was a strong linkage between the ancient Olympics and those in Sarajevo, crystallising in the absence of war. On 6 April 1983 an *Oslobođenje* article further linked Athens and Sarajevo, stating that they were the only two cities in the Balkans that had hosted the Olympics.[60] The author then made the element of peace explicit by noting that, in ancient Athens, the Olympics meant that war stopped at least for the duration of the Games. What is even more interesting is that the author argued that Athens represented the Olympic past, and Sarajevo the Olympic future, invoking the widespread idea that Sarajevo and Yugoslavia were providing the salvation of the Olympic Movement. It is also noteworthy that the author chose to

[57] 'Sarajevska razglednica. Oaza prijateljstva', *Borba* 17.2.1984, 9.

[58] Zoran Mandžuka, 'Oaza mira', *Borba* 21.2.1984, 2.

[59] El. Ka. & B.J., 'Otvorena vrata Olimpijadi', *Oslobođenje* 23.10.1983, 13.

[60] 6 April was a day celebrated in Sarajevo as liberation day, referring to 6 April 1945 when the city was liberated during the Second World War. The article linked 6/4/1945 to 6/4/1978 in Athens.

**Image 5.2** An excerpt from a *Borba* article by Zoran Mandžuka, reading 'in the period of increased international tensions with apparent preferences to suspicion over understanding and the predominance of competing and ideological and other exclusiveness over cooperation and the acceptance of differences, Sarajevo—as everybody unanimously concludes these days—has been an oasis of peace'. (Zoran Mandžuka, 'Oaza mira', *Borba* 21.2.1984, 2)

name the article 'From Myth to Sarajevo'.[61] Phrased this way, Sarajevo appeared the ultimate Olympic host city, even surpassing (modern) Athens.

Athens was far from the only Olympic city that *Oslobođenje* and other Yugoslav newspapers linked to Sarajevo. The host city for the upcoming 1984 Summer Olympics, Los Angeles, was another. Most notably, the day before the official opening of the Sarajevo Games, the mayors of the two 1984 Olympic host cities, Tom Bradley and Uglješa Uzelac, sent a joint message to the Secretary-General of the United Nations, Javier Pérez de Cuéllar in which they claimed that the Olympic Games in Ancient Greece meant a truce between warring parties. 'In keeping this spirit alive' and on behalf of their citizens, the two mayors invited statesmen from around the world to suspend all war campaigns, before asking the Secretary-General and the world to proclaim global peace during the two 1984 Olympic events.[62]

---

[61] B. Radosavljević, 'Od mita do Sarajeva', *Oslobođenje* 6.4.1983, 13.
[62] 'Poruke olimpijskih gradova Sarajeva i Los Anđelesa: Igre mira', *Oslobođenje* 7.2.1984, 13.

Sarajevo was also linked with previous Olympic host cities, such as Austrian Innsbruck, one of the very few cities that had hosted the Olympics twice. For instance, early in the Olympic preparation period, *Oslobođenje* emphasised that Sarajevo should learn from Innsbruck's experience and the Olympic Organising Committee for the Sarajevo Olympics cooperated closely with Innsbruck, not least in relation to building the Olympic venues.[63] In addition, the Mayor of Innsbruck, Alois Lugger, visited Sarajevo in August 1981 and talked to the Committee and Sarajevo's mayor at the time, Ante Sučić and, according to *Oslobođenje*, was very positive about Sarajevo as an Olympic host and expressed strong interest in cooperation between the two cities.[64] Two and a half years later and just a week before the opening of the Olympics, *Oslobođenje* published a page-long article, which again stressed the close relationship between Sarajevo and Innsbruck. This was shortly after criticism by Austrian newspapers and officials of Sarajevo's Olympic venues and the cultural practices of some of the city's population. As already noted, in mid-January 1984, for instance, the Austrian *Kurier* had criticised the haggling in Sarajevo's old quarter *Baščaršija*,[65] while other papers had expressed concern about whether the venues would be ready and whether Sarajevo and Yugoslavia had the capacity to host the Winter Olympics. *Oslobođenje* addressed these issues in the article, which included a lengthy interview with Alois Lugger. The interviewer asked Lugger for his view on the concern expressed by several highly positioned Austrian politicians about Sarajevo's ability to host the Winter Olympics. Lugger, who had served as Mayor of Innsbruck when the city hosted the Winter Olympics in 1964 and 1976, explained that some prominent Austrian politicians had also opposed Innsbruck's Olympic nomination, thereby openly siding with Sarajevo and emphasising that he had always been in favour of Sarajevo's hosting the Games, even before the Bosnian capital won its Olympic bid.[66] Together, the interview and the article left an impression of strong friendship between the two cities and equally strong opposition to those forces that were against both cities' Olympic nominations. Hence, this was not a question

[63] B. Radosavljević, 'Dragocijena iskustva Insbruka', *Oslobođenje* 18.12.1980, 12.

[64] 'Pohvale olimpijskom Sarajevu', *Oslobođenje* 13.8.1981, 10.

[65] Melita Karalić, 'Drugi o Olimpijadi. Duga između svijetova i vjekova', *Oslobođenje* 14.1.1984, 5.

[66] Ekrem Avdić, 'Intervju 'Nedelje': S Olimpijadom u 21. vijek', *Oslobođenje—'Nedelja'*, 28.1.1984, 6.

of Austria versus Yugoslavia, but Olympic Innsbruck and Olympic Sarajevo versus the anti-Olympic forces in both countries.

As we have already seen, reference to international cooperation and friendship was quite common in the Yugoslav press during the Olympic period. One interesting example appeared in an *Oslobođenje* report from its New York correspondent, Kemal Kurspahić, widely regarded as one of the daily's most renowned journalists of all time. A couple of days before the opening of the Sarajevo Olympics, Kurspahić reported on the US coverage of Sarajevo's final pre-Olympic days. Referring to an article published in the *New York Times*, Kurspahić told his readers that the paper's famous sports columnist, Dave Anderson, linked the extraordinarily warm weather in Sarajevo a few days before the start of the Olympics to 'the warmth' of the hosts preparing the city for the Games. According to Kurspahić, Anderson also reminded his readers of 'the trauma' that the Olympic Movement had been undergoing since the killing of eleven members of the Israeli Olympic team at the 1972 Munich Olympics. The Olympic Movement's crisis was further protracted by the Cold War-related tensions about the Soviet invasion of Afghanistan in Lake Placid and the Moscow boycott in 1980. Against this background, according to Kurspahić, Dave Anderson concluded his column by saying how in this situation, 'in Sarajevo, in Tito's Yugoslavia, everybody [felt] welcome'.[67]

On the basis of content in the *New York Times* and several other US newspapers, Kurspahić argued that 'these days, the name Sarajevo is as close to the Americans as names of their American cities: All eyes are these days turned towards *the Olympic stage of friendship*' (emphasis added).[68] 'Even the TV weather forecasts start these days with the forecast for Sarajevo and its surroundings', wrote Kurspahić, before adding that also 'the renowned daily, the *Christian Science Monitor*' had a 'three-page-long article on Sarajevo'. According to the daily's Ross Atkin, continued Kurspahić, due to its cultural diversity and geographical position 'at the crossroads between Paris and Istanbul and Berlin and Athens', Sarajevo had long 'deserved to be an Olympic [host] city'.[69]

[67] Kemal Kurspahić, 'Pogled preko Atlantika. Sarajevsko olimpijsko ruho', *Oslobođenje* 6.2.1984, 2.

[68] Ibid.

[69] Ibid.

Kurspahić's report is interesting on several levels. First, it quite explicitly presents 'Tito's' Yugoslavia and Sarajevo as saviours of the Olympic Movement. We saw in the previous section that, according to Yugoslav officials and the country's media coverage, the Sarajevo Olympics were assisting the crisis-stricken Olympic Movement to recover. For this reason, more than once, *Sport* claimed that Sarajevo was no less than a 'jewel of Olympism'.[70] Another interesting aspect of Kurspahić's report concerns the author's characterisation of the city as an 'Olympic stage'. It has already been suggested in the previous chapters that the Olympic Games are events that can be seen as 'performances' and 'exhibitions' staged in front of a global audience. Yet it is not the audience that is most important in Kurspahić's report, but the stage itself, or as Kurspahić himself put it, the 'Olympic stage of *friendship*', thus transforming Sarajevo into a symbol of friendship and an important 'treasury of peace' in a world filled with Cold War antagonisms.

Furthermore, in Kurspahić's report Sarajevo implicitly appeared as a natural Olympic host, or a host city that should have been awarded the Olympics long before it actually happened. It is noteworthy, in the context of the Olympic Games event, that Sarajevo did not earn this tribute due to its being a winter sports centre. In fact, winter sports were not even mentioned in the report. Rather, Sarajevo's position as Olympic host city was linked to both its own cultural diversity and its geo-historical position as a place where the 'cultures of east and west encountered each other'.[71] Thus, it was due to a focus on politics and culture and not sports that Sarajevo now emerged as an obvious and natural Olympic host city. Finally, Kurspahić's report was also very interesting for what can be seen as its central theme: the Olympics meant that the world now was becoming more interested in Sarajevo. People in the USA had learned about the city. The Olympic host city, and even its weather forecasts, was all over the US media, from newspapers to TV, implying that the city had now gained its place on the world map in the sense that we saw in the chapter 'Putting Sarajevo on the World Tourist Map' discussing this topic.

Gaining global attention had certain cultural connotations specific for Sarajevo, most notably relating to the assassination of the Austrian

---

[70] 'Sarajevo—Dragulj olimpizma', *Sport*, 25.2.1984, 1; Miša Vasiljević, 'Sarajevo '84 i svet. Dragulj olimpizma', *Sport*, 25.2.1984, 7.

[71] Kemal Kurspahić, 'Pogled preko Atlantika. Sarajevsko olimpijsko ruho', *Oslobođenje* 6.2.1984, 2.

Archduke Franz Ferdinand seventy years earlier. In fact, this was the event for which the city was most well-known globally prior to the Olympics. Not surprisingly, during the Olympics many newspapers—Yugoslav and international alike—drew their readers' attention to this anniversary, with the Yugoslav newspapers, once again, often substantiating their stories with references to the international press. One such example was *Nedeljna Borba*'s aforementioned special Olympic supplement published just a few days before the opening of the Olympics. One of the supplement's articles, discussing international press reports of Sarajevo, quoted reportage by Swedish daily *Norrköpings Tidninger* in which it was explained that 'the older generations used to associate Sarajevo with the beginning of the First World War'. However, as the title for the *Nedeljna Borba* article—borrowed from the Swedish paper—had it, the Olympics meant that Sarajevo had now '[s]ecured a place in the history of world sports' instead.[72]

Similarly, a few days later, after the beginning of the Games, *Sport* provided a digest of international reporting on the opening ceremony, including the view in the Belgian newspaper, *Le Soir*, that the Games were an opportunity for Sarajevo to inscribe itself anew in world history, 'seventy years after the assassination on Franz Ferdinand occurred here in the city'. According to *Sport*, *Le Soir* also emphasised that in the troubled world of the early 1980s, Olympic Sarajevo showed a stoicism that accorded with the peacefulness of the Olympic spirit.[73] Although *Sport*'s reportage covered a number of countries and newspapers, it was the Belgian observation that influenced the daily's choice of title, 'Sarajevo, for the second time on the world map'.[74]

Stressing that Sarajevo was on the world map for the second time in the twentieth century implied that the Olympics did not only influence the city by providing it with a new global image. The difference in quality between these two events and the obvious breach between them, which drew global attention to the city, were equally important. The aforementioned *World about Sarajevo*, published shortly after the Olympics by the Sarajevo Olympics Organising Committee, provided an interesting example of this, one borrowed from *The Financial Times* of 23 April 1983. The London-based newspaper argued that Sarajevo long deserved 'to be something more', before raising the story of the 1914 assassination: 'When

[72] 'Upis u istoriju svetskog sporta', *Nedeljna Borba* (Specijalni dodatak povodom 14. Zimskih Olimpijskih Igara), 4–5.2.1984, 6.

[73] 'Sarajevo drugi put na mapi sveta', *Sport* 11.2.1984, 12.

[74] Ibid.

young Gavrilo Princip stopped at that street corner in Sarajevo and fired the fatal shots at Archduke Franz Ferdinand, he once and forever brought himself and the city into world history, and the rest of us into the destruction of the First World War'. The author then reckoned, 'Sarajevo, today, is ready to get into history in a more pleasant way, as the city, during recent months, has been preparing to host the Winter Olympics'.[75]

According to the Sarajevan press, this was also what the city was aiming at, to eradicate 'the malicious' depictions of the city as the place where the First World War started.[76] Accentuating that, in the two years prior to the Olympics, more than 3000 international journalists had visited Sarajevo and thousands and thousands of articles and reports had been written about the city and the 14th Winter Olympics in international newspapers, the Sunday edition of *Oslobođenje*, some three weeks before the opening of the Games, opened its reportage on the international coverage of the Olympics with following words:

> Sarajevo experienced similar global publicity as it is experiencing today when, 70 years ago, Gavrilo Princip's assassination of the prospective successor to the Austrian throne, Franz Ferdinand, was used as an excuse for the First World War. Back then, Sarajevo emerged at the epicentre of the world news. Today, Sarajevo is again at the heart of world media interest, but not any longer as 'the city of the most (in)famous assassination in modern history'.[77]

The newspaper's Melita Karalić went on to list and comment on different examples from the world coverage of the city in those final preparation days, stressing once again that 'it was hardly possible to find a better Olympic host' than Sarajevo, before concluding with a reference to yet another of the international reports:

> One victory has already been secured for all the competitors—a peaceful competition in a city whose ambition for peace has now entered history.[78]

---

[75] Here from Knećević-Čečez et al. (1984, 63).

[76] M. Arapović, 'Postolimpijske misli i... Zov biznisa', *Naši dani* 805, 24.2.1984, 10.

[77] Melita Karalić, 'Drugi o Olimpijadi. Duga između svijetova i vjekova', *Oslobođenje* 14.1.1984, 5.

[78] Ibid.

The contrast between the city associated with the destruction of the First World War and the city 'with ambition for' world peace in the 1980s could hardly be stronger. Sarajevo was no longer a city 'maliciously' associated with the beginning of the First World War but a proof in the troubled post-*Détente* times that the world still 'can live in peace, understanding and friendship', as one source put it, referring to the acting President of the IOC, Juan Antonio Samaranch.[79]

Some of the international reporters put it even more explicitly. For instance, Stewart Powell from the *US News & World Report*, claimed: 'The Winter Olympics' Real Winner Is Sarajevo'. In his report, that carried the same title, Powell named the economic advantages related to the inflow of tourists into the city and the creation of new jobs in the tourism sector as some of the major gains for the city, but he also argued that there was an important benefit beyond the economic one: 'Until now, Sarajevo, a provincial capital of nearly 500,000, has been known mainly as the spot where the 1914 assassination of Austrian Archduke Franz Ferdinand triggered World War I' (Powell 1984, 35). Implied in this statement is the notion that the Olympics changed Sarajevo's global image from the city known for its 1914 assassination to an Olympic city, and that was Sarajevo's principal Olympic victory.

This was also a claim made by the Sarajevan youth periodical, *Naši dani*, whose Miroslav Arapović argued, in the periodical's first post-Olympic issue of 24 February 1984, that the Olympics were a great success because they freed the city from the longstanding and often malicious determinant. 'From now on', continued Arapović, 'people will talk about Sarajevo as the city that organised the best Olympic Games in the history of the event'. Moreover—the periodical's journalist argued—Sarajevo would now be remembered for the Games that brought the host nation, Yugoslavia, its very first Winter Olympic medal. For these reasons, Sarajevo will no longer be only associated with Franz Ferdinand, concluded Arapović.[80]

We see here how the cultural connotations that the Olympics generated were mixed up with the political and sporting outcomes, and, in Powell's view, also the economic results. This is also why the cultural dimension of the Sarajevo Olympics should be addressed in historical analyses of the event. Finally, the same applies to the infrastructural change that the city

---

[79] Branko Tomić, 'Dobro došao svijete', *Oslobođenje* 3.1.1984, 8.

[80] M. Arapović, 'Postolimpijske misli i … zov biznisa', *Naši dani* 805, 24.2.1984, 10.

experienced in relation to the preparations to host the Games. In this respect, the American magazine *Ski* provided an interesting example. In its Olympic portrait of Sarajevo, the magazine had it:

> Sarajevo, a city of nearly half a million inhabitants, is the capital of Bosnia and Herzegovina, one of the six socialist republics that make up modern-day Yugoslavia. An exotic city, Sarajevo was for five centuries the largest, richest and most beautiful city of the Turkish-ruled Balkans. After 40 years of occupation by the Austro-Hungarian empire, the city came dramatically to the attention of the world when visiting Archduke Francis [sic] Ferdinand, heir-apparent to the Austrian throne, was assassinated by a young Bosnian revolutionary, triggering World War I. Sarajevo today is the political, economic, scientific, cultural and sports center of the republic, with museums, galleries, theatres, a university—and an Olympic complex that few could have envisioned five years ago. ('Sarajevo: An Olympic Portrait', *Ski* February 1984, 42–43)

Once again we see that Sarajevo was no longer only associated with the 1914 assassination and the First World War, but also with 'an Olympic complex that few could have envisioned five years ago'. The initial scepticism and doubts concerning the capability of the city to organise such a major global event were now completely gone. Likewise, the historic city of the assassination of Franz Ferdinand and the beginning of the First World War was not the same as contemporary Sarajevo. It is also from this perspective that we should see the opening of the Sarajevo Olympic Museum on the very day of the opening of the Games on 8 February 1984. As *Duga* phrased it in its Olympic issue, Sarajevo was an exception in terms of the Olympic Museum being open before the Games were even finished.[81] Rushing to open the museum, Sarajevo was not only symbolically stating that it now became an Olympic city but also that it was no longer to be associated with the assassination of the Austrian Archduke Franz Ferdinand and the beginning of the First World War.

---

[81] Milomir Marić, 'Sve o zimskoj olimpijadi: Pred početak Olimpijade. Sneško Belić u bosanskom loncu', *Duga 259*, 28.1.1984, 23.

# BIBLIOGRAPHY

BOOKS, ARTICLES, REPORTS, BLOGS AND WEBSITES

Abrams, Roger I. 2013. *Playing Tough: The World of Sports and Politics.* Boston, MA: Northeastern University Press.

Bottici, Chiara. 2007. *A Philosophy of Political Myth.* Cambridge: Cambridge University Press.

Flood, Christopher G. 2002. *Political Myth: A Theoretical Introduction.* New York and London: Routledge.

Houlihan, Barrie. 1994. *Sport and International Politics.* Hemel Hempstead: Harvester Wheatsheaf.

Knežević-Čečez, Gordana, Ljiljana Smajlović, and Mirsad Zorabdić. 1984. *Svijet o Sarajevu. Svjetska štampa, televizija i radio o XIV Zimskim Olimpijskim igrama.* Sarajevo: Organizacioni komitet XIV Zimskih Olimpijskih igara Jugoslavija.

Kolstø, Pål. 2003. Procjena uloge historijskih mitova u modernism društvima. In *Historijski mitovi na Balkanu,* ed. Husnija Kamberović, 11–37. Sarajevo: Institut za istoriju.

Nora, Pierre. 1996. General Introduction: Between Memory and History. In *Realms of Memory: The Construction of the French Past,* ed. Pierre Nora. New York: Columbia University Press.

Pedrotty, Kate Meehan. 2010. Yugoslav Unity and Olympic Ideology at the 1984 Sarajevo Winter Olympic Games. In *Yugoslavia's Sunny Side: A History of Tourism in Socialism (1950s–1980s),* ed. Hannes Grandits and Karin Taylor, 333–363. Budapest and New York: CEU Press.

Powell, Stewart. 1984. Winter Olympics' Real Winner Is Sarajevo. *US News & World Report,* February 13, 1984, 35.

Roche, Maurice. 2000. *Mega-events and Modernity: Olympics, Expos and the Growth of Global Culture.* London: Routledge.

Sarajevo: An Olympic Portrait. *Ski,* February 1984, 42–43.

Sarantakes, Nicholas Evan. 2010. *Dropping the Torch. Jimmy Carter, the Olympic Boycott, and the Cold War.* Cambridge: Cambridge University Press.

Schöpflin, George. 1997. The Functions of Myth and a Taxonomy of Myths. In *Myths and Nationhood,* ed. Geoffrey Hosking and George Schöpflin, 19–35. London: Hurst & Company.

Short, John R. 2012. Globalization, Cities, and the Summer Olympics. In *The Making of Olympic Cities: Critical Concepts in Urban Studies, Volume I: Contexts and Overviews,* ed. John R. Gold and Margaret M. Gold, 235–262. London and New York: Routledge.

Trültzsch, Arno. 2017. *An Almost Forgotten Legacy: Non-Aligned Yugoslavia in the United Nations and in the Making of Contemporary International Law*. Sylff Association, November 16, 2017. Accessed October 31, 2020. https://www.sylff.org/news_voices/23943/.

TSOOC: The Sarajevo Organizing Committee of the XIV Olympic Winter Games Yugoslavia. 1984a. *Sarajevo '84: Tout sur les Jeux / All on the Games / Alles über die Spiele / Sve o igrama*. Sarajevo: Svjetlost.

———. 1984b. *Sarajevo '84. Yugoslavia 8-19.02*. Final Report Published by the Organizing Committee of the XIV Winter Olympic Games 1984 in Sarajevo. Sarajevo: Oslobođenje.

*VGAJ ( Veliki geografski atlas Jugoslavije)*. 1987. Ed. Ivan Bertić. Zagreb: Liber.

Vuic, Jason. 2015. *The Sarajevo Olympics: A History of the 1984 Winter Olympic Games*. Amherst and Boston: University of Massachusetts Press.

# CHAPTER 6

# Framing Olympic Sarajevo as a Truly Yugoslav City

While the situation in the period of the so-called Second Cold War worked well for non-aligned Yugoslavia, things at home were not going smoothly, particularly in terms of the relationship between Yugoslavia's state organisation and the economic deterioration that the country experienced throughout most of the 1980s. As we have seen previously (see Chap. 4), the Yugoslav state was organised in accordance with the theory of workers' self-management, which resulted in overwhelming institutional proliferation, with more or less all institutions having federal, republican and local levels. This also applied to the Party, which was federalised through a process of decentralisation in which the regional branches of the Party became practically independent of each other, serving almost exclusively the interests of their respective republics or autonomous provinces. According to some scholars of Yugoslav history, this development proved to be particularly dangerous when coupled with the economic crisis that hit Yugoslavia at approximately the same time as Sarajevo won its bid for the Olympics. In this situation, the deepening sense of dissatisfaction with the economic performance of the country was increasingly catalysed through the federalised state-system into inter-republic antagonisms; and from there also

Z. Jovanovic, *A Cultural History of the 1984 Winter Olympics,
Modernity, Memory and Identity in South-East Europe*,
https://doi.org/10.1007/978-3-030-76598-9_6

into rising ethnonationalism across Yugoslavia, leading eventually to the dissolution of the country in the early 1990s.[1]

State organisation run on the principle of workers' self-management combined with the economic crisis of the 1980s provide plausible explanations for the origin and causality of the concomitant rise of ethnonationalism in Yugoslavia—and ultimately the dissolution of the country. Yet a more exhaustive understanding of the agency behind Yugoslavia's dissolution calls for the specific identification of the central agents involved. In his study of the notions of ethnicity and identity, Rogers Brubaker (2004, 14–16) argues that we should not treat ethnic groups as the protagonists of the ethnic conflict. The main protagonists of most ethnic conflicts are different ethnic organisations and ethnonational movements. Accordingly, ethnonational elites never represent whole nations, despite their common claims to this effect. In fact, no matter how hard and how well they argue that they reflect the interests of 'their' ethnic groups or nations, conceived of as allegedly enclosed ethnonational wholes, at best they represent their parties or certain branches of ethnonational movements. Similar arguments were presented by those dealing more directly with the political history of Yugoslavia, exemplified in the work of Rudi Klanjšek and Sergej Flere. Based on their examination of Slovenia's secession from Yugoslavia, Klanjšek and Flere (2011, 799) have argued that Yugoslavia's dissolution was not driven by popular 'longing' for mono-national states, but was

[1] This argument was central in the 1990s in among others works of Branka Magaš, *The Destruction of Yugoslavia. Tracking the Break-up 1980–92* (London-New York: Verso, 1993), Susan Woodward, *Balkan Tragedy. Chaos and Dissolution after the Cold War* (Washington, DC, 1995) or John R. Lampe, *Yugoslavia as History. Twice there was a country* (Cambridge: Cambridge University Press, 1996), as well as more recently in Patrick Hyder Patterson's analysis focusing on the rise of consumer culture and the Yugoslav consumerist dream as the central integrative factor in Yugoslav society (Patrick Hyder Patterson, *Bought and Sold: Living and Losing the Good Life in Socialist Yugoslavia* (Ithaca and London: Cornell University Press, 2011)). Meanwhile, Jake Lowinger has explicated in his work how the austerity measures and the economic reforms sponsored by the IMF were linked to the popular upheaval and the rise of ethnonationalism in Yugoslavia (Jake Lowinger, *Economic Reform and the "double movement" in Yugoslavia: An analysis of Labor unrest and ethno-nationalism in the 1980s* (Charleston South Carolina, EEUU, ProQuest, UMI Dissertation Publishing, 2011)). The argument on the linkage between the economic crisis, mass unemployment and austerity measures to the rise of ethnonationalism in the mid- and late 1980s is also central in several of the articles in *Social Inequalities and Discontent in Yugoslav Socialism* (eds. Rory Archer, Igor Duda & Paul Stubbs (Abingdon-New York: Routledge, 2016)), as well as in hopefully soon to be translated from Croatian to English, Sven Cvek, Jasna Račić i Snježana Ivčić, *Borovo u štrajku: rad u tranziciji 1987–1991.* (BRID, Zagreb 2019).

more of a result of the 'political entrepreneurship' of the minority political and cultural elites in the country.

Having said that, it is nevertheless important to keep in mind that there is often a difference between political elites and the different segments of populations, and research in the fields of everyday life history and the history of popular cultures suggests that Yugoslavia provides an excellent example of this. Studies of Yugoslav film, popular music and consumer practices show important discrepancies between elite and popular cultures in Yugoslavia in the 1980s. Thus, the now discredited policy of brotherhood and unity of the different peoples of Yugoslavia, argues Vida T. Johnson (2009), in fact did take root within the country's film world. Likewise, in his seminal book on Yugoslav and post-Yugoslav rock music culture, the Croatian journalist and cultural critic, Ante Perković (2011, 21), has argued that its development away from cultural elites and the political establishment made the country's rock music culture much less ethnonationally oriented than elite cultures in Yugoslavia. Thus, members of Yugoslav rock music culture developed a stronger supranational, extra-territorial sense of pan-Yugoslav belonging than was the case with the country's cultural and political elites, which to a larger extend remained grouped around ethnoregional Academies of Culture and Sciences (in particular in the field of literature).

For this reason, we should be wary of uncritically generalising about inter-ethnic relations in Yugoslavia from the examples and agencies of minority political elites. When dealing with this issue, we should avoid focusing narrowly on Communist Party debates, and disagreements between the leaders of the constituent republics. Moreover, as Dejan Jović (2001, 107–108) has shown in his work on the topic, the situation in Yugoslavia while Sarajevo was preparing for and hosting the Olympics was much more complex than the nationalism narrative insists. According to Jović, the 1970s and 1980s in Yugoslavia should be approached as a period in which the country witnessed a struggle between the forces of integration and fragmentation. Ethnonationalism was on the rise, polarising, fragmenting and pulverising the Yugoslav political community; yet, at the same time, throughout the 1970s and 1980s strong social forces favouring integration also emerged in Yugoslav society. In this regard, as we will see in more detail in this chapter, Jović spoke of the re-emergence of a pan-Yugoslav culture and an incipient 'Yugoslav political nation', both appearing as a reaction to the fragmentation of Yugoslav political and cultural space.

This is also why it is highly problematic to assert that Yugoslavia and its different peoples were only kept together by the force and manipulation applied by the Communist Party and Tito. In relation to the Sarajevo Olympics, it is equally questionable to argue that the happiness and festivity in Sarajevo were possible because the ethnic peace in Yugoslavia at that time was enforced by the iron hand of Tito's regime.[2] Quite contrary to these commonsensical assertions, historian Vjekoslav Perica (2002, 94 et seq.) has shown in his work that it was the patriotic commitment to, and faith in, 'brotherhood and unity' and 'the Yugoslav spirit' among the Yugoslav peoples that made the loose multi-ethnic Yugoslav federation possible. This patriotic commitment was conceived as a counterweight to the ethnic nationalisms that tore the country apart during the Second World War and, according to Perica, was espoused by a large number of citizens in Socialist Yugoslavia, although there were, of course, certain differences between individual regions of the country. Yet, as Klanjšek and Flere (2011, 799) point out, before the final years of the 1980s all Yugoslav ethnic groups and the large majority in all the republics and provinces of the Yugoslav federation exclusively visualised the preservation and progress of their individual republics and provinces as taking place through the preservation and progress of Yugoslavia as a whole.[3] In addition, as Flere (2007, 681–703; 2005, 232) has argued elsewhere, some regions developed an even greater 'love for Yugoslavia', particularly Bosnia and Herzegovina, the northern Serbian autonomous province of Vojvodina and the peninsula of Istria in Croatia. These were multi-ethnic regions which, according to Flere, saw Yugoslavia as a guarantor of their continued existence. Conversely, these regions were often referred to as 'Yugoslavia on a smaller scale' and seen as regions where Yugoslavia was not only an imagined, but also an experienced community, in which the ideological axiom of 'brotherhood and unity' was an important component of everyday life and practice.

Seen from this perspective, and as the capital city of Bosnia and Herzegovina, it is not surprising that Sarajevo was frequently viewed as

[2] Without giving it too much weight, this is the precise phrasing used by Stephan E. Sachs in *Sarajevo: A Crossroads in History*, 1994.

[3] See 'Table 1. Mean level analysis–agreement with the statement "The preservation and progress of all republics depends on the preservation and progress of Yugoslavia as whole"' (Rudi Klanjšek & Sergej Flere, 'Exit Yugoslavia: longing for mononational states or entrepreneurial manipulation?' *Nationalities Papers: The Journal of Nationalism and Ethnicity* Vol. 39: 5, 2011, 799).

one of the most pro-Yugoslav cities in the country. In addition, during the 1970s the city also emerged as the most Yugoslav capital city in terms of the proportion of inhabitants choosing to declare the non-national category 'Yugoslav' in place of ethnic identity in response to the question on nationality at the population census in 1981 (Lampe 1996, 330). Consequently, like no other city in Yugoslavia, Sarajevo was commonly associated with the paradigm of 'unity in diversity', one in which citizens of different ethnic and religious affiliation and background lived in unity, learning to enjoy and take pride in their diversity rather than fear it, as film scholar Pavle Levi (2007, 2) has expressed it. Readings of the city's popular culture also support this argument, indicating a strong critique and rejection of the politics of nationalism, and pronounced pro-Yugoslav stances. According to Dalibor Mišina (2010, 266–267), Sarajevo's musicians were among the first to respond to the climate of increasing *de-Yugoslavisation* and the ethnicisation of the Yugoslav socio-cultural space. The pro-Yugoslav stances and pronounced anti-nationalist agenda would also remain one of the main characteristics of the city's immediate popular-cultural space until the dissolution of the country; or, as Perković (2011, 99) has phrased it, 'as a kind of a black box serving the purpose of preserving all parts of the story, Sarajevo literarily remained in Yugoslavia until the last moment'.

In the light of the foregoing, this chapter looks more closely at the connection between the Olympics and Sarajevo's pronounced Yugoslav character. This Yugoslavness of the city is a rather complex phenomenon and can by no means be reduced to the city's role as the host city for the 1984 Winter Olympic Games. Nonetheless, as a number of sources used in the chapter show, Yugoslavness did have a quite central part in the dominant official discourse of the Sarajevo Olympics. Hence, the chapter seeks to answer the questions how the 1984 winter Olympics influenced Sarajevo's self-representation as a truly Yugoslav city and what were the immediate effects of that. In so doing, the first section of the chapter examines the process of re-identifying Yugoslav unity, occurring in relation to the Olympics. This is then followed, in the chapter's second section, by an analysis of the ways Yugoslavia was performed at the Olympics and also in their aftermath, in particular in the city's youth culture.

## 6.1    Re-identifying Yugoslav Unity
## at the Sarajevo Olympics

Although at times showing strong authoritarian tendencies, the Yugoslav communist regime nevertheless always depended on popular support. The Communist Party of Yugoslavia (CPY) came to power through its position as the leader of the so-called National War of Liberation (Narodnooslobodilačka borba, shortened to NOB). Through the NOB, the communists achieved substantial popular legitimacy, and therefore enjoyed more of a mandate to implement radical social change, in the immediate post-war years, than their counterparts elsewhere in Eastern and Central Europe. In practice, this meant that the country's new communist leaders were free to concentrate on copying the policies of Moscow, policies that would, according to the Party's ideological presuppositions, eventually lead Yugoslavia into communism. While the so-called Stalinist period of the immediate post-war years, from 1945 to 1948, was generally considered the most authoritarian period of the Yugoslav socialist state, we need to remember that, even at this time, the CPY leaders were not just ideologues committed to a Marxist-Leninist vision of the future but also very practical power politicians.

As Carol S. Lilly (2001) shows in her work on the topic, in the first stage of Yugoslavia's post-war development, from the liberation of Belgrade in October 1944 up to the November 1945 elections, the CPY concentrated primarily on achieving power. In this period it adopted a 'people's democratic' vocabulary, assuring Yugoslav citizens that it was willing to cooperate with 'all progressive forces' in the country. Only after attaining power in the 1945 elections, did the CPY begin to focus on introducing the foundations of socialism through its persuasive policies. With this shift, the CPY's rhetoric became more rigid, and state-society relations increasingly one-sided, effectively terminating debate. By late 1947 the CPY's control was firmly established, allowing the more complex tasks of ideological re-education and indoctrination to begin. As a result, during early 1948 the party leaders began to pay more attention to the issue of ideology, yet again to be interrupted and delayed by the Soviet-Yugoslav split in June 1948 (Lilly 2001, 3).

As Carol Lilly (2001, 252) also argues, in the period after the Soviet-Yugoslav split, the CPY's leaders gradually relegated the transformation of society and culture to the distant future, when it would be achieved not by the CPY's leaders' heroic efforts but by the inevitable forces of history, in line with the teachings of Historical Materialism. Therefore, the main task for the CPY—which in 1952 was renamed the League of Communists of Yugoslavia (LCY)—was to stay in power and ensure social ownership of the means of production long enough for those forces of history to develop. However, this required the LCY to promote other, less ideological, sources of legitimacy, such as a higher standard of living, greater freedoms, and last but not least, the gradual decentralisation of power.

Raising the standard of living was a priority because, in addition to being one of the least developed countries in Europe prior to the Second World War, Yugoslavia also suffered heavily during the course of the war in terms of destruction of infrastructure and industrial plants. Moreover, after rejecting Marshall Plan help for ideological reasons, the (re)building of the country's economy after the war was additionally slowed down in 1948 by the socialist countries' economic blockade following the Soviet-Yugoslav split. This resulted in the majority of Yugoslavia's population still living in deep poverty at the beginning of the 1950s. However, after five years of economic stagnation caused by the blockade, Yugoslavia started to experience rapid modernisation in the mid-1950s, accompanied by a steady rise in the standard of living and two and a half decades of uninterrupted economic growth, enjoying one of the highest growth rates in the world during the 1960s (Bojičić 1996, 30–31). Due to this development, '[a]fter a quarter of a century of power in the post-war state, Tito and the League of Communists could look with understandable pride and satisfaction at their achievements', as historian of Yugoslav film, Daniel J. Goulding, puts it (2002 [1985], 111). Along with this development, Goulding further argues, by the late 1960s and early 1970s, Yugoslavia had accomplished a remarkable transition, from a predominantly rural and small-town-based culture built on an agrarian economy to an increasingly modern, urbanised and industrial state. Yugoslavia of the early 1970s— that is, at the time when Sarajevo started seriously considering its Olympic nomination—had become blessed with blocks of concrete high-rise and traffic jams. As Goulding observes, despite backward areas and the still-present poverty, unemployment and inequality that the socialist system had promised to abolish, life in general was improving steadily. New towns and suburbs sprang up around the major cities to accommodate the steady influx of people from the countryside, consumer goods proliferated, the university system was greatly expanded, new roads were built and political and economic freedoms were greater than in any other communist country. Not everything was rosy though. Yugoslavia had an unfavourable balance of payments, inflation, housing shortage, and suffered from the inability to absorb the increasing numbers of professionally and university-educated young people into the economy. Rural and small-town values were assaulted and agriculture neglected. The regional differences were marked by the rising inequality between an underdeveloped south and the more prosperous north. Nevertheless, at a general level, as another scholar has argued (Ramet 1984, 3), the feeling of living in a functioning and increasingly prosperous country boosted the optimism, satisfaction and self-confidence of Yugoslavs.

By the late 1970s, however, the first signs of an economic crisis became apparent, and by the early 1980s the country was in serious trouble. The optimism of the 1960s and 1970s was now replaced by gloom, pessimism and resignation (Ramet 1984, 3). The economic crisis of the 1980s would prove to be a crucial element in the break-down of the loose Yugoslav federation, as the economic downturn, in this situation, was increasingly being identified with particular republics or regions—most notably Serbia, Kosovo and the Krajina region in Croatia. In crisis-ravaged regions people started seeing themselves as victims of unfair development policies in the socialist federation, causing a deepening sense of dissatisfaction. Meanwhile, in the more well-off regions, especially Slovenia, a strong narrative of exploitation was emerging, based on claims that its wealth was being transferred to the poorer areas (Patterson 2011, 48). In this atmosphere, intellectuals in all parts of the country increasingly began to question previously widely accepted political myths centred on the resistance movement during the Second World War, and the socialist revolution during and after the war, as well as the very idea of Yugoslav unity (Ramet 1984, 3 & 6).

This was the general situation in Yugoslavia while Sarajevo was preparing to host the Olympics, one that was among others, reflected in debates concerning Olympic financing. Kate Meehan Pedrotty has analysed these debates in the aforementioned article, 'Yugoslav unity and Olympic ideology at the 1984 Sarajevo Winter Olympic Games'. Resonating with the discussion in Part I of this book, Pedrotty (2010, 337) argued in her article that Yugoslav Olympic and tourist organisations used the image of peace-loving Yugoslavia in order to promote the country abroad and increase tourist revenues at a time of growing domestic economic crisis. These organisations stressed the presumed natural harmony of the country's non-alignment, along with international Olympic brotherhood. Pedrotty aptly argues that woven into this image was the implication that Yugoslavia's people lived this universalism on a daily basis in their 'brotherhood and unity' country. Analysing this image as an ideological construct, however, she then points out that the Sarajevo Olympics in reality opened a Pandora's box of inter-ethnic rivalries, suspicion of corruption and financial malfeasance, accusations of nationalism and displeasure with the federal system—all issues that would become tragically unworkable by the end of the decade.

Providing a valuable interpretation of the political elite's disagreements over Olympic financing, Pedrotty (2010, 347) offers an argument that while non-aligned Yugoslavia might have seemed like an ideal stage for performing international cooperation, 'on the domestic stage "brotherhood and unity" was wearing dangerously thin'. While relating her analysis of disputes and accusations between political leaders in the country to the rise of regional and inter-ethnic rivalries and increasing exasperation with the federal system on the political level, Pedrotty ultimately produces a somewhat exaggerated picture of inter-ethnic quarrels in Socialist Yugoslavia in the early 1980s. Eager to connect the dissolution of the country with the disagreements over Olympic financing plaguing the narrow circle of political elites, Pedrotty goes too far and argues that 'brotherhood and unity' was, in fact, wearing dangerously thin. She bases this argument exclusively on generalisations from debates prior to the Games, which seems somewhat arbitrary, given that the Olympics were ultimately quite a success for Yugoslavia, both economically and in terms of sporting results.

As we will see shortly, this success had the potential to influence the sense of relatedness and unity among Yugoslavs in a positive way. In fact, as Nicolas Moll (2015, 135) puts it in his more recent work on the topic, when in the end the Olympics proved an enormous success, they instantly became a memory site and symbol with positive connotations, one which could be presented as a prestige success for Yugoslavia and as a successful illustration of its brotherhood and unity ideology. Moreover, even before the Olympic Games event started, *Oslobođenje* claimed in its last pre-Olympic Sunday edition that the Olympics fulfilled its 'goal even before the start' of the sporting events. In a turn of the common phrase of everyone achieving well-being and success and no one being harmed, the daily chose to open its article with a claim of 'Vučko—the wolfy—being fed and the sheep being whole'.[4] Two weeks prior to this, the daily brought an arguably even stronger claim, referring to the international press with some US observers commenting how the Sarajevo Olympics was a 'gold mine' for the Yugoslav economy. Evoking thereby the sense of economic crisis in Yugoslavia, the observers nonetheless also insisted that the now already secured Olympic success was fuelling pride among the hosts—a 'pride that bridges the differences'.[5]

Not seeking to reject Pedrotty's argument altogether, but rather to provide the other side of the story, in the remainder of this section, I call attention to some of the sporting and economic results of the Sarajevo Olympics and address their potential impact on inter-ethnic and interregional relations in the country as a whole and in particular at the local city level of Sarajevo. To begin with, I would like to present two important theoretical arguments. The first concerns the process of identity-formation processes and was offered by Gerd Baumann (1999, 95). According to this argument, 'identity' is inextricably connected to the notion of difference, meaning that identity-formation should be understood as two interconnected processes: differentiation and identification. Following the same stream of argument, Baumann points out that our personal and collective identities emerge in a double movement: bonding, or the building of the solidarity around the common 'we' and bordering, that is, separating 'us' from 'others'. According to the second argument, originally proposed by Pierre Bourdieu, subjects do not, strictly speaking, know that what they are doing has more meaning than they assert (Pierre Bourdieu 1977, 79).

Building upon these two theoretical arguments, I want to offer a further argument relating to Yugoslavia's most important sporting result at the Sarajevo Olympics. As noted, the Sarajevo Olympics brought Yugoslavia its first ever Winter Olympic medal when, on 14 February 1984, a Slovenian, Jure Franko, won a silver medal in the giant slalom. Fulfilling the prophecy of *Naši dani* journalist Senad Avdić, who in 1982 argued that all Yugoslavs would celebrate if a Slovenian skier won a medal or an important international competition,[6] Yugoslav media—stunned by

---

[4] Zoran Kurtović, 'Cilj prije starta', *Oslobođenje Nedjelja* 4.2.1984, 5.

[5] 'Strana sredstva informisanja o pripremama Sarajeva za ZOI: Ponos spaja razlike', *Oslobođenje* 15.1.1984, 2.

[6] Senad Avdić, 'Jugosloven(c)i,' *Naši dani* 736, 5.2.1982, 3.

the success—whole-heartedly and proudly celebrated Franko's and the country's Olympic first. Avdić's statement had appeared as the Yugoslav alpine ski team started attracting more attention among the country's ski-sports enthusiasts in the early 1980s. Previously holding a rather minor position in world skiing, at the turn of the 1980s Yugoslav skiers began to acquire significant international success in competitions such as the World Cup and the World Championship. As explained before, the Yugoslav alpine ski team was at that time composed exclusively of Slovenian skiers, and the Yugoslav Alpine Skiing Union was consequently located in Slovenia's capital, Ljubljana. However, as the previously mostly unnoticed Yugoslav skiers—more specifically, Slovenian skiers—started achieving notable international results, alpine skiing gained wider popularity all over Yugoslavia, a trend intensified by the prospect of the country's imminent hosting of the Winter Olympics.

As I have argued elsewhere (Jovanovic 2017, 774), in this situation in the early 1980s, dissonance between the increased popularity of alpine skiing and the federalised media space of Yugoslavia became apparent: international alpine skiing competitions were mostly only directly transmitted on Slovenian TV, while the TV centres in the other Yugoslav republics and autonomous provinces at best provided shortened and delayed reportage. Interestingly, with the rising popularity of the discipline and the Olympics in sight, Avdić wrote an article during the 1982 Alpine Skiing World Cup in the Austrian winter sport resort, Schladming, criticising this practice and demanding nation-wide transmissions of the competitions. Wittily naming the article, 'Yugo(Slovenians)', Avdić argued against the logic that, because the Yugoslav team was wholly Slovenian, only Slovenians watched skiing competitions. He countered this by insisting, 'the hearts of all Yugoslavs will tremble equally when they hear the Yugoslav national anthem [signalling] that one of the *Yugo(Slovenian)* skiers has won a medal' (emphasis added).[7] Interestingly, exactly as its journalist Avdić had predicted a couple of years earlier, when Jure Franko won the Olympic silver, the youth periodical was exclamatory in its celebration of the Slovenian skier, calling him proudly '*naš* Jure Franko', that is, 'our Jure Franko'. The periodical did not stop there but in its typical jesting manner exclaimed 'Jurek, pa onda burek!', that is, Jure Franko before burek,

---

[7] Senad Avdić, 'Jugosloven(c)i,' *Naši dani* 736, 5.2.1982, 3.

widely considered the most favourite dish of Yugoslavs (Image 6.1).[8] In a similar manner sports daily, *Sport*, chose to name its article covering Franko's success 'Jure Franko wins first "blue" silver', referring to the common nickname of the Yugoslav national team.[9]

This development epitomises sport's capability to group people in categories other than those of ethnonational affiliation and, by doing so, creating unifying experience across ethno-cultural and regional boundaries. This capability comes often most clearly to fruition at important events or when a national team attains prominent results. This was exactly what happened when Franko won his silver, as exemplified by an article in the high-circulating *Politika* (16 February 1984), which provided a report from the medal-award celebration outside the Skenderija Olympic sports centre. It will serve to illustrate the point. In his coverage, *Politika*'s reporter told readers that 'the first Yugoslav ever to win a medal at the Winter Olympics, Jure Franko, had a group of supporters who contributed in their own way to the general celebratory atmosphere, here in Sarajevo'.[10] Franko's friends and supporters, congregating at the Skenderija to celebrate the giant-slalom silver medallist, were soon joined by many Sarajevans. Lasting into the late hours, the celebration started with Slovenian *popevkas* but ended with a *kolo* dance that, according to the daily, incorporated everybody from the gathered mass.[11] Discursively linking *popevka*, a Slovenian popular musical genre with influences from schlager, canzona and swing, and *kolo*, a traditional Balkan circle dance, the daily's reporter symbolically embraced all Yugoslavia in this interesting depiction of the celebration in Sarajevo, constructing, thereby, a common Slovenian-Sarajevan-Yugoslav 'we'.

This episode of medal-award celebration outside is equally interesting in the context of the dissolution of Yugoslavia and Slovenia's push for independence, which would take place just a few years after the Olympics. As Gregor Starc and Vlado Kotnik show in their respective studies, during the years at the turn of the 1990s, skiing became a marker of Slovenian distinction from 'the Balkanic' Yugoslavs.[12] Yet, in relation to Pedrotty's

---

[8] M. Arapovich & Z.O. Milanović, 'Novi prilozi za biografiju ZOI 84. Jurek, pa onda Burek!', *Naši dani* 804, 18.2.1984. 8–9.

[9] 'Jure Franku prvo "plavo" srebro', *Sport* 15.2.1984, 8–9.

[10] Vladimir Dedić, 'Popevke i kolo pred Skenderijom', *Politika* 16.2.1984, 12.

[11] Ibid.

[12] On this issue see Gregor Starc, 'Skiing memories in the Slovenian national mnemonic scheme: An anthropological perspective', *Anthropological Notebooks*, 12 (2) 2006, 5–22; and

**JUREK, PA ONDA BUREK!**

U trenutku dok smo završavali ovaj broj obradovao nas je naš Jure Franko, osvojivši drugo mjesto u veleslalomu, i tako našoj zemlji donio prvu medalju otkad se takmičimo na zimskim olimpijskim igrama. Nedostajalo mu je samo par stotinki sekunde pa da se okiti i zlatom. Svejedno, i to je veliki uspjeh za ovog 22-godišnjeg Novogoričanina. Uspjeh Franka ipak izgleda da smo naslutili, počevši od poznatog proroka Mladena Delića, koji je to predvidio nekoliko dana unaprijed, do svih onih gledalaca pored staze koji su kad se Jure pojavio na stazi bili najbučniji i skandirali njegovo ime oburužani transparentima na kojima je listom pisalo:

»Volimo Jureka više od bureka«

**Image 6.1**  Very much in the spirit of the city's youth culture of the 1980s, ironically claiming Jure Franko's superiority to Yugoslavia's favourite dish, burek, Sarajevo youth periodical *Naši dani* framed a still to this day iconic reference to the Sarajevo Olympics: 'We love Jure[k] even more than we love burek'. (M. Arapovich & Z. O. Milanović, 'Novi prilozi za biografiju ZOI '84', *Naši dani* 804 18.2.1984)

argument, I want to stress that on the continuum between rupture and continuity posited by historians since the emergence of the modern historical discipline, this development was clearly more rupture than continuation. In fact, the historical record strongly indicates that in the immediate

Vlado Kotnik, 'Sport and nation in anthropological perspective: Slovenia as land of skiing nationhood', *Antropologija* (7) 2009, 56–78.

post-Olympic years, a genuine Yugoslavisation of Slovenian alpine skiing occurred. This Yugoslavisation went both ways: Slovenian skiers felt strongly a part of the larger Yugoslav community, while other Yugoslavs identified strongly with the Slovenian skiers. Accordingly, both saw the Slovenian skiers as sportsmen representing first and foremost Yugoslavia. This was also the general impression presented in *Naši dani*'s 1987 interview with the coach of the Yugoslav alpine skiing team at the time, Tone Vogrinc.[13] Neither Vogrinc nor the Sarajevo youth periodical saw anything contradictory in claiming simultaneously that alpine skiing was a Slovenian national sport, while speaking of it as 'Yugoslav skiing'. This was interestingly apparent in the title, 'Tone Vogrinc: Skiing is Slovenian plebiscite' accompanied by the subheading, 'The manager of national alpine skiing team talks about the breakthrough of the Yugoslav skiing into the world elite'.[14]

As the subheading of the Vogrinc interview implies, the 'breakthrough' was closely related to the golden age of Yugoslav skiing, the catalyst for which, according to Vogrinc, was the moment when Bojan Križaj won the junior competition of the European Cup in 1975. This result spurred the popularity of alpine skiing among young Slovenians, producing better results year by year, before finally culminating in the immediate post-Olympic years. It is noteworthy that, during this period—arguably, at least indirectly, also due to Franko's medal and Yugoslavia's Olympic success—Yugoslav-wide transmissions of skiing competitions became a norm. All the while—to borrow Avdić's wording one last time—the Yugo(Slovenian) skiers were obtaining better results than ever before. It thus makes sense to argue that from the late 1970s and at least until 1987—that is, while Yugoslav political space was fragmenting—alpine skiing in the country was going through a phase of a genuine Yugoslavisation. Consequently, the case of alpine skiing strongly supports Dejan Jović's argument touched on at the start of this chapter—an argument that Yugoslavia of the 1970s and 1980s was experiencing fragmentation and integration at the same time. It likewise exemplifies why generalising about the general situation in 1980s Yugoslavia on the basis of the narrow agency of the country's political elites is deeply problematic.

---

[13] Juso Prelo & Radmilo Milanović, 'To ti kažem: Tone Vogrinc. Smučanje je slovenački plebiscit', *Naši dani* 912, 27.3.1987, 8–9.
[14] Ibid.

The sporting aspect of the Sarajevo Olympics did not only affect the sense of connectedness among Yugoslavs through event results. As Philip A. D'Agati argues in his work on the relationship between the Olympics and nationalism, due to their festival nature, the Olympics inevitably have cultural connotations and therefore cultural ramifications, including the power to affect culture and, more importantly, cultural understanding(s). As D'Agati (2011, 5) puts it, the Olympics are a stage with an international audience, upon which culture, history, heritage, legitimacy and the origin of the host nation are all carefully displayed. This in turn implies that the Olympics have a powerful ability to assist in the process of re-identifying society through the process of reinventing tradition, in Hobsbawm's sense of that term.

Following this stream of thought, it makes sense to look more closely at the process of re-identifying Yugoslav society in relation to the reinvention of Sarajevo's winter sports tradition during the Olympic period. There are a few things in this respect that we need to recall from earlier discussions. As we saw in the previous chapters, the idea of Sarajevo's Winter Olympics nomination was not the result of the city's position as a winter sports resort, but rather an attempt to explore new avenues of tourism development in Bosnia and Herzegovina. As illustrated in Part I of this book, just a couple of decades before the Olympics no one seriously associated Sarajevo with winter sports, let alone the Winter Olympics. As discussed, the official English translation of the city's tourist guide in 1966 did not even mention skiing or other winter sports in its section on sport, linking the mountains surrounding the Bosnian capital city exclusively to their outstanding mountaineering potential (Tihić 1966, 31–33). Sarajevo was simply not a winter sport centre at that time. Consequently, when the city won its bid for the Olympics in 1978, most of the necessary Olympic infrastructure was missing.

The absence of infrastructure and substantial winter sports traditions meant that when construction of the Olympic venues started in the city, it was accompanied by the construction of winter sports traditions for the city. Once again, we need to remember Slovenia's dominant position as the leading centre of Yugoslavia's winter sports: not only as the Yugoslav republic producing the majority of Yugoslav winter sports competitors, but also having by far the most developed winter sports infrastructure. Moreover, as *Ski* magazine's Seth Masia (1984, 48) argued, Slovenian villagers had a long tradition of using skis as a means of daily transportation in this mountainous region. Interestingly, in the context of this chapter's discussion, Masia talked exclusively about Slovenia in the article and yet chose to name it, 'Yugoslavia: First Alpine Nation on Skis'. This was arguably because Slovenia's skiing tradition considerably overshadowed that of any other part of the country. There is nothing exceptionally Yugoslav in this. Nations frequently construct their traditions on the basis of practices, customs and heritage common only in small and delimited parts of their territory. Yet, in an interesting twist in the process of inventing Sarajevo's Winter Olympics tradition by appropriating the Slovenian winter sports tradition, the Slovenian practice of building winter sport venues was reinvented as a Yugoslav tradition and then appropriated as Sarajevo's (Winter Olympics) tradition as well. This process corresponded closely with Socialist Yugoslavia's official ideological axiom of 'brotherhood and unity' and related cultural policies. Existing research on the topic of popular culture has extensively mapped how, according to the axiom, all the specific characteristics of the different regions of Yugoslavia had to be interpreted as being 'the property of all the peoples of Yugoslavia' (Ceribašić 1998, 127).

This reflects what happened during Sarajevo's preparation to host the XIV Olympic Winter Games, when the city's and Yugoslavia's winter sport traditions were constructed in accordance with the country's ideological axiom of 'brotherhood and unity'. Sarajevo's *Oslobođenje* provides an interesting example of the linkage between the two spheres in its cultural section, 'KUN', 7 November 1981, which carried an article dealing with what the daily's journalist described as 'Winter Olympics architecture'. Discussing the new generation of Sarajevan architects who were contributing to building the venues for the 1984 Winter Olympics, the 'KUN' article chose to present them as members of the 'Yugoslav school of ski-jump building'. Pointing explicitly to the *Planica* ski jumping hills in Slovenia, constructed in 1936 as the first of its kind in the world, the article referred to this school as both 'world-renowned' and 'one of the oldest in the world'.[15] This example demonstrates marvellously the work of reinventing subnational traditions as national which, along with claiming their antiquity, is rather typical of the invention of tradition more broadly. Yet again, in the context of the Yugoslav brotherhood and unity policies, it is noteworthy that the ski jumps built in Slovenia in the 1930s were presented not only as a part of a non-temporal pan-Yugoslav 'school',

---

[15] Aleksandar Trumić, 'Majstori ostaju nepoznati,' *Oslobođenje—kulturni dodatak 'Kultura Umjetnost Nauka'* 22, 7.11.1981, 1–2.

but also directly linked to a new generation of young Sarajevo architects in the 1980s. What we see at work here is the Olympics' assisting in the re-identification of Yugoslav 'brotherhood and unity' society, by reinventing the *Slovenian* winter sports tradition as a *Yugoslav*—and thereby also *Sarajevan*—Winter Olympics tradition. In this way Slovenia, Yugoslavia and Sarajevo were connected in one common, transgenerational 'we', not dissimilar to the transcultural 'we' described in relation to Olympic Sarajevo's celebrating Jure Franko's silver with *popevka* and *kolo*.

Elsewhere, Jure Franko's Olympic success was presented as a common 'pan-Yugoslav success occurring as the Bosnian *objects* conjoined with the Slovenian *subject'*, as one of the leading Yugoslav columnists of the time wittily put it. It can be argued that this symbolic framing, offered by Zagreb-based *Start* journalist, Veselko Tenžera,[16] marks an incarnation of multiculturalist Yugoslavism and its ideological axiom of 'brotherhood and unity', according to which the goal of the country's nationality policies should not be the creation of a common Yugoslav national identity. Rather, it sought to strengthen the idea that all Yugoslavs, regardless of their nationality, would profit from a common faith in 'unity in diversity'. Thus, in Tenžera's symbolism, Slovenian sportsmen profited from Bosnian Olympic venues—and vice versa—culminating in a common all Yugoslav success.

Yugoslav Olympic success was not limited only to sports results. Financially, the Sarajevo Olympics were also rather successful, ending, according to the final report (TSOOC 1984b, 182–183, 185), with a rela-tively large surplus. Furthermore, they provided a platform from which to market the country's products and enterprises. In fact, according to gen-eral opinion during the Olympic period, voiced in the final report (TSOOC 1984b, 170–171), Yugoslav enterprises did a good job, courtesy of the Yugoslav advertising industry, in terms of the promotion of their products in both old and new markets, although advertising was particularly directed towards Western markets. In seeking to improve their position and eventually increase their sales in the West, Yugoslav enterprises received enormous support from the Yugoslav Olympic Committee and especially the Organising Committee of the Sarajevo Olympics. Indeed, the promoters of different Yugoslav enterprises aligned themselves closely with these two bodies, as well as with local and national tourism

---

[16] As cited in M. Arapović, 'Postolimpijske misli i … Lov biznisa,' *Naši dani* 805, 24.2.1984, 10.

promoters. A very interesting example of how this alliance materialised could already be seen at one of the earliest promotions of the Sarajevo Olympics, which took place at the 1980 Lake Placid Winter Olympics.

As we saw in the Part I, Lake Placid was the first major milestone in the project of turning Sarajevo into a global tourism centre in that it was here that it was officially promoted as an 'Olympic city'; at the same time, the country's enterprises also saw a chance to go global. Hence, in Lake Placid, the Olympic Organising Committee, the Sarajevo Tourism Association and the Slovenian ski producer Elan appeared together, supporting and enforcing each other on the global stage—or 'in front of the eyes of the world' in Maurice Roche's sense of that phrase. As *Oslobođenje* explained in its report from the Lake Placid Olympics, Elan used this opportunity to promote its products in hopes of gaining ground in the otherwise remote—and generally not so easy to penetrate North American ski equipment market.[17] As we will see shortly, other companies soon followed Elan's example, regarding the Olympics as a springboard for a more long-term business development. Yugoslav sporting and political elites likewise perceived the Sarajevo Olympics as a golden business opportunity, and offered strong institutional support to the companies. Hence, very early in the Olympic preparation process, the Yugoslav Olympic Organising Committee had already established an advertising section that sought to help promote Yugoslav companies globally.

It does, therefore, not come as a surprise that the first post-Olympic Sunday issue of the federal government's daily *Borba* also reserved a whole page of its 'Society section' to a discussion of the topic of Olympic advertising and sponsorship. Published under the headline, 'The Olympic Recap' (*Olimpijski bilansi*), it comprised three articles, accompanied by an illustration by one of the leading political cartoonists in the country, Predrag Koraksić Corax. The lead article of the three was built on an interview with the director of the Olympic marketing service, Vladimir Postnikov. Of note is that the article was named 'The World Has Seen What We Can', implying the extent to which the Sarajevo Olympics—true of Olympics in general—were an exhibition presented to a global audience. Very much in the manner of Maurice Roche's (2000, 6) previously discussed argument on the issue, the article told the story of how the

---

[17] (Kemal Kurspahić, Alija Resulović, Boro Radosavljević, Tanjug et al.), 'Olimpijski dnevnik. Ime na karti svijeta', *Oslobođenje* 19.2.1980, 15.

Olympics provided a stage on which to exhibit Yugoslavia (and hence its enterprises) as a strongly business-minded nation.

According to Postnikov, the Olympic marketing service played an important role in terms of providing institutionalised support for the promotion of Yugoslav enterprises, which, in their capacity as official Olympic sponsors, in turn helped the organisation of the Games financially. Arguing that the business results of the Olympics surpassed all expectations, Postnikov provided a number of examples of enterprises—mostly Bosnian and Slovenian—that had already profited from the sponsorship they had provided during the Olympic period. One of them was the aforementioned Elan, which, according to Postnikov, climbed from number six to number three in ski equipment sales in the North American market in the course of the Olympic period. Another was the Sarajevo-based Energoinvest discussed in Chap. 3, which had begun to engage in international cooperation to install ropeways and ski-lifts around the world. This said, according to Postnikov and to the interviewing journalist, Enver Demirović, the ultimate results of the promotional efforts made by enterprises during the Olympic period would only be fully apparent post-Olympics.[18] This view was cultivated throughout the preparation period, as right from the point of winning the bid, the Sarajevo Olympics were commonly viewed as an extraordinary opportunity for the country and its enterprises to 'step out into the world of business'.[19]

The Olympic promotional bulletin, *Olimpijski informator* (The Olympic Guide)—launched by the Yugoslav Olympic Committee and the Organising Committee of the Sarajevo Olympics in 1981—also wrote regularly, in a similar vein, about the potential economic implications of the Olympics for those enterprises sponsoring them. In one piece it rephrased the common proverb, 'As you sow so shall you reap', to apply to what was sown in the form of sponsorship during the Olympic preparation period would give results post-Olympics, naming the article, 'The Spring of Marketing'.[20] Thus, the Olympics were more than simply an exhibition showing the world Yugoslavia's mastery. The whole Olympic episode, from winning the bid to the closing of the Games, became 'the admission test' to a bigger playing field in post-Olympic times, a period

[18] Enver Demirović, 'Svijet je vidio šta možemo', *Nedeljna Borba* 25–26.2. 1984, 3.

[19] Zoran Kurtović, 'Cilj prije starta', *Oslobođenje Nedjelja* 4.2.1984, 5.

[20] Husein Hujić, 'Proljeće marketinga (The Spring of Marketing)', *Olimpijski informator* 11 (March 1982).

supposedly qualitatively different from that in pre-Olympic and contemporary Olympic Yugoslavia. Indeed, *Borba*'s Demirović spoke of the just finished Olympics as 'the big exam' that the country had successfully completed, implying thereby that the Olympics were a stage on which Yugoslavia and its enterprises had performed in order to gain admission to the world of global business markets.[21]

The second article, dealing with major Slovenian Olympic sponsors left the same impression, which the very title of the article witnessed: '*Dobra ulaznica*' (A Good Ticket). The article's main argument was that although it was still too early to know the final economic impact of the Olympics, Slovenian businessmen were already more than satisfied with the results achieved. Several enterprises were discussed, ranging from the aforementioned manufacturer of skis and ski binders Elan and the sportswear brand Toper to the domestic appliance manufacturer Gorenje and the soft drinks and mineral water brand Radenska. While some of these enterprises used the Olympics to make explicit business contracts, others only expected to experience the results of their Olympic performance in the aftermath of the Games.[22]

Meanwhile, it must be remembered that all this did not occur in a vacuum, but in the specific situation of severe economic crisis that hit the country just as Sarajevo won its Olympic candidacy. This was a crisis from which Yugoslavia never recovered, one that led to reciprocated accusations between the political elites in the country's federal units and, according to the argument in this chapter, proved to be central in the final dissolution of the loose Yugoslav federation. In this situation, the Olympics had the potential to strengthen bonds between Yugoslav republics and provinces and prolong common faith in the Yugoslav project.

In this respect, and resonating with the chapter's discussion on the building of a common 'we' for Bosnians and Slovenians in terms of sport, it is interesting to note that a similar process occurred in terms of business promotion. Some scholars have argued that Bosnia and Herzegovina on the one hand, and Slovenia on the other, presented two opposite poles in terms of the Yugoslav republics' relationships with multicultural Yugoslavism. While Bosnia and Herzegovina was widely viewed as the most pro-Yugoslav republic and commonly represented as 'Yugoslavia on a smaller scale', Slovenia was usually perceived as being most at odds with

[21] Enver Demirović, 'Svijet je vidio šta možemo', *Nedeljna Borba* 25–26.2. 1984, 3.
[22] Smail Festić, 'Dobra Ulaznica', *Nedeljna Borba* 25–26.2. 1984, 3.

the multinational federated Yugoslav state (Tomc 2006, 447). At the Sarajevo Olympics, they came together—resulting, according to *Borba*'s Demirović, in universal Yugoslav business-promotion success.[23] This argument was fully in accordance with the main discourse concerning the Sarajevo Olympics which, according to Nicolas Moll's work on the topic, mentioned in the introduction, can be summarised as 'Sarajevo and its Olympics bringing all of Yugoslavia together, and Sarajevo and Yugoslavia bringing the whole world together' (Moll 2015, 131).

Corax' aforementioned cartoon caught this perfectly. Combining the mascot and the symbol of the Sarajevo Olympics—respectively Vučko and Pahulja—Corax' illustration produced a message in which Vučko, the little wolf, introduced himself to the world by opening windows out of the geometrically stylised Olympic symbol, Pahulja, the Snowflake. It is very symbolic that Vučko opened the windows outwards, towards the world. In this image Sarajevo and Yugoslavia were displayed to the global audience. Given that it was placed in the section dealing with Yugoslav advertising and business promotion during and after the Olympics, it implied that for Yugoslavs—or at least *Borba*'s readership—Yugoslav unity was closely related to the economic performance of the country (Image 6.2).

This perception had a particularly strong implication at the local level in Sarajevo. Given the degree of investment in infrastructural works relating to the Games, they had great potential to maintain the sense of continuing economic prosperity from the 1970s well into the 1980s. As noted in the first chapter, hosting the Olympic Games and tourism development go hand in glove. Consequently, one of the main impacts the Olympics have on their host cities is the short and long-term economic gain generated by the ensuing flow of tourists. Sarajevo, as we saw in the previous chapter, had a more marked rise in tourist numbers than Belgrade and Zagreb at the time, indicating that the city had indeed profited in this area as a result of hosting the Olympics.

Furthermore, according to *The Final Report* (TSOOC 1984b, 183, 191–192), the Sarajevo Winter Olympics ended with a surplus of ten million dollars. Even more importantly, around 9000 new jobs had been created in the city as a result of the Games. One media source argues that the numbers were even higher, counting no less than 11,000 temporary and 4000 permanent jobs (Powell 1984, 35). As we saw in Chap. 4 dealing with the changes—however temporary—in consumption patterns

---

[23] Enver Demirović, 'Svijet je vidio šta možemo', *Nedeljna Borba* 25–26.2. 1984, 3.

**Image 6.2** An early post-Olympic article by *Nedeljna Borba* contending that while not all results of the just finished Olympics were known by that time, there was not any doubt that when Yugoslavs perform united they also attain best results. ('Svijet je vidio šta možemo', *Nedeljna Borba* 25–26.2.1984, 1)

connected with the Olympics, these jobs offered young Sarajevans previously unimaginable income at a time of economic crisis and rising unemployment in the nation as a whole.[24] For this reason, as the Zagreb youth weekly *Polet* explained in its 9 February 1984 issue, Yugoslavs from all over the country made their way to Sarajevo during the Olympics in the

---

[24] Veso Đorem, 'Nađi mi babo strenžera!', *Naši dani* 805, 24.2.1984, 11.

hope of making some fast money.[25] In fact, as other sources also point out, good job opportunities in Olympic Sarajevo made Yugoslavs from different parts of the country come together. In its opening day issue *Sport* told its readers that chefs from all parts of Yugoslavia came to Sarajevo to work in the city's restaurants, hotels and canteens; while buses and bus drivers from many different Yugoslav cities arrived in Sarajevo to help transport athletes, visitors and locals to the Olympic venues. Finally, young people from some thirty different Yugoslav cities came to Sarajevo, where their proficiency in different foreign languages was in high demand.[26]

In addition to the influx of tourists and their hard currency, and the creation of thousands of new jobs (some of which, as we have seen, were rather well paid), the huge number of new apartments left behind by the Olympics also had an important impact in a period of harsh austerity measures and the downsizing of public expenditure all over the country. According to the post-Olympic pamphlet, *Sarajevo—The Olympic City*, published by the Sarajevan branch of the aforementioned SSRN of Yugoslavia, 2640 new apartments were built in the Olympic and media villages of Dobrinja and Mojmilo to house journalists and competitors (SSRNBiH 1984, 21). *The Final Report* (TSOOC 1984b, 106) put the number even higher, claiming that the 'residential facilities' of Mojmilo and Dobrinja comprised 2750 flats. Whichever of the two claims is right, these apartments were surely one of the major reasons why Sarajevo's population grew much faster than the population of other major Yugoslav cities in the 1980s. Of eight Yugoslav metropoles with official city status, Sarajevo's growth of 17.3% in the period from 1981 to 1991 was unparalleled by the other seven. In fact, it is very pertinent in this context that Sarajevo's nearest rival was the Croatian city of Split, which experienced growth of 12% and which, as we saw, hosted the 1979 Mediterranean Games, followed by the Croatian capital Zagreb that, as we will see in more detail in the next section, hosted the 1987 Zagreb Universiade.[27]

---

[25] Zoran Simić, 'Poletov bob dvosjed u Sarajevu', *Polet* 251, 9.2.1984, 13.

[26] 'Gori vatra od Jahorine do Bjelašnice', *Sport* 8.2.1984, 8.

[27] Zagreb experienced growth of 8.6%, followed by the Macedonian capital of Skopje, which in the slightly longer period of 1981–1994 grew 7.9% (the 1991 census of population was not completed in Macedonia due to an Albanian boycott; hence the full census only took place three years later). Ljubljana, Novi Sad and Belgrade experienced growth of 5.9%, 5.8% and 5.7% respectively, while Slovenia's second city and one of Yugoslavia's major industrial centres, Maribor, grew less than 1%. (All figures computed on the basis of the last two Yugoslav censuses in 1981 and 1991.)

The fact that it was these three cities that experienced the biggest growth in Yugoslavia's last decade implies that sport, particularly major sporting events, played an important role in many aspects of Yugoslav society. This phenomenon provides further impetus for urging that greater attention be paid to sport in Socialist Yugoslavia. Some scholars have already pointed out this linkage; for instance ethnologist and scholar on Yugoslavia's late socialism, Dean Duda (2006, 95–96, n1), who chronologically framed what he called 'the period of Yugoslavia's decedent socialism' by these three international sporting events: the 1979 Mediterranean Games in Split, the 1984 Winter Olympics in Sarajevo and the 1987 Universiade in Zagreb.

The macroeconomic developments—the growth in the tourism industry, the creation of new jobs and the increase in residential apartments—were only part of the economic impact of the Sarajevo Olympics. The general impression of the city in the years leading up to the Olympics was equally important in that it evaded the otherwise omnipresent sense of harsh economic crisis in Yugoslavia. As noted, according to general perceptions, the city had never developed so fast as during the preparations for the Olympics.

In addition to the new apartments which the Sarajevans inherited after the Games, the Olympics also left an important legacy in terms of architecture, facilities and infrastructure, while their prominent urban dimension contributed substantially to urban and social policies in the city. Infrastructural projects resulted in new sports stadia and hotels, improved public transport and road networks and a cleaner urban environment. All this added to the general sense of continuing prosperity. Moreover, as described, Sarajevo's shops were very well supplied immediately before and during the Olympic period, provoking comments among journalists and visitors from other parts of the country that the city felt like a 'leftover oasis from the Yugoslavia of the prosperous 1970s', according to Belgrade's *Duga*,[28] or an 'oasis of Yugoslavia from ten years earlier' as Zagreb's *Polet* claimed that many of the interviewed visitors described Sarajevo.[29] This interesting metaphor used by both *Duga* and *Polet* was impregnated with the idea of 'the good old days' of the prosperous 1970s, which were, according to Pedro Ramet, blessed with optimism and

---

[28] Milomir Marić, 'Pred početak olimpijade. Sneško belić u bosanskom loncu', *Duga*, 28.1.1984, 22–23.

[29] Zoran Simić, 'Poletov bob dvosjed u Sarajevu', *Polet* 251, 9.2.1984, 13.

enthusiasm (Ramet 1984, 3). Against this background it makes sense to assert that at least for a short period during the Olympics and in the immediate post-Olympic period, the otherwise omnipresent sense of economic crisis that was strangulating Yugoslavia in the mid-1980s seemed to be absent in Sarajevo where the Olympic years were associated with the prosperous times of the previous decade. It is, therefore, reasonable to argue that herein lay the 1984 Winter Olympics' capacity to prolong Sarajevo's 'love for Yugoslavia', which Sergej Flere talks about.

This development—the protraction of the city's pronouncedly Yugoslav orientation relating to the absence of the sense of crisis that was elsewhere weakening support for the Yugoslav project—should also be seen from the perspective of the argument proposed by historian Robert J. Donia in his *Sarajevo. A Biography* (2006, xi). Donia points out that '[o]n the spectrum between experience and imagination expounded by Benedict Anderson, Sarajevo [was] more an experienced than an imagined community'. This is a very important observation, because—as we will see in the next section—the dominant representation in the Olympic period linked Sarajevo to Yugoslavia and stressed its position as a truly Yugoslav city.

## 6.2   Performing Yugoslavia During and After the Sarajevo Olympics

Discussing the relationship between the Olympics and nationalism in his 2011 book, *Nationalism on the World Stage: Cultural Performance and the Olympic Games*, Philip A. D'Agati draws attention to the way national and subnational identities are performed at the Games. Operating with the concepts of stage, display and cultural performance, D'Agati argues that the Olympics, by their very nature as a cultural festival, carry important cultural connotations and should thus be considered beyond the framework of sporting competitions and narrow political and economic results. According to D'Agati (2011, 5), the Olympics constitute a stage with an international audience, upon which culture, history, heritage, legitimacy and origin are carefully displayed. For this reason, he writes, the Olympics could be approached as a cultural performance, which he defines as the artistic display of national and subnational identity through the deliberate use of cultural elements such as icons, narratives and so on.

Against this theoretical backdrop, D'Agati presents several thematic chapters, one of which deals with the Sarajevo Olympics (149–161).

Named 'Exalting the Core', it offers a comparative perspective from which the author discusses how the host nations of the 1980 Moscow Summer Olympics, 1984 Sarajevo Winter Olympics and 2000 Sydney Summer Olympics, respectively, staged Soviet, Yugoslav and Australian national and subnational identities. In his analysis, D'Agati focuses on the opening and closing ceremonies of these Games, proposing that, at the Sarajevo Winter Olympics, Yugoslav state-level elites performed their regime's concept of a non-national Yugoslav identity by stressing the technical aspects of the ceremonies and marginalising any expression of the identities of the country's ethnonational groups. Following this line of reasoning, D'Agati defines this favoured non-national identity as a core that was being exalted at the ceremonies, and the allegedly marginalised ethnonational identities as peripheries that were being cut away from that core. Stressing that the 1984 Winter Olympics occurred in 'an atmosphere of anti-nationalist rhetoric within the tumultuous period after the death of Socialist Yugoslavia's president for life, Josip Broz Tito', D'Agati (2011, 154 & 159–160) argues that 'it makes much sense that Sarajevo's exaltation of the core was as devoid of ethnic presentations as possible'.

To support his argument, D'Agati (2011, 154–156) draws attention to the clothing worn by the Yugoslav Olympic team at the opening and closing ceremonies—futuristic solid-white costumes with no connection to any ethnic or national tradition in Yugoslavia—and also to the limiting of ethno-cultural connotations in the performances to ethnic dress and cultural dances. Yet, according to D'Agati, even these were greatly constrained, with the audience being presented with the traditional *kolo* dance performed to modern music and with modernised steps, thereby underplaying its ethnic origins. Moreover, writes D'Agati, although dressed in the traditional costumes of the different ethnic groups of Yugoslavia, the procession of Yugoslavs escorting the Olympic flag at the opening ceremony was led by flag bearers wearing the solid-white Yugoslav team clothing, thereby diminishing ethnic connotations. Based on these observations, D'Agati concludes (2011, 154–155 & 159–160) that the Sarajevo Games directly restricted demonstration of ethnonational identities that could conflict with Yugoslavia's decentralised style of governance.

While D'Agati's analysis contributes some valuable theoretical insights in terms of the performance of national identities at the Olympics and offers a very interesting interpretation of Sarajevo's opening and closing ceremonies, it is nonetheless problematic on several levels. Most notably, the argument about the marginalisation of ethnonational identities seems somewhat exaggerated and some important facts that could compromise it are elided. Importantly, D'Agati misses one of the central moments at the opening ceremony in Sarajevo: the opening speech given by the Slovenian alpine skier, Bojan Križaj. As we saw earlier in the chapter, Križaj was assumed to be directly responsible for the growing popularity of alpine skiing in Yugoslavia, and the international skiing press had named Križaj the second most likely medal winner in the alpine disciplines (Fry 1984, 40). For this reason, *Oslobođenje* explained in its 25 January issue, there was never any doubt that Križaj was going to read the Olympic oath at the opening ceremony. However, while Križaj, due to his sporting results and success, appeared the natural choice for this role, a selection of language was not as obvious. *Oslobođenje* presented three options. As the audience was going to be international, one option was English, which would not be a problem, as Križaj was fluent in the language. However, as the Olympics were 'not being held in England' but in Yugoslavia, *Oslobođenje* offered a second option: Serbo-Croatian. This was the official language in Sarajevo and, numerically, the most widely spoken in Yugoslavia. Yet, the daily asked, why should Križaj do it in Serbo-Croatian? Yugoslavia is a federation in which all nationalities have equal rights; Križaj is a Slovenian and logically, therefore, should do it in his own mother tongue, Slovenian, concluded *Oslobođenje*.[30] Ultimately, this was also the choice made by Križaj and the Olympic Organising Committee, which was mainly constituted of representatives from Bosnia and Herzegovina. Thus, on 8 February, at the opening ceremony, Križaj read the Olympic oath in Slovenian—a language not fully intelligible to most Bosnians and to a large majority of other non-Slovenian Yugoslavs (Image 6.3).

The fact that the Olympic opening speech was given in Slovenian complicates D'Agati's allegation that the demonstration of ethno-cultural identities was restricted during the Games. As different scholars have argued, language was always one of the most visible and potent markers of ethno-cultural identities in the multi-ethnic and multilingual Yugoslav Federation, particularly among Slovenians (Jovanovic 2014, 51). Analysing the topic of nationalism and federalism in late socialist Yugoslavia, Ramet (1984, 44) has illustrated with several cases from the 1960s through to the 1980s how the language always served as a central indicator of Slovene distinctiveness vis-à-vis the rest of the country and thereby as a powerful feature of Slovenian national identity. Likewise, as Predrag Matvejević

---

[30] Z. Odić, 'Jezik olimpijske zakletve', *Oslobođenje* 26.1.1984, 11.

**Image 6.3** 'The Language of the Olympic Oath', an *Oslobođenje* article insisting that the Olympics are more than just a sporting event and explaining that the choice of the language in which the Olympic oath was to be conducted in Sarajevo was exemplary thereof. Arguing for the choice of Slovenian over Serbo-Croatian would be a manifestation of equality and brotherhood and unity among the people of Yugoslavia. (Z. Odić, 'Jezik olimpijske zakletve', *Oslobođenje* 26.1.1984, 11)

(1982, 98 & 103 et seq.) argued in his 1982 book on the topic of Yugoslavism, in the early 1980s Slovenian was, vis-à-vis Serbo-Croatian, at the centre of national debates in Slovenia. Finally, language proved to be the most important single element of nationalist mobilisation in Yugoslavia's northernmost republic in the late 1980s (Ramet 2006, 314–315; Jovanovic 2014, 134–135). Against this socio-politico-historical context, it makes as much sense to argue that Križaj's reading of the Olympic oath in Slovenian was in fact, to use D'Agati's terminology, an act of exalting and not of marginalising subnational identities at the opening ceremony.

Moreover, contrary to the impression that D'Agati's interpretation may leave, this episode of expression of ethnonational identity should not be seen as being in conflict with Yugoslavia's nationality policies but very much in line with them. Several scholars, among them Rogers Brubaker

(1996, 7–8, 23–54) and Husnija Kamberović (2018), have argued that the Communist Party elites in Eastern Europe in general and in Yugoslavia in particular were not anti-national. As Steven L. Burg and Michael L. Berbaum argued in 1989 (1989, 538), the nationalities policies in Socialist Yugoslavia could best be defined as pro-national and not 'non-national', as D'Agati claims. Yet this did not mean that the Yugoslav Socialist Government had given up on the idea of creating a sense of common pan-Yugoslav identity altogether, in the way that D'Agati phrases it. Paradoxically while insisting on the complexity of the situation regarding inter-ethnic relations in Yugoslavia, D'Agati ends up providing an overly abstract and simplified socio-politico-historical contextualisation of the event in terms of Yugoslavia's nationality policies and inter-ethnic relations. Thus, he speaks of unspecified 'state-level elites' that were allegedly performing the 'regime's non-national Yugoslav identity' at the Sarajevo Olympics. However, given Yugoslavia's decentralised style of governance—mentioned by D'Agati himself—the notion of 'state-level elites' becomes a highly problematic abstract. This applies both to the inter-republican debates about Olympic financing that Pedrotty has pointed to in her study and to the factual composition of the Sarajevo Olympic Organising Committee. The latter was, as pointed out above and as explained in the *Final Report* for the Sarajevo Olympics (TSOOC 1984b, 92) constituted by two thirds of people appointed by the Sarajevo City Assembly and the last third from different Yugoslav and Bosnian sports and socio-political organisations.

Furthermore, explicitly criticising Susan Woodward's claim of a strong sense of inter-ethnic solidarity among Yugoslavs by suggesting that the Yugoslav government had ceased its efforts to create a single cohesive sense of national identity, D'Agati (2011, 153–154) leaves the impression that a sense of pan-Yugoslav (supra)national identity never emerged. I argue, on the other hand, that, although the nationalities policy in Socialist Yugoslavia could be defined as pro-national, that did not mean that its government had given up on the idea of creating a sense of common pan-Yugoslav identity altogether. As Andrew Baruch Wachtel (1998, iii), a historian of Yugoslavia's literature, argues in his study of the phenomenon of Yugoslavism, after abandoning the creation of a single national Yugoslav identity, the socialist regime focused its cultural policy on what can be called *multicultural Yugoslavism*. This was crafted in a spirit that emphasised the common faith of all Yugoslavs regardless of their nationality, that is, the faith in 'unity in diversity'. In this context, it was the latter that defined the transnational pan-Yugoslav identity that emerged alongside the more familiar, ethnonational notions of group belonging. A similar argument was offered by a number of scholars, with Vjekoslav Perica (2002, 94 et seq.), for example, claiming that a patriotic commitment to 'brotherhood and unity' and 'the Yugoslav spirit' developed among the Yugoslav peoples as a counterweight to the ethnic nationalism that tore Yugoslavia apart during the Second World War. In Socialist Yugoslavia, according to Perica, this spirit was espoused by a large number of Yugoslavs and even resulted in the emergence of a new Yugoslav nationality.

This development confronts D'Agati's claim that there was no sense of pan-Yugoslav identity or strong inter-ethnic solidarity among Yugoslavs. As we saw in the introduction to this chapter, Dejan Jović (2001, 107–108) suggested that inter-ethnic integration among Yugoslavs emerged as a reaction to the fragmentation of Yugoslav political and cultural space. Hence, when Sarajevo was preparing for the Olympics, Yugoslavia was experiencing what Jović has called *New Yugoslavism*. This constituted part of an emergent social force in Yugoslav society in the early to mid-1980s that went against nationalist polarisation and resulted, as Jović and other researchers have argued, in a significant growth in the number of people identifying as 'Yugoslavs-nationally undeclared'. The growing popularity of such Yugoslav self-identification occurred precisely at the time Sarajevo started seriously preparing for the Olympics. In consequence, in the 1981 Yugoslav census, the number of people opting to classify themselves as 'Yugoslavs-nationally undeclared' was five times greater than in the census ten years earlier.[31] This phenomenon triggered considerable discussion in Yugoslav society, including debates on whether it was a desirable development or not.[32] Eric Gordy (1999, 6) has argued that the phenomenon suggests that people were seeking and finding alternatives to a narrow national identity, and the 'Yugoslav' option was proving increasingly popular. I have argued elsewhere (Jovanovic 2014, 28–53) that this was closely related to different aspects of socio-economic modernisation, most notably urbanisation and the spread of education. Constituting an emergent force in the early to mid-1980s, *New Yugoslavism* did not mean that a new 'national group' was emerging in the country; rather, it indicated a societal development in which ethnonational identification was losing its

---

[31] Computed on the basis of the censuses in 1971 and 1981.
[32] On this topic see for instance Jovanovic (2014, 30 et seq.).

appeal, particularly for those segments of the population that were most exposed to the effects of socio-economic modernisation.

This development should be seen from the perspective offered by some scholars, which argues that, while giving up on crafting a single national identity, Yugoslavia's communist authorities based their nationality policies on the ideological assumption that socio-economic modernisation of the country, and the accompanying subprocesses of urbanisation, mass education and the emancipation of women, would weaken the political force of nationalism and ultimately result in strengthening the sense of Yugoslav unity (Sekulić et al. 1994). Following this stream of logic, the idea of Yugoslav unity was built not upon the images of a common ethnic origin or past, but was related to the future that Socialist Yugoslavia promised to achieve. It therefore makes sense to argue that the image of a modern, non-national Yugoslavia so clearly expressed in the futurism of the Yugoslav Olympic uniforms was born out of this idea of a pan-Yugoslav future.

Acknowledging this socio-cultural situation makes it difficult to read the focus on technology, futurism and the modernised subnational identities of the country's ethnic groups at the Olympics' opening and closing ceremonies, as solely a diversion in the 'tumultuous period after Tito's death', as D'Agati puts it. Barrie Houlihan (1994, 13) argues in his discussion of the relationship between sport and ideology in authoritarian states that probably its most common element is that sport, in the broadest sociological sense of the term, becomes a vehicle for projecting an image of the state and its political and ideological priorities. Seen from such a perspective, it makes sense to argue that futurism, modernity and updated subnational identities were emphasised at the Olympic ceremonies because they were seen as tools for crafting a sense of Yugoslavness, both at the Olympics and beyond, thereby reflecting the prevailing ideological assumption in Yugoslav society and among the communist authorities that modernity was the solution for the country's 'national question', and not simply a diversion, as D'Agati's analysis implies.

D'Agati's general discussion of identity in Yugoslavia leaves likewise an impression that the author is asserting that Yugoslav identity—whether seen as supranational or transnational—and the country's ethnonational identities were mutually exclusive and that, therefore, a pan-Yugoslav inter-ethnic solidarity and sense of connectedness required a strong single and cohesive pan-Yugoslav national identity. Yet the historical record points very much in the opposite direction, supported by existing research on the topic (Flere 1986, 131–149) that includes an extensive sociological study of 'national identity' among Yugoslav youth carried out by a consortium of Yugoslav sociological institutes in late 1985 and early 1986. Aware of the possible duality, and even multiplicity, of identification, the researchers conducting this study distinguished between what they called 'declared' and 'preferred' nationality in the study's questionnaires. 'Declared' nationality was most commonly seen as the 'objective' national identity inherited from one's parent(s), while 'preferred' nationality corresponded most often to a 'subjectively chosen' (national) identity. The results showed that while 15.6% answered that their 'declared' identification was 'Yugoslav', another 36.2% chose 'Yugoslav' as their 'preferred' national identification.

This situation indicates a fluidity in national identification in the immediate period after the Sarajevo Olympics. Three years earlier, in 1982, when Sarajevo was preparing to host the Games, sociologist Esad Čimić (1982, 74) wrote that Yugoslavism should not be equated merely with people opting for the 'Yugoslav' category in a census. As he argued, some people experienced their Yugoslavness as a common consciousness of belonging to a broader Yugoslav community. Thence, those people felt no need to declare 'Yugoslav' identity because they already saw themselves as Yugoslavs by virtue of being Serbs, Croats, Slovenes, Muslims and so on. *Oslobođenje*'s aforementioned comment on the language of Bojan Križaj's opening speech at the Sarajevo Olympics resonates with Čimić's argument, giving the impression that, by presenting his speech in Slovenian, Križaj in fact was expressing his Yugoslavness.

It is also noteworthy that in his theoretical considerations D'Agati draws attention to the process of re-identifying Yugoslavia as a country of brotherhood and unity that occurred during the Sarajevo Olympics. Yet this was closely related to the cultural reproduction of Sarajevo's image as a miniature Yugoslavia. During the country's socialist period, for a variety of reasons, the Socialist Republic of Bosnia and Herzegovina was, as noted, commonly referred to as 'Yugoslavia on a smaller scale'. The logic behind this drew on the republic's multi-ethnic composition, one that was not dominated by any single nationality, its geographical location in the middle of the country,[33] and finally its being the region of the country

---

[33] In fact, the geographical centre of Yugoslavia was commonly assumed to be in the village of Rakovica in Sarajevo's vicinity (less than 20 km west of the city).

most strongly associated with the NOB, an association that was painstakingly reproduced through Yugoslav popular culture.

As already touched on briefly, in its capacity as Bosnia and Herzegovina's capital and by far its largest city, Sarajevo shared this image of a miniature Yugoslavia. This image was diligently reproduced during the Olympic period. One example of this can be seen in the aforementioned *Borba* article published in the immediate post-Olympic days under the title, 'Oasis of Peace', in which the author argued that Sarajevo was both Yugoslavia 'on a smaller and a larger scale'.[34] A similar example may be found in *Sport*, which, while covering the various cultural events in Sarajevo during the Olympics, claimed that 'Yugoslavia on a smaller scale [is] in every corner [of the city]'.[35] Here, just like in many other cases, the city became the country in miniature or, in Dalibor Mišina's wording (2010, 267), 'Yugoslavia condensed into a single city'. This image was also the most likely reason why it was common practice in the Bosnian-Herzegovinian newspapers to present Sarajevo and Yugoslavia as having the same agency in the Olympic period, leaving Bosnia and Herzegovina out of contention and linking Sarajevo directly to Yugoslavia. This was most notably the case in the majority of official documents about the Olympics, when a frequently used formula was 'Sarajevo—Yugoslavia', although the triptych 'Sarajevo, Bosnia and Herzegovina and Yugoslavia' also appeared (Moll 2015, 132).

It is not unimportant that this Yugoslav dimension of the Olympics was not only promoted by the central Yugoslav authorities, but also, and even more eagerly, by the Olympic Organising Committee, which was, as we saw, largely consisting of persons from Bosnia and Herzegovina, and which emphasised that Sarajevo organised the Olympics 'as a representative of entire Yugoslavia', as Nicolas Moll puts it (2015, 132). This kind of representation came to fruition in the 'KUN' article 'Open to All Sides of the World' discussed in the previous chapter. Published approximately twenty months before the Olympics, the article (as explained in the previous chapter) analysed the political messages and connotations of the Snowflake symbol—the simple, outward-opening quadratic shape of which, it claimed, stood for Sarajevo's openness to the world. Yet, before drawing this conclusion, the author argued that it was also not without significance to the city of Sarajevo and its ethnonational character. Rather,

---

[34] Zoran Mandžuka, 'Oaza mira', *Borba* 21.2.1984, 2.
[35] V. Kočović, 'Za svačiji merak,' *Sport*, 2.2.1984, 10.

the Snowflake emphasised the universalist character of the city, its republic Bosnia and Herzegovina and Yugoslavia as a whole, where people of different religious and ethnic affiliations lived side by side in unity.[36]

We saw in the previous chapter that Olympic success provided Yugoslavia and Sarajevo with an opportunity—a symbolic power—to present themselves as the ideal Olympic hosts, meaning that, in the Yugoslav press, Sarajevo and Yugoslavia were equated with the Olympic ideology. This came as a culmination of the process that had already started during the Olympic preparation period. In the example from 'KUN', we see that, by constructing Yugoslavia as a 'natural' Olympic host nation, it was simultaneously re-identified as a country of brotherhood and unity, which was extrapolated from Sarajevo to Yugoslavia in a rather interesting way, once again reflecting the city's image as a miniature Yugoslavia. This is also the point made by Pedrotty in her article. I will however go even further and suggest—in line with D'Agati's argument that due to their festival nature the Olympics inevitably have the power to affect culture and cultural understandings (D'Agati 2011, 5)—that the 1984 Winter Olympics caused further proliferation of this image—and on several levels.

In this respect, reviewing the city's and Yugoslav press' writings about the official cultural events happening in Sarajevo during the Olympics (different exhibitions, concerts, theatre & ballet performances etc.) imply that they often had a pronouncedly pan-Yugoslav focus and pan-Yugoslav character. Hence, as for instance Divna Pervan wrote in 'KUN' on the opening day for the Olympics, in the musical sense the languages and styles of all Yugoslav national groups were to be represented in the Olympic musical programmes.[37] It is as well noteworthy that Yugoslav news agencies—in, as we have seen, an otherwise strongly decentralised Yugoslav media space—agreed jointly to cover the Sarajevo Olympics, taking ownership and responsibility for different Olympic press centres during the Games event. Artists and cultural workers from all over the country followed the same path, having for instance their paintings and sculptures displayed at the newly opened Olympic Museum. Finally, the National theatres from Sarajevo, Belgrade and Zagreb jointly produced a ballet for the Olympic

---

[36] Radomir Vuković, 'Simbol i znak. Otvoren za sve strane svijeta', *Oslobođenje—kulturni dodatak 'KulturaUmjetnostNauka'* 50, 29.5.1982, 1.

[37] Divna    Pervan,    'Jezik    svih    naroda',    *Oslobođenje—kulturni    dodatak 'KulturaUmjetnostNauka'* 8.2.1984, 7.

audience (and in continuation of that planned on touring Yugoslavia in the immediate aftermath of the Olympics).[38]

Having shown these examples, I will nevertheless underline that this was neither an exception for the Sarajevo Olympics nor something odd in the Yugoslav context. Jasenko Zekić's work on the 1987 Zagreb Universiade, occurring some three-and-a-half years after the Sarajevo Olympics, shows the same development in the Croatian capital city in relation to the city's position as host city of that event. This is arguably also the reason why Zekić (2007) chose to call his article, 'The 1987 Universiade—The Second Illyrian Coming' (Univerzijada '87—drugi ilirski preporod), clearly referring to the Illyrian movement, an intellectual movement in the Croatia of the 1830s and 1840s, from which the idea of Yugoslav unity would subsequently develop.[39] During the Olympics in Sarajevo *Oslobođenje* quite explicitly pursued the narrative of Yugoslav unity, when it more than once explained to its readership how Vučko, the Olympic mascot, was designed by a Slovene, the Olympic symbol, Snowflake, by a Sarajevan, the Olympic pictograms by a Belgrader and finally 'the Olympic cantata' by a composer from Zagreb.[40]

Even on a rather banal level, activities like opening restaurants or serving food from different parts of the country, very common during the Sarajevo Olympics, had the potential to strengthen both the world's and Sarajevans' feeling that the city was 'a miniature Yugoslavia'. For the event and 'the Olympics guests' a broad variety of food and specialties from all Yugoslav regions was secured; whether it was by offering 'cheeses from six different Yugoslav regions',[41] or preparing individual restaurants to be able to serve food from 'the Bosnian-Herzegovinian, the Serbian, the Slovenian, Zagorje and the Dalmatian cuisine' (to offer just a couple of examples).[42]

The historical record from the immediate post-Olympic period indicates that this practice and the official, pronouncedly pro-Yugoslavian, Olympic discourse had a strong potential to substantially influence

---

[38] Branka Miličević-Mašić, 'Svijetla obraza svijetu (Olimpijada zajedništva)', *Oslobođenje Nedjelja* 7.1.1984, 9.

[39] On this issue see Dejan Djokić, 'Introduction: Histories, Myths, Concepts,' in *Yugoslavism. History of a Failed Idea*. Ed. Djokić, Dejan. (London: Hurst and Company, 2003).

[40] Branka Miličević-Mašić, 'Svijetla obraza svijetu (Olimpijada zajedništva)', *Oslobođenje Nedjelja* 7.1.1984, 9.

[41] G. Logar, 'Sarajevski meni za "džet-set" društvo', *Borba* 19.1.1984, 10.

[42] E. Isaković, 'I ručak uz muziku', *Oslobođenje* 21.4.1982, 9. NB: Zagorje is a cultural region in northern Croatia, not far from the capital Zagreb.

Sarajevans' self-representation and self-knowledge. Thus, approximately two years after the Olympics, in 1986, this discourse got its pop musical expression in the lyrics of a very popular song, 'Entire Yugoslavia One Courtyard' (*Cijela Juga jedna avlija*) by the local band Merlin.[43] In very cosmopolitan language the song linked a series of Yugoslav cities to a united Yugoslavia and then, by stressing the inter-ethnic coexistence in their own city, Sarajevo, left the impression that Sarajevo and Yugoslavia were bringing not only Yugoslavia, but the whole world together: 'Belgrade is dancing, Novi Sad is dancing/Tuzla, Sombor, Zagreb, Titograd/entire Yug(oslavi)a one courtyard/Serbs, Bosnians, Blacks and Albanians/were never strangers in my city' (Merlin 1986).

The 1984 Winter Olympics, it could therefore be argued, sparked a pronounced sense of Yugoslavness in Sarajevo—a trait that characterised the city in the 1980s. Throughout Yugoslavia's socialist era, Sarajevo had always had the image of being one of the most Yugoslav cities in the country. Yet, with the rise of ethnonationalism across the country in the 1980s, this image became even more pronounced, due to the opposite trend in other major Yugoslav cities.[44] In line with this, research on the topic implies that, in the immediate post-Olympic years, the city's youth culture was very vocal and even bold about its pro-Yugoslav orientation (Levi 2007; Mišina 2010). As Croatian journalist and cultural critic Ante Perković (2011, 37) wrote in his book on Yugoslav and post-Yugoslav rock music culture, during these years, Sarajevo pop and rock bands linked Yugoslavia to different themes in their songs in ways that were borderline bizarre. However, and as I have argued elsewhere (Jovanovic 2017, 767–768), the fact that it made sense for these bands to bring Yugoslavia-related issues into their music, even their love songs, says a great deal about the sense of Yugoslavness in Sarajevan youth culture in the mid-1980s. This makes it possible to argue that the city's youth culture was, to a substantial degree, defined by its *banal Yugoslavism*, in political theorist

---

[43] The name Merlin alludes to Marilyn Monroe, as Merlin stands for the Serbo-Croatian transliteration of the actress's name. This is expressed on the cover of Merlin's debut album, which juxtaposed a picture of Marilyn Monroe and the first half of the title, *It is Difficult with You*, on the front and the picture of young female Partisan hero Marija Bursać and the second half of the title, *but Even More So without You*, on the back.

[44] Hence, for instance, while elsewhere in Yugoslavia the fandom in especially football became more and more closely interconnected with nationalism in the late 1980s, in Sarajevo the members of 'Horde Zla' (The Evil Hordes), supporters of FC Sarajevo, still as late as in December 1990 proudly emphasised their Yugoslavness and their Yugoslav orientation (Neven Anđelić, 'Iz drugog ugla: "Horde zla" - "Furamo se na jugoslovenstvo"', *Ven*, December 1990).

Michael Billig's sense of the term 'banal nationalism'. It is nevertheless important to keep in mind that these pronounced feelings were by no means confined to the city's youth culture. As Dalibor Mišina (2010, 267) observes, Sarajevo was commonly viewed as being 'Yugoslavia condensed into a single city' and considered a model of what the whole country was supposed to be: multicultural, open, and unsuspicious of 'others'.

A number of media outlets in the city also emerged as some of the most pro-Yugoslav in the country. According to *Polet*'s Hajrudin Redžović, 'due to the multiethnic composition of Bosnia and Herzegovina, which doomed Sarajevan journalists to a Yugoslav orientation' Sarajevo's journalism was regarded as the most objective in Yugoslavia at the end of the 1980s.[45] With the rise of new ethnonationalist dogmas and nationalist exclusiveness, the Yugoslav orientation meant that Sarajevan journalism became the most open to integrating different views. This understanding of pro-Yugoslav orientation corresponds very closely with the concept of Yugoslavness utilised by anthropologist Stef Jansen in his work on antinationalism and cosmopolitanism in post-Yugoslavia. Jansen argues that Yugoslavness could best be understood as a discursive space with a distinct, diverse, open character. According to Jansen (2009, 80), this Yugoslavness was not necessarily openly 'Yugoslavist' but rather more about open interethnic boundaries, often assuming a pronouncedly tolerant, anti-nationalist and cosmopolitan form. Understood this way, Yugoslavness becomes the opposite of nationalist segregation and exclusiveness.

The Yugoslavness of Sarajevo's media space was demonstrated by the case of YUTEL (short for Yugoslav Television). Conceived as a pan-Yugoslavian TV channel, YUTEL was initiated by the country's last Prime Minister Ante Marković. It was transmitted from Sarajevo and not from the federal capital Belgrade, as might have been expected. Established in 1990, the concept behind YUTEL's programming was to show different points of view, thereby fighting the nationalist atomisation that was taking place in Yugoslav media space (Kurspahić 2003, 56–59). Transmitting until the start of the war in Sarajevo in April 1992, YUTEL is today best remembered for the big peace concert the channel organised in Sarajevo on 28 July 1991, called 'YUTEL for Peace' (YUTEL *za mir*). With strong, if unintended, symbolism, the concert took place in the Olympic Hall Zetra. It was supposed to be transmitted live to the whole country, but

---

[45] Hajrudin Redžović, 'Sarajevski Omladinski radio: pogled iz bliza. Mujo kuje mali megaherz', *Polet* 413, 29.9.1989, 20.

could in the end only be watched by audiences in Bosnia and Herzegovina and Macedonia, as the political and media leaderships in other republics refused to broadcast it. Some of the most notable participants from Sarajevo were Crvena jabuka, Plavi orkestar, Hari Mata Hari, Merlin, Goran Bregović of Bijelo dugme and several leading protagonists of the subcultural movement of New Primitivism, including the singer of Zabranjeno pušenje, Dr Nele Karajlić. It was part of a larger anti-war movement active in Bosnia in the period from the outbreak of the war in Croatia in June 1991 until war spread to Bosnia some nine months later. The anti-war movement was whole-heartedly supported by the Sarajevan media, which provided space for anti-war messages offered by well-known cultural personalities from Sarajevo, and covered the movement's activities. During those nine months, a number of big peace rallies were organised across Bosnia and Herzegovina, attracting tens of thousands of participants in different Bosnian-Herzegovinian cities and towns.[46] Mostly ignored by the Western media, the movement reached its zenith at the beginning of March 1992, when, according to Belgrade sociologist Dušan Janjić (1992, 281), large demonstrations in Sarajevo forced nationalist leaders to call off the planned beginning of the war. However, soon after the more than three-year long merciless bombardment and the destruction of the city started, and the Holliday Inn, Trebević and Zetra became globally associated with the war—the image that these Olympic venues paradoxically were supposed, once and forever, to erase.

## Bibliography

### Books, Articles, Reports, Blogs and Websites

Baumann, Gerd. 1999. Culture: Having, Making, or Both? In *The Multicultural Riddle, Rethinking National, Ethnic, and Religious Identities*, 81–96. New York: Routledge.

Bojičić, Vesna. 1996. The Disintegration of Yugoslavia: Causes and Consequences of Dynamic Inefficiency in Semi-command Economies. In *Yugoslavia and After, a Study in Fragmentation, Despair and Rebirth*, ed. David A. Dyker and Ivan Vejvoda, 28–47. London: Longman.

---

[46] For more on the movement see Steven L. Burg & Paul S. Shoup, 'The Descent into War' in *The War in Bosnia-Herzegovina: Ethnic conflict and international intervention* (M.E. Sharpe, London 2000), 62–127.

Bourdieu, Pierre. 1977. Structures, Habitus and Practices. In *Outline of a Theory of Practice*, 78–87. Cambridge: Cambridge University Press.

Brubaker, Rogers. 1996. Nationhood and the National Question in the Soviet Union and Its Successor States: An Institutionalist Account. In *Nationalism Reframed: Nationhood and the National Question in the New Europe*, 23–54. Cambridge: Cambridge University Press.

———. 2004. Ethnicity without Groups. In *Ethnicity without Groups*, 7–27. Cambridge, MA: Harvard University Press.

Burg, Steven L., and Michael L. Berbaum. 1989. Community, Integration, and Stability in Multinational Yugoslavia. *The American Political Science Review* 83 (2): 535–554.

Ceribašić, Naila. 1998. Heritage of World War II in Croatia: Identity Imposed Upon and by Music. In *Music, Politics, and War: Views from Croatia*, ed. Svanibor Pettan, 109–129. Zagreb: Institute of Ethnology and Folklore Research.

Čimić, Esad. 1982. *Politika kao sudbina: prilog fenomenologiji političkog stradalništva*. Beograd: Mladost.

D'Agati, Philip A. 2011. *Nationalism on the World Stage. Cultural Performance and the Olympic Games*. Lanham, MD: University Press of America.

Donia, Robert J. 2006. *Sarajevo. A Biography*. Ann Arbor: University of Michigan Press.

Duda, Dean. 2006. 'Užas je moja furka': Socijalistički urbani imaginarij Branimira Štulića. In *Devijacije i promašaji. Etnografija domaćeg socijalizma*, ed. Lada Čale Feldman and Ines Prica, 95–120. Zagreb: Institut za etnologiju i folkloristiku.

Flere, Sergej. 1986. Odnos mladih prema etnosu. In *Položaj, svest i ponašanje mlade generacije Jugoslavije. Preliminarna analiza razultata istraživanja*. Ed. Srđan Vrcan et al., 131–149. Beograd-Zagreb: IDIS.

———. 2005. The Atheist Civil Religion in Communist Yugoslavia: The Broken Convent of Tito's People. *Jahrbuch für Historische Kommunismusforschung Enthält* 18: 216–232.

———. 2007. The Broken Covenant of Tito's People: The Problem of Civil Religion in Communist Yugoslavia. *East European Politics and Societies* 21 (4): 681–703.

Fry, John. 1984. Gold Medal Picks. *Ski*, February 1984, 40.

Gordy, Eric D. 1999. *The Culture of Power in Serbia: Nationalism and the Destruction of Alternatives*. University Park, PA: Pennsylvania State University Press.

Goulding, Daniel J. 2002 [1985]. *Liberated Cinema. The Yugoslav Experience, 1945–2001*. Bloomington, IN: Indiana University Press.

Houlihan, Barrie. 1994. *Sport and International Politics*. Hemel Hempstead: Harvester Wheatsheaf.

Janjić, Dušan. 1992. Civil War and Possibilities for Peace in Bosnia and Herzegovina. In *Ex-Yugoslavia: From War to Peace*, ed. Randha Kumar and Josep Palau, 267–303. Madrid: Generalitat Valenciana.

Jansen, Stef. 2009. Cosmopolitan Openings and Closures in Post-Yugoslav Antinationalism. In *Cosmopolitanism in Practice*, ed. Magdalena Nowicka and Maria Rovisco, 75–92. Farnham, England and Burlington, VT: Ashgate.

Johnson, Vida T. 2009. From Yugoslav Cinema to New Serbian Cinema. *KinoKultura* (Special Issue 8: Serbian Cinema) http://www.kinokultura.com/specials/8/serbian.shtml.

Jovanovic, Zlatko. 2014. *'All Yugoslavia Is Dancing Rock and Roll'. Yugoslavness and the Sense of Community in the 1980s Yu-Rock*. PhD Thesis, Faculty of Humanities, University of Copenhagen.

———. 2017. The 1984 Sarajevo Winter Olympics and Identity-Formation in Late Socialist Sarajevo. *The International Journal of the History of Sport* 34 (9): 767–782.

Jović, Dejan. 2001. The Disintegration of Yugoslavia. A Critical Review of Explanatory Approaches. *European Journal of Social Theory* 4 (1): 101–120.

Kamberović, Husnija. 2018. Džemal Bijedić i afirmacija muslimanske nacije tokom 1960-ih i 1970-ih godina. *Yu historija*. http://www.yuhistorija.com/serbian/jug_druga_txt01c8.html.

Klanjšek, Rudi, and Sergej Flere. 2011. Exit Yugoslavia: Longing for Mononational States or Entrepreneurial Manipulation? *Nationalities Papers: The Journal of Nationalism and Ethnicity* 39 (5): 791–810.

Kurspahić, Kemal. 2003. *Prime Time Crime: Balkan Media in War and Peace*. Washington, DC: USIP Press.

Lampe, John R. 1996. *Yugoslavia as History: Twice There Was a Country*. Cambridge: Cambridge University Press.

Levi, Pavle. 2007. *Disintegration in Frames: Aesthetics and Ideology in the Yugoslav and Post-Yugoslav Cinema*. Stanford, CA: Stanford University Press.

Lilly, Carol S. 2001. *Power and Persuasion: Ideology and Rhetoric in Communist Yugoslavia 1944–1953*. Boulder, CO: Westview Press.

Masia, Seth. 1984. Yugoslavia: First Alpine Nation on Skis. *Ski*, February 1984, 48.

Matvejević, Predrag. 1982. *Jugoslovenstvo danas: Pitanja kulture*. Zagreb: Globus.

Mišina, Dalibor. 2010. 'Spit and Sing, My Yugoslavia': New Partisans, Social Critique and Bosnian Poetics of the Patriotic. *Nationalities Papers* 38 (2): 265–289.

Moll, Nicolas. 2015. An Integrative Symbol for a Divided Country? Commemorating the 1984 Sarajevo Winter Olympics in Bosnia and Herzegovina from the 1992–1995 War Until Today. *Croatian Political Science Review* 51 (5): 127–156.

Patterson, Patrick Hyder. 2011. *Bought and Sold: Living and Losing the Good Life in Socialist Yugoslavia*. Ithaca and London: Cornell University Press.

Pedrotty, Kate Meehan. 2010. Yugoslav Unity and Olympic Ideology at the 1984 Sarajevo Winter Olympic Games. In *Yugoslavia's Sunny Side: A History of Tourism in Socialism (1950s–1980s)*, ed. Hannes Grandits and Karin Taylor, 333–363. Budapest and New York: CEU Press.

Perica, Vjekoslav. 2002. United We Stand, Divided We Fall. The Civil Religion of Brotherhood and Unity. In *Religion and Nationalism in Yugoslav States*, ed. Balkan Idols, 89–108. Oxford and New York: Oxford University Press.

Perković, Ante. 2011. *Sedma republika. Pop kultura u YU raspadu.* Zagreb-Beograd: Novi liber/Glasnik.

Powell, Stewart. 1984. Winter Olympics' Real Winner Is Sarajevo. *US News & World Report*, February 13, 1984, 35.

Ramet, Pedro. 1984. *Federalism and Nationalism 1963–1983.* Bloomington and Indianapolis: Indiana University Press.

Ramet, Sabrina Petra. 2006. *The Three Yugoslavias: State-Building and Legitimation, 1918–2005.* Washington, DC: Woodrow Wilson Center Press.

Roche, Maurice. 2000. *Mega-events and Modernity: Olympics, Expos and the Growth of Global Culture.* London: Routledge.

Sekulić, Duško, Garth Massey, and Randy Hodson. 1994. Who Were the Yugoslavs? Failed Sources of a Common Identity in the Former Yugoslavia. *American Sociological Review* 59 (1): 83–97.

SSRNBiH (Gradska konferencija SSRNBiH Sarajevo). 1984. *Sarajevo—Olimpijski grad: Ljudi i akcija.* Sarajevo: NIŠRO Oslobođenje.

Tihić, Smail. 1966. *Tourist Guide Through Sarajevo.* Beograd: Turistička štampa.

Tomc, Gregor. 2006. We Will Rock YU. Popular Music in the Second Yugoslavia. In *Impossible Histories, Historical Avant-Gardes, Neo-Avant-Gardes, and Post-Avant-Gardes in Yugoslavia, 1918–1991*, ed. Dubravka Djurić and Miško Šuvaković, 442–465. Cambridge, MA: The MIT Press.

TSOOC: The Sarajevo Organizing Committee of the XIV Olympic Winter Games Yugoslavia. 1984b. *Sarajevo '84. Yugoslavia 8-19.02.* Final Report Published by the Organizing Committee of the XIV Winter Olympic Games 1984 in Sarajevo. Sarajevo: Oslobođenje.

Wachtel, Andrew Baruch. 1998. *Making a Nation, Breaking a Nation: Literature and Cultural Politics in Yugoslavia.* Stanford: Stanford University Press.

Zekić, Jasenko. 2007. Univerzijada '87.—drugi ilirski preporod. *Časopis za suvremenu povijest* 39 (2): 299–318.

RECORDS (DISCOGRAPHY)

Merlin. 1986. Cijela Juga jedna avlija. *Teško meni sa tobom (a još teže bez tebe).* Sarajevo: Diskoton.

# CHAPTER 7

# Conclusion: Sarajevo's Olympic Benchmark

## 7.1 More Than a Sporting Event

As emphasised in the introductory remarks, this book was a goal-specific case study of the 1984 Sarajevo Winter Olympics. Zooming in on the capital of Bosnia and Herzegovina in the period from the mid-1960s through to the mid- to late 1980s, throughout the book I have approached it both as a location and as a trope, telling the story of the great infrastructural, socio-cultural and political transformations occurring in this period—in the city itself, in Yugoslavia and in the global Olympic culture. The then Yugoslav city of Sarajevo, however, formed the core of the study, primarily in terms of the different representations of Sarajevo in the years surrounding the Olympics. With this background in mind, I have carried a number of analyses based on a wide range of primary sources. My point of departure was the hypothesis that Sarajevo has become impossible to imagine without its 'Olympic identity'. In studying this 'Olympic identity', I have directed my analytical focus towards the processes of (re)making the image of Sarajevo in relation to its position as the Olympic host city. Accordingly, in the preceding five chapters I have explored the crafting of different urban, socio-cultural and political (including geopolitical) images of the city in relation to local, national and international developments. In these five chapters I have placed emphasis on the promotion of specific types of desirable self-images of Sarajevo and socialist,

© The Author(s), under exclusive license to Springer Nature Switzerland AG 2021
Z. Jovanovic, *A Cultural History of the 1984 Winter Olympics,
Modernity, Memory and Identity in South-East Europe*,
https://doi.org/10.1007/978-3-030-76598-9_7

self-managing Yugoslavia. Methodologically, the study revolved around a series of representational analyses concerning the tropes and ideas relating to, among other things, the city's cultural *otherness* and emerging environmental sensitivity, consumption-related modernity in socialist, self-managing Yugoslavia, and the pronounced Yugoslav character of Sarajevo. Equally, as we saw in a number of examples, both the city and the country—that is, their elites—put considerable effort into promoting themselves as guarantors of world peace in the troubled times of the late Cold War world.

Although being a goal-specific case study, I have time and again placed the Sarajevo Olympics and the developments in socialist, self-managing and non-aligned Yugoslavia in the context of different global trends, including that of the relationship between the Olympics and modernity. In doing so, my analytical approach was shaped by the theoretical assumption of *intertextuality*, stressing that a text can only communicate its meanings when situated in relation to other texts and to the larger issues, as the meaning of texts always 'arises' between the texts and in particular context. Following this theoretical approach, I let texts and images 'talk to each other' and offered my interpretation of the relation between them.

The analysis has shown that the contemporaneous Sarajevan and Yugoslav press frequently stressed in their writings that the Sarajevo 1984 Winter Olympics were much more than just a sporting event. Political and economic elites, at both the local and the Yugoslav level, as well as tourism promoters in Bosnia and Herzegovina, saw the Sarajevo Olympics as primarily serving economic development. They assumed the Olympic Games event to be an extraordinary opportunity to further develop tourism on all levels, from local Sarajevan to Bosnian-Herzegovinian and Yugoslav. Their ideas and strategies emerged from the suggestion offered in the late 1960s by the transnational intergovernmental economic organisation the OECD. Meanwhile, on the international level, the Yugoslav political establishment also saw the 1984 Winter Olympics as a chance to emphasise the country's geopolitical specificity and strengthen its neutralist position in the bipolar Cold War world of the early 1980s. Concurrently, on the local level, the Olympic Games were associated with several large infrastructural projects and the flourishing youth subcultural scene in the city. Meanwhile, for the city's youth the Olympics became a bearer of their identity, a marker of their sense of belonging to and their identification with the city, that is, their *Sarajevanness*.

## 7.2    Sarajevo Before and After the Olympics

In this monograph's three parts, I have examined what the 1984 Olympics meant for Sarajevo's image in relation to three different dimensions of the event: the local/non-local dimension, the modern/non-modern dimension and the national/non-national dimension. In terms of the local/non-local dimension, detailed examination of different local and global aspects of the Sarajevo Olympics has shown that the logic behind the city's Olympic bid was first and foremost economic. The idea behind the Olympic nomination was inseparably interlaced with the hope for turning Sarajevo into a travel destination, the focal element of which would be winter sports tourism. In relation to this logic, the Sarajevo Olympics became an important temporal reference for local elites and the city's political regime. For the political establishment, the Olympics provided a new direction in the city's development, while members of the local political and economic elites hoped that the Olympics would bring more foreign tourists to the city. Nonetheless, despite the strictly economic logic and strategy, several important cultural ramifications became apparent with the Games. First, its position as Olympic host city provided Sarajevo with an opportunity to (re-)position itself in the world of global intercity comparison and economic competition. In this respect, Olympic preparations became inseparable from the promotion of different positive images of the city, which resulted in some important changes in its representations: for example, in the official tourist monographs. Most notably, in these monographs the city was gradually constructed as a 'natural' winter sports centre.

Second, examination of the debates concerning the desired economic implications of the Olympics demonstrated that they were structured around the assertion that hosting the Olympics was less about the event itself and more about the post-Olympic future. Accordingly, in cultural terms the Olympics announced the beginning of a new, qualitatively different era for the city. Hence, the Olympics emerged as an epoch-making event in the city's development. As we have seen throughout the book, this idea rested mostly on the inherent ability of the Olympic Games to trigger the sense of a break with the past, a sense that was often as much or even more imagined than real. Based on the analyses of the studied source material, I have also suggested that the Olympics became a lens through which the city's youth saw the world around them. Thus, in the everyday lives of young Sarajevans the Olympics became a tool that they could use to position themselves in the popular-cultural space of Yugoslavia and the world. In continuation of that, as the analysis has shown, despite being about economics, the Olympics—and the Olympic period as such—emerged as an inescapable temporal and cultural reference point in the city.

Third, when examining the cultural implications of the relationship between Olympic universalism and Sarajevo's uniqueness, I found out that, despite being a global event, the Olympics made the local population and urban elites more aware of local peculiarities and the city's distinctiveness. In this situation some interesting ideas about the city's Ottoman past surfaced and came to play a rather important role in this regard. One of my main conclusions on this issue was that through this process the image of the city's *otherness* and *Ottomanness* was turned from a perceived disadvantage into an asset that could be used for tourism purposes. Once again, as we saw in the analysis, this was not only the case for political and cultural elites, but was also evident in the sphere of youth subcultures. Hence, *Nju primitivizam*, the major subcultural movement that sprung up in Sarajevo during the Olympic preparation period, readily appropriated the city's cultural particularity and included it into the repertoire, positioning itself, from the perspective of their city's position as Olympic host city, vis-à-vis the cultural scenes in other major cultural centres in the country.

In relation to the modern/non-modern dimension of the Olympics, we saw how bidding for, and then being awarded the right to host the Olympics, helped unleash different physical and social urban imaginaries in Sarajevo. A number of analysed sources showed that, during the preparations for the Olympics event, rather dramatic changes occurred in representations and self-representations of Sarajevo. Most notably, the Olympics made it possible for the city to re-imagine itself and construct a (self-)image as a particularly environmentally progressive city. The environment and *the greening* of the city became some of the most central themes of the Olympic discourse. It is in this context important to repeat, in line with findings more generally, that this reflects the general assumption that the Olympics constituted a major break in Sarajevo's history, almost creating two different cities: one pre-Olympic and one (post-)Olympic. I have nevertheless argued that, despite this general assumption and the fact that this development was closely associated with the Olympics, the Games themselves did not cause or initiate it, but rather enhanced it, making it more marked and urgent.

The analysis further showed that while the city's elites and political leadership saw the Olympics as an opportunity for important infrastructural renovations and enormous environmental improvements in the city, they also stressed that these projects were only one side of the necessary prerequisites for the Games' ultimate success. They argued that in order for the success to be complete, the host city's populace also had to improve and modernise their social conduct. In other words, the elites asserted that it was not enough just to make Sarajevo modern for the Olympics, its inhabitants must also change. Only then, they believed, could Sarajevans become 'proper hosts for the Olympics'. As we saw, to this end, in 1983, the city's leading daily newspaper, *Oslobođenje*, launched a project, lasting more than six months, during which it took the central role in inculcating the residents with desirable forms of social behaviour, or, to put it more bluntly, in *disciplining* them for the Olympics.

In relation to the modernity dimension of the Sarajevo Olympics, I have as well paid considerable attention to Socialist Yugoslavia's consumer culture as a benchmark and proof of its modernity. In this regard, I stressed the ever-present notion and self-understanding in the Balkans and Eastern Europe of a need to economically and culturally successfully catch up to the West. As in the rest of the book, the analysis was placed in a global context. Accordingly, in the context of global Capitalist system I emphasised the similarities and differences both across and within communist East and capitalist West. As we saw, sources frequently excluded Yugoslavia from the communist world. Likewise, for instance in terms of Olympic financing, Yugoslavia had more in common with most Olympic host countries in the West, than those same countries had in common with the USA. This was particularly the case in that the Games' financing was carried out on the basis of contracts with different Yugoslav and international sponsors and the sale of TV rights to Western broadcasting companies.

Another interesting finding in this respect was that the Sarajevo Olympics disclosed some important generational differences in the city. In the emergent Olympic discourse, young people in general were perceived as primary agents of change and modernisation. In the globally emerging neoliberal language of 'entrepreneurship', the Yugoslav media began to depict Sarajevan youth as an entrepreneurial and business-minded generation, counterposing the new Sarajevan generations to the presumably dominant Balkan and Ottoman economic 'traditionalisms' and the backward character of the city prior to the Olympics. In this way, Sarajevo's peculiarities could at one and the same time be seen as an asset and as a disadvantage in the global(ising) tourism competition.

Finally, in relation to the national/non-national dimension of the Olympics, the analysis has shown that on the international level Yugoslavia found the Olympics a valuable tool in attempting to establish its international leadership based on its position as one of the leaders of the Non-Aligned Movement. The analysis further showed that in a period of rising East-West tensions in the post-*Détente* years of the late 1970s and early 1980s, non-aligned Yugoslavia's political elites stressed that it was not a coincidence that Yugoslavia was hosting the Olympics. Rather, they argued, this position rested on the fact of Yugoslavia being a particularly peace-loving country in these troubling years. Arguing further that the Olympic movement was closely associated with peace, they presented the country as 'the best possible Olympic host'; an image that was equally promoted by the Yugoslav media, by the country's and the city's local political leaderships and by the Olympic Organising Committee. Stressing the newly won international recognition of the country's neutralist policies during the immediate pre-Games period, they claimed Sarajevo and Yugoslavia to be not only an ideal but even a 'natural' Olympic host.

As we saw in the first chapter of Part III (which dealt with this topic), this image of Yugoslavia as a particularly peace-loving nation and the ideal and natural Olympic host was frequently used to counterpose the previously dominant image of Sarajevo as the city in which the shooting of Archduke Ferdinand in 1914 allegedly initiated WWI. Emerging from the new Olympic discourse was an image of Sarajevo as an oasis of peace in the period of renewed Cold War tensions; the period sometimes called 'the Second Cold War'. In the re-making of the image of Sarajevo, the Olympic Organising Committee chose 'the Snowflake' as the Olympic symbol; a shape designed to stress Sarajevo's and Yugoslavia's supposed cosmopolitanism and openness to all sides of the world. In crafting this image, Sarajevan and Yugoslav media several times aligned Olympic Sarajevo with other Olympic host cities, such as Athens, Los Angeles and not least the Austrian city of Innsbruck. When doing this, the media usually pointed out friendship between the past and present Olympic cities, localising different *agents of Olympism* in these cities. In doing so, they implicitly emphasised Sarajevo's multi-ethnic character, cosmopolitanism and openness.

Exploring the nationality dimension of the Olympics, the monograph's final chapter examined the cultural ramifications of processes of re-identification of the host society's ideological priorities, highlighting the specifically Yugoslav relationship between modernity and national identities in the country. As we saw, the Olympics provided an opportunity—most notably at the Olympic opening and closing ceremonies—to perform Yugoslavia and the Yugoslavness of Sarajevo. In this regard, I have argued that this was carried out very much in line with the official nationality policies which prioritised the notion of 'unity in diversity' and its ideological axiom of 'brotherhood and unity' among different Yugoslav peoples over the need to craft a common Yugoslav national identity. In this situation, according to the analysed sources, during the process of inventing Sarajevo's Olympic and winter sports traditions, the organisers sought to enhance a sense of their multicultural pan-Yugoslav character, in accordance with the official nationality policies of brotherhood and unity. In accordance with these policies all the specific characteristics of the different regions and national groups of Yugoslavia were presented as belonging to all the peoples of the country in common. The result thereof was, as we saw, a strengthening of the image of Sarajevo as a truly Yugoslav city. This development proved to be particularly important for the post-Olympic period, in which the city's pronounced Yugoslavness was emphasised time and again, at the time Yugoslavia started experiencing the rise of ethnonationalism among its peoples. The infrastructural works and related investments in the city in relation to hosting of the Olympics also had an important impact on the city and its pronounced Yugoslav image. This development was momentous because, as several scholars—to whose works I referred throughout the chapter—have argued, Yugoslavia's subsequent dissolution was closely related to the economic crisis of the 1980s. According to this argument, the crisis weakened the sense of unity in Yugoslavia. Seen from this perspective, the Olympics had a substantial potential to postpone the sense of the crisis in the city, thereby prolonging Sarajevo's 'love for Yugoslavia' and, consequently, contributing to Sarajevo in several ways appearing as 'the last leftover oasis of Yugoslavia' in the early 1990s.

These findings from the book's three parts and five chapters indicate that the Olympics created the impression that there were *two Sarajevos*: one that existed before the city won its bid for the 1984 Winter Olympic Games and another that emerged with the Olympics. As we have seen in a number of examples, the Olympic period was in Sarajevo regarded as being radically beyond and qualitatively different from the pre-Olympic one. This view was also voiced by the then President of the IOC, Juan Antonio Samaranch. According to the *Christian Science Monitor*, a couple of days after the Sarajevo Games finished Samaranch contended that from then on 'the history of Sarajevo [would] be spoken of as before or after the XIV Winter Olympics' (Atkin 1984). In other words, the Olympics emerged as an important temporal and cultural reference point for the city. This was so not least in respect of the city's aforementioned youth subcultures, but also in more general cultural representations and the common understanding of Olympic economics.

### 7.3    THE URBAN DIMENSION OF THE SARAJEVO OLYMPICS: LOCAL AND GLOBAL TRENDS

As argued in the introduction, Olympic events have an important urban dimension and serve as catalysts of urban change. Not least in terms of financial outcomes and economic after-effects; legacies in architecture, facilities and infrastructures relating to sport, communication, transport and housing; and impacts on tourism and city image. The urban dimension of the late twentieth-century Olympic Games that Maurice Roche talks about in his discussion on the topic have substantially contributed to the broader urban social and economic policies of their host cities (Roche 2000, 138–143). This was, as this volume's analysis has clearly shown, also the case in Olympic Sarajevo. As we saw throughout this study, local planners, tourism promoters and political elites in Sarajevo were all from the very beginning well aware of the urban dimensions of the late twentieth-century Olympic games events. In his broader argumentation concerning the Olympics in general, Roche argues that, while the Olympic Games events derive their income from various sources, since the mid-1980s, selling the rights to transmit the Games to American and other regional TV companies has provided a large share of Olympic funding. As we saw, Sarajevo was exemplary in this regard, with a large percentage of Olympic financing coming from a single source, the US TV giant, ABC. Money for the Olympics, Roche further suggests, also came from corporate sponsorship, ticket sales, lotteries and through taxes and the public sector. In Sarajevo, the introduction of extra taxes served to finance infrastructural improvement, the lottery was an element in financing plans from the beginning, and the sponsorship of domestic and international corporations made considerable contributions. The economic impact of the Sarajevo Olympics also featured in the creation of short- and long-term employment for the local and national population, creating several thousand jobs in the crisis-ridden Yugoslav economy of the early 1980s.

In terms of the events' urban dimension, according to Roche, though costly, and commonly financed through taxes and public funding, the broader infrastructural spending on transport, housing and communication involved in staging the events often substantially improved the infrastructural situation of host cities. Furthermore, the construction or reconstruction of Olympic venues, such as the main stadiums and complexes, produced important architectural heritage for the host cities, with the sports venues sometimes becoming recognisable international symbols of the host cities. The Sarajevo Olympics confirmed this rule too. The so-called Project for Environmental Protection, which was commonly seen as a precondition for Sarajevo's Olympic nomination, already completely changed the city. With the completion of the project, many of the long-standing problems with sewage and air and water pollution were reduced. In that way, the Olympics made it possible to solve some problems predating even the idea of Olympic nomination. As we further saw in the analysis, infrastructural projects relating directly to the Olympics also had a strong urban impact on the city. So strong that some sources claimed that they made the city almost unrecognisable. For instance, the tram transportation was modernised, and trolleybuses introduced into the city; new roads were built, the train station and the airport expanded, and the 'Olympic mountains' in the city's vicinity were connected with the urban centre. At the same time, the Olympic Hall Zetra and its outdoor speed skating ring became synonymous with Sarajevo's Olympic heritage.

Besides these infrastructural impacts, Roche (2000, 138–140) stresses that different studies of the Olympics' urban dimension have demonstrated that building the facilities and complexes often had strong social impacts. For example, the Olympics have a pronounced effect on the housing market, either positively due to facilities, such as Olympic villages, providing new apartments, or more negatively as the Olympic infrastructure and facilities affected housing markets and land value. In some cases, the construction of facilities even led to housing relocation because of the compulsory purchase of land for clearance and building. In Sarajevo, the Olympics resulted in several thousand new apartments for Sarajevans, at a time of harsh public expenditure cuts all over the country. The Olympic villages of Mojmilo and Dobrinja became new urban neighbourhoods connected to the city centre by modern means of transportation, and quickly turned into sought-after city districts. That said, this development came at a cost for some, as the original village of Dobrinja had to be cleared to make space for the new apartment buildings. Ultimately, however, the general feeling was—as the *Christian Science Monitor* had it in its early post-Olympic issue—that the city 'leaped years ahead with new roads and buildings' (Atkin 1984).

Roche (2000, 140) has additionally pointed out that one of the main impacts the Olympic Games are assumed to have on their host cities is the short- and long-term economic effect on the inflow of domestic and foreign tourists. The number of overnight stays in Sarajevo more than doubled in the ten-year period from 1975 to 1984 (Bertić 1987, 86). Besides, according to some arguments proposed in the analysis (cf. Pedrotty 2010, 358), the Sarajevo Olympics contributed to a rise in tourist numbers in Yugoslavia more broadly, something that also happened in other places—most notably in South Korea after the 1988 Seoul Summer Olympics. However, as Roche (2000, 140–141) states with reference to different research on the topic, it is rather difficult to estimate even the short-term net effects of an Olympic event. A rise in tourism, he argues, may also be a result of general development or longer-term strategies that cannot be reduced to the Olympics alone. In Sarajevo's case, we also have to take into account the general socio-economic crisis in Yugoslav society, which affected further investments in tourism promotion so strongly that the number of visitors plummeted in the post-1987 period. Yet, in this respect, we must not fall into what Roche calls the 'short-termism of most studies of the touristic impacts of Olympic events' (Roche: 141). The improved infrastructure and positive media coverage on the global level sometimes have delayed touristic impact. Sarajevo was unfortunate in this regard, as the rise of ethnonationalism in Yugoslavia in the late 1980s, leading to the bloody wars of the 1990s, erased this opportunity for the city and in fact for Yugoslavia as whole.

Finally, and as Roche (2000, 140) also points out, besides the economic and social impacts, the Olympic Games also have important short- and long-term cultural significance for the image of host cities nationally and internationally. According to this argument, the Olympics represent key occasions on which the host cities can construct and present images of themselves on the global stage (D'Agati 2011, 149–161). As we saw, other scholars—most notably John R. Short (2012, 255–256)—have argued that winning the bid for the Olympics in itself is a notable success providing opportunities to market positive images of the host city. However, in order to retain these positive images, the host cities must host Games that are successful from beginning to end. In fact, frequently Olympic events have been remembered negatively. This certainly holds true of the 1972 Munich Summer Olympics due to the killing of Israeli athletes, the 1996 Atlanta Summer Olympics due to the Olympic Park bombings, the 2008 Beijing Summer Olympics due to the bad air quality, the 1980 Lake Placid Winter Olympics due to the traffic chaos, and the 1986 Mexico City and 1988 Seoul Summer Olympics due to the harsh treatment of student demonstrators.

Sarajevo, on the other hand, as, among others, historian Jason Vuic (2015) showed in his work, emerged as an absolute success, transmitting an unequivocally positive image of the city and Socialist Yugoslavia. In fact, the Bosnian capital exceeded all expectations and surprised the world. Accordingly, as we saw in the analysis, Aziz Hadžihasanović from the Sarajevo Olympics Organising Committee and journalists from Sarajevo's leading youth periodical, *Naši dani*, also claimed that, in the face of 'some malicious' reporters, Sarajevo did an excellent job of hosting the Olympics. Finally, also the then President of the IOC, Juan Antonio Samaranch, will be remembered—and equally greatly loved in Sarajevo—for claiming that the Sarajevo Olympics were the best Olympic Games held up to that date, while, according to the *Christian Science Monitor*'s Ross Atkin, the Sarajevo experience helped spark a renewed interest elsewhere in the world in hosting the Winter Games. Atkin recalled how not long before the Sarajevo Olympics basically no one wanted the Games, but after February 1984 at least six communities had already 'thrown their ski hats into the ring for 1992' (Atkin 1984).

Besides being momentous in terms of the re-emergence of the interest in hosting the Winter Olympic Games event, the Sarajevo Games also marked the beginning of the new phase in urban transformation relating to the Winter Olympic Games. As noted in the introduction, arguing that the 1984 Winter Olympic Games became an opportunity to modernise the city of Sarajevo, Stephen Essex and Brian Chalkley (217–223) coined this phase 'large-scale urban transformation'. The widespread impression that preparations for the Games event changed Sarajevo to the extent of being unrecognisable strongly supports Essex's and Chalkley's argument. Conclusively, the conjuncture of the infrastructural transformation of the city and particularities of the historical moment, in which the Olympics were held, turned the 1984 Winter Olympics into an event which is a benchmark in Sarajevo's history. And this is in fact typical of the very process through which Olympic events around the world are becoming markers around which people reflect and periodise their biographies. They do so in the same way as they do in relation to other readily identifiable and memorable public events, such as wars and revolutions; and that is what makes the Olympics relevant to study, despite the fact that they have often been perceived as unimportant, trivial and populist cultural ephemera.

BIBLIOGRAPHY

BOOKS, ARTICLES, REPORTS, BLOGS AND WEBSITES

Atkin, Ross. 1984. Olympics Had Moments of Brilliance Plus a Good Host in Sarajevo. *Christian Science Monitor*, February 21, 1984. https://www.csmonitor.com/1984/0221/022107.html.

D'Agati, Philip A. 2011. *Nationalism on the World Stage. Cultural Performance and the Olympic Games.* Lanham, MD: University Press of America.

Pedrotty, Kate Meehan. 2010. Yugoslav Unity and Olympic Ideology at the 1984 Sarajevo Winter Olympic Games. In *Yugoslavia's Sunny Side: A History of Tourism in Socialism (1950s–1980s)*, ed. Hannes Grandits and Karin Taylor, 333–363. Budapest and New York: CEU Press.

Roche, Maurice. 2000. *Mega-events and Modernity: Olympics, Expos and the Growth of Global Culture.* London: Routledge.

Short, John R. 2012. Globalization, Cities, and the Summer Olympics. In *The Making of Olympic Cities: Critical Concepts in Urban Studies, Volume I: Contexts and Overviews*, ed. John R. Gold and Margaret M. Gold, 235–262. London and New York: Routledge.

*VGAJ ( Veliki geografski atlas Jugoslavije).* 1987. Ed. Ivan Bertić. Zagreb: Liber.

Vuic, Jason. 2015. *The Sarajevo Olympics: A History of the 1984 Winter Olympic Games.* Amherst and Boston: University of Massachusetts Press.

# BIBLIOGRAPHY

## NEWSPAPERS AND JOURNALS REFERENCED

*Borba*
*Duga*
*Naši dani*
*Oslobođenje*
*Polet*
*Politika*
*Sport*
*Start*
*Ven*

## ARCHIVAL MATERIAL

### ARHIV JUGOSLAVIJE

[The Archives of Yugoslavia], Belgrade, Serbia
Jugoslovenski Olimpijski Komitet [Yugoslav Olympic Committee], JOK—832/
    F-10 & JOK—832/F-11.

© The Author(s), under exclusive license to Springer Nature
Switzerland AG 2021
Z. Jovanovic, *A Cultural History of the 1984 Winter Olympics,
Modernity, Memory and Identity in South-East Europe*,
https://doi.org/10.1007/978-3-030-76598-9

## HISTORIJSKI ARHIV SARAJEVO

Izvršno vijeće Skupštine Socijalističke Republike Bosne i Hercegovine [The Executive Council of the Assembly of Bosnia and Herzegovina].
Organizacioni Komitet XIV Zimskih Olimpijskih Igara '84 [The Sarajevo Olympic Organising Committee].
Letters to the Mayor of Sarajevo.
[Sarajevo Historical Archives], Sarajevo, Bosnia and Herzegovina.

## INTERNET PORTALS REFERENCED

Agencija Fena, Otvorena izložba. 2010. Olimpijski umjetnici olimpijskom Sarajevu. June 3, 2010. Accessed November 7, 2020. https://www.sarajevo.ba/en/article/2807/otvorena-izlozba-olimpijski-umjetnici-olimpijskom-sarajevu.
'Dom mladih'. Skederija. Accessed January 12, 2021. https://www.skenderija.ba/index.php/dommladih.
'Gras Sarajevo'. *Wikipedia* https://bs.wikipedia.org/wiki/GRAS_Sarajevo.
Jelin-Dizdar, Tina. 2012. Povratak olimpijskog duha u Sarajevo. *Radio Slobodna Evropa*, December 10, 2012. Accessed February 1, 2021. https://www.slobodnaevropa.org/a/povratak-olimpijskog-duha-u-sarajevo/24794660.html.
'Svečano otvoren EYOF'. 2019. Olimpijski duh se vratio u Sarajevo. *Radio Sarajevo*, February 10, 2019. Accessed February 1, 2021. https://www.radiosarajevo.ba/vijesti/bosna-i-hercegovina/otvoren-eyof-2019-u-sarajevu-nakon-35-godina-zapaljen-olimpijski-plamen/326819.
Tanović, Muamer. 2019. Jure Franko: Život dijelim na onaj prije i onaj poslije Sarajeva '84. *AlJazeera*, February 6, 2019. Accessed February 1, 2021. http://balkans.aljazeera.net/vijesti/jure-franko-zivot-dijelim-na-onaj-prije-i-onaj-poslije-sarajeva-84.

## BOOKS, ARTICLES, REPORTS, BLOGS AND WEBSITES

Abrams, Roger I. 2013. *Playing Tough: The World of Sports and Politics*. Boston, MA: Northeastern University Press.
Anderson, Raymond H. 1972a. Diners Club or Just Dinars, Yugoslav Consumer Is King. *The New York Times*, August 16, 1972. https://www.nytimes.com/1972/08/16/archives/diners-club-or-just-dinars-yugoslav-consumer-is-king.html.
———. 1972b. Yugoslav Enterprise Prospers. *The New York Times*, October 7, 1972, 43. https://www.nytimes.com/1972/10/07/archives/yugoslav-enterprise-prospers-stress-on-efficiency-builds-a.html.

Atkin, Ross. 1984. Olympics Had Moments of Brilliance Plus a Good Host in Sarajevo. *Christian Science Monitor*, February 21, 1984. https://www.csmonitor.com/1984/0221/022107.html.

Barney, Robert Knight, Stephen R. Wenn, and Scott G. Martyn. 2002. Monique Berlioux Zenith: Sarajevo and Los Angeles Television Negotiations. In *Selling the Five Rings. The International Olympic Committee and the Rise of Olympic Commercialism*, ed. Robert Knight Barney, Stephen R. Wenn, and Scott G. Martyn, 181–202. Salt Lake City: University of Utah Press.

Baum, Drago. 2002. *Emerik Blum. Monografija*. Sarajevo: Sahinpašić.

Baumann, Gerd. 1999. Culture: Having, Making, or Both? In *The Multicultural Riddle, Rethinking National, Ethnic, and Religious Identities*, 81–96. New York: Routledge.

Bayly, C.A. 2004. *The Birth of the Modern World 1780–1914. Global Connections and Comparisons*. Malden, MA: Blackwell.

Beattie, Bob. 1984. Sarajevo. A TV Olympics. *Ski*, February 1984, 36.

Berg, Adam P. 2016. *Denver '76: The Winter Olympics and the Politics of Growth in Colorado during the Late 1960s and Early 1970s* (Doctor of Philosophy, The Pennsylvania State University).

Betts, Paul, and Katherine Pence. 2008. Introduction. In *Socialist Modern. East German Everyday Culture and Politics*, ed. Paul Betts and Katherina Pence, 1–34. Ann Arbor: University of Michigan.

Billig, Michael. 2009 [1995]. *Banal Nationalism*. London: Sage.

Blasius, Martin. 2017. FC Red Star Belgrade and the Multiplicity of Social Identifications in Socialist Yugoslavia: Representative Dimensions of the 'Big Four' Football Clubs. *The International Journal of the History of Sport* 34 (9): 783–799.

Bockman, Johanna. 2011. *Markets in the Name of Socialism: The Left-Wing Origins of Neoliberalism*. Stanford, CA: Stanford University Press.

Bojičić, Vesna. 1996. The Disintegration of Yugoslavia: Causes and Consequences of Dynamic Inefficiency in Semi-command Economies. In *Yugoslavia and After, a Study in Fragmentation, Despair and Rebirth*, ed. David A. Dyker and Ivan Vejvoda, 28–47. London: Longman.

Bottici, Chiara. 2007. *A Philosophy of Political Myth*. Cambridge: Cambridge University Press.

Bourdieu, Pierre. 1977. Structures, Habitus and Practices. In *Outline of a Theory of Practice*, 78–87. Cambridge: Cambridge University Press.

Bren, Paulina, and Mary Neuburger. 2012. Introduction. In *Communism Unwrapped: Consumption in Cold War Eastern Europe*, ed. Paulina Bren and Mary Neuburger, 3–19. Oxford: Oxford University Press.

Brentin, Dario. 2013. 'A Lofty Battle for the Nation': The Social Roles of Sport in Tudjman's Croatia. *Sport in Society* 16 (8): 993–1008.

————. 2016. Ready for the Homeland? Ritual, Remembrance, and Political Extremism in Croatian Football. *Nationalities Papers* 44 (6): 860–876.

Brentin, Dario, and Andrew Hodges. 2018. Fan Protest and Activism: Football from Below in South-Eastern Europe. *Soccer and Society* 19 (3): 329–336.

Brubaker, Rogers. 1996. Nationhood and the National Question in the Soviet Union and Its Successor States: An Institutionalist Account. In *Nationalism Reframed: Nationhood and the National Question in the New Europe*, 23–54. Cambridge: Cambridge University Press.

————. 2004. Ethnicity without Groups. In *Ethnicity without Groups*, 7–27. Cambridge, MA: Harvard University Press.

Burg, Steven L., and Michael L. Berbaum. 1989. Community, Integration, and Stability in Multinational Yugoslavia. *The American Political Science Review* 83 (2): 535–554.

Burg, Steven L., and Paul S. Shoup. 2000. The Descent into War. In *The War in Bosnia-Herzegovina: Ethnic Conflict and International Intervention*, 62–127. London: M.E. Sharpe.

Ceribašić, Naila. 1998. Heritage of World War II in Croatia: Identity Imposed Upon and by Music. In *Music, Politics, and War: Views from Croatia*, ed. Svanibor Pettan, 109–129. Zagreb: Institute of Ethnology and Folklore Research.

Chappelet, Jean-Loup. 2012. From Lake Placid to Salt Lake City: The Challenging Growth of the Winter Games Since 1980. In *The Making of Olympic Cities. Critical Concepts in Urban Studies, Volume I: Contexts and Overviews*, ed. John R. Gold and Margaret M. Gold, 74–93. London and New York: Routledge.

Čihák, Jan. 2016. *Tramvaji i trolejbusi / Tramvaje a trolejbusy*. Ústí na Labem: Jan Čihák.

Čimić, Esad. 1982. *Politika kao sudbina: prilog fenomenologiji političkog stradalništva*. Beograd: Mladost.

Čolović, Ivan. 1996. Football, Hooligans and War. In *The Road to War in Serbia: Trauma and Catharsis*, ed. Nebojša Popov, 373–396. Budapest: Central European University Press.

————. 2013. Balkanist Discourse and Its Critics. *Hungarian Review* 4 (2): 70–79. http://www.hungarianreview.com/article/balkanist_discourse_and_its_critics.

Cvek, Sven, Jasna Račić, and Snježana Ivčić. 2019. *Borovo u štrajku: rad u tranziciji 1987–1991*. Zagreb: BRID.

D'Agati, Philip A. 2011. *Nationalism on the World Stage. Cultural Performance and the Olympic Games*. Lanham, MD: University Press of America.

Dabac, Tošo. 1953. Ing. Juraj Neodhardt: Ovako ćemo izgraditi Sarajevo u budućnosti. *Mozaik*, September 1953. http://www.yugopapir.com/2013/08/ing-juraj-neidhardt-ovako-cemo.html.

Djokić, Dejan. 2003. Introduction: Histories, Myths, Concepts. In *Yugoslavism. History of a Failed Idea*, ed. Dejan Djokić, 1–10. London: Hurst and Company.

Donia, Robert J. 2006. *Sarajevo. A Biography*. Ann Arbour: University of Michigan Press.

Duda, Dean. 2006. 'Užas je moja furka': Socijalistički urbani imaginarij Branimira Štulića. In *Devijacije i promašaji. Etnografija domaćeg socijalizma*, ed. Lada Čale Feldman and Ines Prica, 95–120. Zagreb: Institut za etnologiju i folkloristiku.

Duda, Igor. 2017. Everyday Life in Both Yugoslavias. Catching up with Europe. In *Yugoslavia From a Historical Perspective*. Eds. Latinka Perović et al., 391–408. Belgrade: Helsinki Committee for Human Rights in Serbia.

Edwards, Paul N. 2003. Infrastructure and Modernity: Force, Time, and Social Organization in the History of Sociotechnical Systems. In *Technology and Modernity*, eds. Thomas J. Misa, Philip Brey, and Andrew Feenberg, 185–226. Cambridge: MIT Press.

Elias, Norbert. 1994. *The Civilizing Process*. Oxford: Blackwell.

Essex, Stephen, and Brian Chalkley. 1998. Olympic Games: Catalyst of Urban Change. *Leisure Studies* 17 (3): 187–206.

———. 2004. Mega-Sporting Events in Urban and Regional Policy: A History of the Winter Olympics. *Planning Perspectives* 19 (2): 201–232.

Fehérváry, Krisztina. 2013. *Politics in Color and Concrete: Socialist Materialities and the Middle Class in Hungary*. Bloomington and Indianapolis, IN: Indiana University Press.

Flere, Sergej. 1986. Odnos mladih prema etnosu. In *Položaj, svest i ponašanje mlade generacije Jugoslavije. Preliminarna analiza razultata istraživanja*. Ed. Srđan Vrcan et al., 131–149. Beograd-Zagreb: IDIS.

———. 2005. The Atheist Civil Religion in Communist Yugoslavia: The Broken Convent of Tito's People. *Jahrbuch für Historische Kommunismusforschung Enthält* 18: 216–232.

———. 2007. The Broken Covenant of Tito's People: The Problem of Civil Religion in Communist Yugoslavia. *East European Politics and Societies* 21 (4): 681–703.

Flood, Christopher G. 2002. *Political Myth: A Theoretical Introduction*. New York and London: Routledge.

Fry, John. 1984. Gold Medal Picks. *Ski*, February 1984, 40.

Gaudette, Marilyne, Romain Roult, and Sylvain Lefebvre. 2017. Winter Olympic Games, Cities, and Tourism: A Systematic Literature Review in This Domain. *Journal of Sport & Tourism* 21 (4): 287–313.

Gilbert, Andrew. 2017. Tri vjere, jedna nacija, država Tuzla! Football Fans, Political Protest and the Right to the City in Postsocialist Bosnia–Herzegovina. *Soccer & Society* 19: 1–27.

Gordy, Eric D. 1999. *The Culture of Power in Serbia: Nationalism and the Destruction of Alternatives.* University Park, PA: Pennsylvania State University Press.

Goulding, Daniel J. 2002 [1985]. *Liberated Cinema. The Yugoslav Experience, 1945–2001.* Bloomington, IN: Indiana University Press.

Grabrijan, Dušan. 1984. *The Bosnian Oriental Architecture in Sarajevo: With Special Reference to the Contemporary One.* Ljubljana: Tiskarna Tone Tomšič.

Gracyk, Theodore. 2001. *I Wanna be Me: Rock Music and the Politics of Identity.* Philadelphia: Temple University Press.

Hadžihasanović, Aziz. 2010. *1984. Olimpijada trijumfa i šansi.* Sarajevo: Rabic.

Hall, Stuart. 2005. Representation and Media, 6. https://www.mediaed.org.

Harvey, David. 1996. The Cities or Urbanization? *City: Analysis of Urban Trends, Culture, Theory, Policy, Action* 1 (1–2): 38–61.

Hodges, Andrew. 2018. *Fan Activism, Protest and Politics. Ultras in Post-Socialist Croatia.* London: Routledge.

Holubec, Stanislav, Włodzimierz Borodziej, and Joachim von Puttkamer. 2014. Introduction. In *Mastery and Lost Illusions: Space and Time in the Modernization of Eastern and Central Europe,* ed. Włodzimierz Borodziej, Stanislav Holubec, and Joachim von Puttkamer, 1–14. Munich: Walter de Gruyter GmbH.

Houlihan, Barrie. 1994. *Sport and International Politics.* Hemel Hempstead: Harvester Wheatsheaf.

Hughson, John, and Fiona Skillen, eds. 2014. *Football in Southeastern Europe: From Ethnic Homogenization to Reconciliation.* London: Routledge.

Janjetović, Zoran. 2011. *Od 'Internacionale' do komercijale: Popularna kultura u Jugoslaviji 1945–1991.* Beograd: Institut za noviju istoriju Srbije.

Janjić, Dušan. 1992. Civil War and Possibilities for Peace in Bosnia and Herzegovina. In *Ex-Yugoslavia: From War to Peace,* ed. Randha Kumar and Josep Palau, 267–303. Madrid: Generalitat Valenciana.

Jansen, Stef. 2009. Cosmopolitan Openings and Closures in Post-Yugoslav Antinationalism. In *Cosmopolitanism in Practice,* ed. Magdalena Nowicka and Maria Rovisco, 75–92. Farnham, England and Burlington, VT: Ashgate.

Johnson, Vida T. 2009. From Yugoslav Cinema to New Serbian Cinema. *KinoKultura* (Special Issue 8: Serbian Cinema) http://www.kinokultura. com/specials/8/serbian.shtml.

Jokić, Gojko. 1984. Gradovi-Metropole - Sarajevo. In *Čudesna Jugoslavija.* Svjetlost, 250–253.

Jovanovic, Zlatko. 2014. *'All Yugoslavia Is Dancing Rock and Roll'. Yugoslavness and the Sense of Community in the 1980s Yu-Rock.* PhD Thesis, Faculty of Humanities, University of Copenhagen.

———. 2017. The 1984 Sarajevo Winter Olympics and Identity-Formation in Late Socialist Sarajevo. *The International Journal of the History of Sport* 34 (9): 767–782.

Jović, Dejan. 2001. The Disintegration of Yugoslavia. A Critical Review of Explanatory Approaches. *European Journal of Social Theory* 4 (1): 101–120.

———. 2003. Communist Yugoslavia and Its Others. In *Ideologies and National Identities*, ed. John Lampe and Mark Mazower, 277–302. New York, NY: Central European University Press (CEU Press).

Kamberović, Husnija. 2018. Džemal Bijedić i afirmacija muslimanske nacije tokom 1960-ih i 1970-ih godina. *Yu historija*. http://www.yuhistorija.com/serbian/jug_druga_txt01c8.html.

Klanjšek, Rudi, and Sergej Flere. 2011. Exit Yugoslavia: Longing for Mononational States or Entrepreneurial Manipulation? *Nationalities Papers: The Journal of Nationalism and Ethnicity* 39 (5): 791–810.

Klasić, Hrvoje. 2016. The Tito-Stalin Football War. *RADOVI—Zavod za hrvatsku povijest* 48: 387–404.

———. 2017. How Falcons Became Partizans. *The International Journal of the History of Sport* 34 (9): 832–847.

Klumbytè, Neringa, and Gulnaz Sharafutdinova. 2012. Introduction: What Was Late Socialism? In *Soviet Society in the Era of Late Socialism, 1964–1985*, ed. Neringa Klumbytè and Gulnaz Sharafutdinova, 1–14. Lanham, MD: Lexington Books.

Knežević-Čečez, Gordana, Ljiljana Smajlović, and Mirsad Zorabdić. 1984. *Svijet o Sarajevu. Svjetska štampa, televizija i radio o XIV Zimskim Olimpijskim igrama*. Sarajevo: Organizacioni komitet XIV Zimskih Olimpijskih igara Jugoslavija.

Kolanović, Maša. 2011. *Udarnik! Buntovnik? Potrošač...: Popularna kultura i hrvatski roman od socijalizma do tranzicije*. Zagreb: Naklada Lievak.

Kolstø, Pål. 2003. Procjena uloge historijskih mitova u modernism društvima. In *Historijski mitovi na Balkanu*, ed. Husnija Kamberović, 11–37. Sarajevo: Institut za istoriju.

Kostelnik, Branko. 2004. *Moj život je novi val: Razgovori s prvoborcima i dragovoljcima novog vala*. Zaprešić: Fraktura.

Kotnik, Vlado. 2007. Sport, Landscape, and the National Identity: Representations of an Idealized Vision of Nationhood in Slovenian Skiing Telecasts. *Journal of the Society for the Anthropology of Europe* 7: 19–35.

———. 2009. Sport and Nation in Anthropological Perspective: Slovenia as Land of Skiing Nationhood. *Antropologija* 7: 56–78.

Krylova, Anna. 2014. Soviet Modernity: Stephen Kotkin and the Bolshevik Predicament. *Contemporary European History* 23 (2): 167–192.

Kulić, Vladimir. 2014. The Scope of Socialist Modernism: Architecture and State Representation in Postwar Yugoslavia. In *Sanctioning Modernism: Architecture and the Making of Postwar Identities*, ed. Vladimir Kulić, Timothy Parker, and Monica Penick. Austin, TX: University of Texas Press.

Kurspahić, Kemal. 2003. *Prime Time Crime: Balkan Media in War and Peace*. Washington, DC: USIP Press.

Lampe, John R. 1996. *Yugoslavia as History: Twice There Was a Country*. Cambridge: Cambridge University Press.

Levi, Pavle. 2007. *Disintegration in Frames: Aesthetics and Ideology in the Yugoslav and Post-Yugoslav Cinema*. Stanford, CA: Stanford University Press.

Levinston, Charles. 2013. East-West Trade and the Unions. In *International Trade Unionism*, 142–202. London: Routledge.

Liao, Hanwen, and Adrian Pitts. 2006. A Brief Historical Review of Olympic Urbanization. *The International Journal of the History of Sport* 23 (7): 1232–1252.

Ličina Ramić, Aida. 2017. Od ekološke katastrofe do olimpijskog grada—Sarajevo 1971–1984. In *Poplava, zemljotres, smog: prilozi ekohistoriji Bosne i Hercegovine u 20. stoljeću: zbornik radova*, ed. Amir Duranović, 115–147. Sarajevo: Udruženje za modernu historiju/Udruga za modernu povijest (Edicija Zbornici; knj. 3).

Lilly, Carol S. 2001. *Power and Persuasion: Ideology and Rhetoric in Communist Yugoslavia 1944–1953*. Boulder, CO: Westview Press.

Lowinger, Jake. 2011. *Economic Reform and the 'Double Movement' in Yugoslavia: An Analysis of Labor Unrest and Ethno-nationalism in the 1980s*. Charleston (South Carolina, EEUU), ProQuest, UMI Dissertation Publishing.

Luthar, Breda, and Maruša Pušnik. 2010. Introduction: The Lure of Utopia: Socialist Everyday Spaces. In *Remembering Utopia: The Culture of Everyday Life in Socialist Yugoslavia*, ed. Breda Luthar and Maruša Pušnik, 1–33. Washington, DC: New Academia Publishing.

Magaš, Branka. 1993. *The Destruction of Yugoslavia. Tracking the Break-Up 1980–92*. London and New York: Verso.

Masia, Seth. 1984. Yugoslavia: First Alpine Nation on Skis. *Ski*, February 1984, 48.

Matvejević, Predrag. 1982. *Jugoslovenstvo danas: Pitanja kulture*. Zagreb: Globus.

Miljković, Marko. 2017. Blind-Alleys on the Road to Communism: 'Isms' of the Automobile Sport in Socialist Yugoslavia, 1945–1992. *The International Journal of the History of Sport* 34 (9): 815–831.

Mills, Richard. 2009. 'It All Ended in an Unsporting Way': Serbian Football and the Disintegration of Yugoslavia, 1989–2006. *International Journal of the History of Sport* 26: 1187–1217.

———. 2010. Velež Mostar Football Club and the Demise of 'Brotherhood and Unity' in Yugoslavia, 1922–2009. *Europe-Asia Studies* 62 (7): 1107–1133.

———. 2016a. Cold War Football: Soviet Defence and Yugoslav Attack following the Tito–Stalin Split of 1948. *Europe-Asia Studies* 68 (10): 1737–1741.

———. 2016b. The Pitch Itself Was No Man's Land': Siege, Željezničar Sarajevo Football Club and the Grbavica Stadium. *Nationalities Papers* 44 (6): 877–903.

———. 2017. Laying the Foundations of Physical Culture: The Stadium Revolution in Socialist Yugoslavia. *The International Journal of the History of Sport* 34 (9): 729–752.

———. 2018. *The Politics of Football in Yugoslavia: Sport, Nationalism and the State*. London: IB Tauris.

Mišina, Dalibor. 2010. 'Spit and Sing, My Yugoslavia': New Partisans, Social Critique and Bosnian Poetics of the Patriotic. *Nationalities Papers* 38 (2): 265–289.

Moll, Nicolas. 2015. An Integrative Symbol for a Divided Country? Commemorating the 1984 Sarajevo Winter Olympics in Bosnia and Herzegovina from the 1992–1995 War Until Today. *Croatian Political Science Review* 51 (5): 127–156.

Morrison, Kenneth. 2016. *Sarajevo's Holiday Inn on the Frontline of Politics and War*. Palgrave Macmillan.

Nora, Pierre. 1996. General Introduction: Between Memory and History. In *Realms of Memory: The Construction of the French Past*, ed. Pierre Nora. New York: Columbia University Press.

Patterson, Patrick Hyder. 2011. *Bought and Sold: Living and Losing the Good Life in Socialist Yugoslavia*. Ithaca and London: Cornell University Press.

Pedrotty, Kate Meehan. 2010. Yugoslav Unity and Olympic Ideology at the 1984 Sarajevo Winter Olympic Games. In *Yugoslavia's Sunny Side: A History of Tourism in Socialism (1950s–1980s)*, ed. Hannes Grandits and Karin Taylor, 333–363. Budapest and New York: CEU Press.

Perica, Vjekoslav. 2001. United They Stood, Divided They Fell: Nationalism and the Yugoslav School of Basketball, 1968–2000. *Nationalities Papers: The Journal of Nationalism and Ethnicity* 29 (2): 267–291.

———. 2002. United We Stand, Divided We Fall. The Civil Religion of Brotherhood and Unity. In *Religion and Nationalism in Yugoslav States*, ed. Balkan Idols, 89–108. Oxford and New York: Oxford University Press.

Perković, Ante. 2011. *Sedma republika. Pop kultura u YU raspadu*. Zagreb-Beograd: Novi liber/Glasnik.

Petrov, Ana. 2017. How Doing Sport Became a Culture: Producing the Concept of Physical Cultivation of the Yugoslavs. *The International Journal of the History of Sport* 34 (9): 753–766.

Poblocki, Kacper. 2012. 'Knife in the Water' Competitive Consumption in Urbanizing Poland. In *Communism Unwrapped: Consumption in Cold War Eastern Europe*, ed. Paulina Bren and Mary Neuburger, 68–86. Oxford: Oxford University Press.

Pogačar, Martin. 2010. Yugoslav Past in Film and Music: Yugoslav Interfilmic Referentiality. In *Remembering Utopia: The Culture of Everyday Life in Socialist Yugoslavia*, ed. Breda Luthar and Maruša Pušnik, 199–224. Washington, DC: New Academia Publishing.

Powell, Stewart. 1984. Winter Olympics' Real Winner Is Sarajevo. *US News & World Report*, February 13, 1984, 35.

Prohić, Kasim, and Sulejman Balić. 1975. *Sarajevo*. Sarajevo: Turistički savez Sarajevo.

———. 1983. *Sarajevo*. Sarajevo: Turistički savez Sarajevo.

Ramet, Pedro. 1984. *Federalism and Nationalism 1963–1983*. Bloomington and Indianapolis: Indiana University Press.

———. 1985. Apocalypse Culture and Social Change in Yugoslavia. In *Yugoslavia in the 1980s*, ed. Pedro Ramet, 3–26. Boulder, CO: Westview.

Ramet, Sabrina Petra. 2006. *The Three Yugoslavias: State-Building and Legitimation, 1918–2005*. Washington, DC: Woodrow Wilson Center Press.

Roche, Maurice. 2000. *Mega-events and Modernity: Olympics, Expos and the Growth of Global Culture*. London: Routledge.

Sachs, Stephan E. 1994. *Sarajevo: A Crossroads in History*. https://www.stevesachs.com/papers/paper_sarajevo.html.

Sack, Allen L., and Zeljan Suster. 2000. Soccer and Croatian Nationalism: A Prelude to War. *Journal of Sport and Social Issues* 24: 305–320.

Sakac, Boris. 2008. 'From the Mediterranean Games Split 1979 to the Beijing 2008 Olympic Games' in the Report for the IOC and the ORIS (Olympic Result and Information Services), 99–108 (Conference Paper).

*Sarajevo, Bosnia and Herzegovina, Yugoslavia. General Questionnaire*. n.d.

Sarajevo: An Olympic Portrait. *Ski*, February 1984, 42–43.

Sarantakes, Nicholas Evan. 2010. *Dropping the Torch. Jimmy Carter, the Olympic Boycott, and the Cold War*. Cambridge: Cambridge University Press.

Sbetti, Nicola. 2017. Like a Bridge Over Troubled Adriatic Water: The Complex Relationship between Italian and Yugoslavian Sporting Diplomacy (1945–1954). *The International Journal of the History of Sport* 34 (9): 800–814.

Schaap, Dick. 1984. *The 1984 Olympic Games: Sarajevo/Los Angeles* (The Official Book of the US Olympic Committee).

Scherrer, Jutta. 2014. 'To Catch Up and Overtake' the West: Soviet Discourse on Socialist Competition. In *Competition in Socialist Society*, ed. Melanie Ilic and Katalin Miklóssy, 10–22. Abingdon and New York: Routledge.

Schöpflin, George. 1997. The Functions of Myth and a Taxonomy of Myths. In *Myths and Nationhood*, ed. Geoffrey Hosking and George Schöpflin, 19–35. London: Hurst & Company.

Sekulić, Duško, Garth Massey, and Randy Hodson. 1994. Who Were the Yugoslavs? Failed Sources of a Common Identity in the Former Yugoslavia. *American Sociological Review* 59 (1): 83–97.

Short, John R. 2012. Globalization, Cities, and the Summer Olympics. In *The Making of Olympic Cities: Critical Concepts in Urban Studies, Volume I: Contexts and Overviews*, ed. John R. Gold and Margaret M. Gold, 235–262. London and New York: Routledge.

Shuker, Roy. 2008 [1994]. *Understanding Popular Music Culture*. London and New York: Routledge.

*Social Inequalities and Discontent in Yugoslav Socialism.* 2016. Eds. Rory Archer, Igor Duda and Paul Stubbs. Abingdon and New York: Routledge.

*Sport in Socialist Yugoslavia.* 2018. Ed. Dario Brentin and Dejan Zec. London: Routledge.

SSRNBiH (Gradska konferencija SSRNBiH Sarajevo). 1984. *Sarajevo—Olimpijski grad: Ljudi i akcija.* Sarajevo: NIŠRO Oslobođenje.

Stankovič, Peter. 2005. Soccer and Nationalism in Slovenia. *Ethnologia Balkanica* 9: 305–320.

Starc, Gregor. 2002. Skiing Memories in the Slovenian National Mnemonic Scheme: An Anthropological Perspective. *Anthropological Notebooks* 12: 5–22.

Tagshold, Christian. 2012. Modernity, Space and National Representation at the Tokyo Olympics 1964. In *The Making of Olympic Cities. Critical Concepts in Urban Studies, Volume III: Critical Concepts in Urban Studies,* ed. John R. Gold and Margaret M. Gold, 26–37. London and New York: Routledge.

*TEJ (Turistička enciklopedija Jugoslavije I).* 1958. Eds. Ljubica D. Trajković. Beograd: Turistička štampa.

Ther, Philipp. 2016 [2014]. *Europe since 1989: A History* (Orig.: *Die neue Ordnung auf dem alten Kontinent: eine Geschichte des neoliberalen Europa.* Translated by Charlotte Hughes-Kreutzmüller). Princeton, NJ: Princeton University Press.

Tihić, Smail. 1966. *Tourist Guide Through Sarajevo.* Beograd: Turistička štampa.

Todorova, Maria. 1997. *Imagining the Balkans.* Oxford and New York: Oxford University Press.

Tomc, Gregor. 2006. We Will Rock YU. Popular Music in the Second Yugoslavia. In *Impossible Histories, Historical Avant-Gardes, Neo-Avant-Gardes, and Post-Avant-Gardes in Yugoslavia, 1918–1991,* ed. Dubravka Djurić and Miško Šuvaković, 442–465. Cambridge, MA: The MIT Press.

Trentmann, Frank. 2006. Knowing Consumers—Histories, Identities, Practices: An Introduction. In *The Making of the Consumer: Knowledge, Power and Identity in the Modern World,* ed. Frank Trentmann, 1–27. Oxford: Berg.

Trültzsch, Arno. 2017. *An Almost Forgotten Legacy: Non-Aligned Yugoslavia in the United Nations and in the Making of Contemporary International Law.* Sylff Association, November 16, 2017. Accessed October 31, 2020. https://www.sylff.org/news_voices/23943/.

TSOOC: The Sarajevo Organizing Committee of the XIV Olympic Winter Games Yugoslavia. 1984a. *Sarajevo '84: Tout sur les Jeux / All on the Games / Alles über die Spiele / Sve o igrama.* Sarajevo: Svjetlost.

———. 1984b. *Sarajevo '84. Yugoslavia 8-19.02.* Final Report Published by the Organizing Committee of the XIV Winter Olympic Games 1984 in Sarajevo. Sarajevo: Oslobođenje.

Underwood, Paul. 1960. Credit Cards' Gain: Yugoslavia Acting to Ease Exchange Troubles for the American Tourist. *The New York Times*, February 28, 1960. https://www.nytimes.com/1960/02/28/archives/credit-cards-gain-yugoslavia-acting-to-ease-exchange-troubles-for.html.

*U znaku Sarajeva. Kako su xiv zimske olimpijske igre opisane u jugoslovenskoj štampi i JRT.* 1984. Eds. Zlatan Husarić, Dušan Paravac, Dževad Tašić, Hidajet Delić, Ante Jelavić and Velimir Jojić. Sarajevo: Organizacioni komitet XIV zimskih olimpijskih igara.

*VGAJ (Veliki geografski atlas Jugoslavije).* 1987. Ed. Ivan Bertić. Zagreb: Liber.

von Puttkamer, Joachim. 2014. Mastery of Space and the Crises of Modernity in Central and Eastern Europe. In *Mastery and Lost Illusions. Space and Time in the Modernization of Eastern and Central Europe*, ed. Włodzimierz Borodziej, Stanislav Holubec, and Joachim von Puttkamer, 17–29. Munich: Walter de Gruyter GmbH.

Vrcan, Srđan. 1990. *Sport i nasilje danas u nas i druge studije iz sociologije sporta.* Zagreb: Naprijed.

———. 2002. The Curious Drama of the President of a Republic versus a Football Fan Tribe. *International Review for the Sociology of Sport* 37: 59–77.

Vrcan, Srdjan, and Drazen Lalic. 1999. From Ends to Trenches, and Back: Football in the Former Yugoslavia. In *Football Cultures and Identities*, eds. Gary Armstrong and Richard Giulianotti, 176–185. New York: Palgrave Macmillan.

Vuic, Jason. 2015. *The Sarajevo Olympics: A History of the 1984 Winter Olympic Games.* Amherst and Boston: University of Massachusetts Press.

Vuletić, Dean. 2008. Generation Number One: Politics and Popular Music in Yugoslavia in the 1950s. *Nationalities Papers* 36 (5): 861–879.

Wachtel, Andrew Baruch. 1998. *Making a Nation, Breaking a Nation: Literature and Cultural Politics in Yugoslavia.* Stanford: Stanford University Press.

Wolff, Larry. 1997. *Inventing Eastern Europe: The Map of Civilization on the Mind of the Enlightenment.* Stanford: Stanford University Press.

Woodward, Susan. 1995. *Balkan Tragedy: Chaos and Dissolution after the Cold War.* Washington, DC: The Brookings Institution.

Yurchak, Alexei. 2005. *Everything Was Forever, Until It Was No More.* Princeton, NJ: Princeton University Press.

Zec, Dejan, and Miloš Paunović. 2015. Football's Positive Influence on Integration in Diverse Societies: The Case Study of Yugoslavia. *Soccer & Society* 16 (2–3): 236–237.

Zekić, Jasenko. 2007. Univerzijada '87.—drugi ilirski preporod. *Časopis za suvremenu povijest* 39 (2): 299–318.

———. 2016. Mediteranske igre u Splitu—odrazi političke dimenzije u tiskanim medijima. *Časopis za suvremenu povijest* 48 (1): 97–117.

Zhuk, Sergei I. 2011. The 'Closed' Soviet Society and the West - The Consumption of Western Cultural Products, Youth and Identity in Soviet Ukraine During the 1970s'. In *The Crisis of Socialist Modernity. The Soviet Union and Yugoslavia in the 1970s*, eds. Marie-Janine Calic, Dietmar Neutatz and Julia Obertreis, 87–117. Göttingen/Oakville, CT: Vandenhoeck & Ruprecht.

Zimmerman, William. 1987. *Open Borders, Nonalignment, and the Political Evolution of Yugoslavia*. Princeton, NJ: Princeton University Press.

Zubok, V.M. 2009. *Zhivago's Children: The Last Russian Intelligentsia*. Cambridge, MA: Belknap Press of Harvard University Press.

## RECORDS (DISCOGRAPHY)

BB (Bonton Baya). 1983. Sarajevo, Texas, Nashville, Tennessee. *Elpi*. Sarajevo: Diskoton.

EJK (Elvis J. Kurtovich). 1984. Baščaršy hanumen. *Mitovi i legende o kralju Elvisu*. Ljubljana: RTV Ljubljana.

Merlin. 1986. Cijela Juga jedna avlija. *Teško meni sa tobom (a još teže bez tebe)*. Sarajevo: Diskoton.

ZP (Zabranjeno pušenje). 1984a. Abid. *Das ist Walter*. Zagreb: Jugoton.

———. 1984b. Anarhija All over Baščaršija. *Das ist Walter*. Zagreb: Jugoton.

———. 1984c. Šeki's on the Road Again. *Das ist Walter*. Zagreb: Jugoton.

## VIDEOS

ZOI 84. 1984a. *ZOI 84 Promotivni spot 1—Branko Đurić Đuro*. Accessed January 29, 2021. https://youtu.be/p4GgMGTFhjs.

———. 1984b. *ZOI 84 Promotivni spot 2—Branko Đurić Đuro*. Accessed January 29, 2021. https://youtu.be/fs5U1A1h5Js.

# INDEX[1]

[1] Note: Page numbers followed by 'n' refer to notes.

© The Author(s), under exclusive license to Springer Nature
Switzerland AG 2021
Z. Jovanovic, *A Cultural History of the 1984 Winter Olympics,
Modernity, Memory and Identity in South-East Europe*,
https://doi.org/10.1007/978-3-030-76598-9

Printed by Printforce, the Netherlands